THE 101 SCARIEST MOVIES EVER MADE

THE 101 SCARIEST MOVIES EVER MADE

by
Christopher Wayne Curry
David C. Hayes
Charles E. Pratt, Jr.
Andrew J. Rausch
R.D. Riley

BearManor Media
2017

The 101 Scariest Movies Ever Made

BearManor Media
P. O. Box 71426
Albany, GA 31708

bearmanormedia.com

Typesetting and layout by John Teehan

Published in the USA by BearManor Media

ISBN—978-1-62933-172-0

Table of Contents

FOREWORD

by Herschell Gordon Lewis

Any listing that evaluates anything—automobiles, apples, inventions, cataclysms, seminal years—runs a risk: Accusers point out either prejudice or omissions.

A skeptic or a self-appointed "authority" would run a more profound risk by rashly attacking the careful compilation the authors give us here. Candidates for inclusion include early, early silent films, such as *Nosferatu* (1922) and contemporary ventures such as *Drag Me to Hell* (2009). Anyone and everyone who's even peripherally attached to a love or history of horror films will find a huge batch of offerings.

Even rambling through the list is a treat. Wow—there's *Diabolique* (1955), number 31 (the original, not the remake). Half a century after that French masterpiece saw its first release, nobody who ever saw it—nobody—could ever forget that marvelous scene of the ostensibly drowned body eerily rising from under bathtub water. There's the first *Invasion of the Body Snatchers* (1956), number 30, a film that was the progenitor of hundreds of plot-borrowing imitators.

As a scuba diver, I was stupefied by the denouement of *Open Water* (2003), number 98...and still have that impossible final scene in my mind when just the title comes up. And here's a bone thrown to those whose memories don't carry back—*Saw* (2004), number 100, the natural bastard-child of all that went before.

The 101 Scariest Movies Ever Made deserves more than a permanent position in the history of motion pictures. It also deserves a permanent position in the library of anyone who recognizes that the very history of motion pictures themselves...and the fascinating development of special effects and the constant evolving to cope with audience sophistication doesn't damage the historical value of those that went before.

Treasure this book. You'll join horror hounds like me. And we're a group worth joining, aren't we?

Thank you to the authors of this book for inviting us to your mesmerizing world of horror film history!

INTRODUCTION

by Darryl Mayeski

Who doesn't love a good scare?

Back when I published *Screem Magazine* #18, we delved into this subject with an entire issue dedicated to "Films That Scarred Us for Life." Our writers reminisced about fright flicks that gave them the creeps as youngsters: *The Blob* (1958), *Tourist Trap* (1979), *The Exorcist* (1973), *Jaws* (1975), and *Chitty Chitty Bang Bang* (1968) (a kid's worst nightmare—the creepy Child Catcher!). I would think that most fans began their love of horror films at a young age, our most impressionable years. Some of my earliest memories involve sitting in front of a TV watching *Chiller Theatre* on WPIX, Channel 11 out of New York. *Horror Hotel* (a.k.a *The City of the Dead*, 1960), *Black Sunday* (1960), *The Crawling Eye* (a.k.a *The Trollenberg Terror*, 1958), *Curse of the Demon* (1957), *The Werewolf* (1956), *Carnival of Souls* (1962), and *Night of the Living Dead* (1968) were just a few of the films that have been etched into my brain since I was a boy. I still love them, and I'll even admit that these motion pictures still give me chills to this day. In my adolescent years, *The Exorcist*, *The Wicker Man* (1973), *The Texas Chainsaw Massacre* (1974), *Jaws*, *Halloween* (1978), *Alien* (1979), *Friday the 13th* (1980), and *The Shining* (1980) raised the scare bar even higher, with more graphic and realistic terror.

Finding ways to frighten a new audience in today's cinema may be more of a challenge, as many of this generation's youth are so desensitized to violence. But there are several recent movies that still pack a good scare punch—*The Descent* (2005), *Martyrs* (2008), *The Conjuring* (2013), and *The Babadook* (2014). It's a challenge to put together a book with a listing of just what are the scariest films of all time, but this collection is a worthy start for those who are looking to find a quick thrill at night … the only time you should watch any of these horrific gems!

#1 The Exorcist (1973)

Something beyond comprehension is happening to a little girl on this street, in this house. A man has been called for as a last resort to try and save her. That man is The Exorcist.

Why it made the list:

Including *The Exorcist* on a list of the scariest films ever made is a no-brainer, as it tops, or comes close to topping, nearly every such list that has been fashioned. *The Exorcist* is truly the most frightening film ever made, and it still holds up. Today, even with the advent of CGI technology and advanced filmmaking methods, *The Exorcist* remains the pinnacle of the genre. Not only is this film unbelievably scary, but it's masterfully crafted. It received 10 Academy Award nominations—a feat quite rare for a horror film—and won two for its sound and screenplay.

Synopsis:

Actress Chris MacNeil (Ellen Burstyn) begins to notice some unusual behavior from her 12-year-old daughter Regan (Linda Blair). She then has the young girl evaluated, and Regan undergoes a battery of tests. During this period, Regan displays unusual powers, such as inhuman strength and levitation, and she starts to speak blasphemously in a male demonic voice. Chris initially believes that her daughter is reacting to the recent divorce of her parents but comes to suspect something much darker. She eventually contacts Father Damien Karras (Jason Miller), a Georgetown priest. Karras interviews the young girl and ultimately comes to the conclusion that she may be possessed. Father Lankester Merrin (Max von Sydow), an experienced exorcist, is then called in to perform an exorcism. Once Merrin and Karras begin the ritual, it becomes apparent that

WILLIAM PETER BLATTY'S
THE EXORCIST
Directed by WILLIAM FRIEDKIN
ELLEN BURSTYN MAX VON SYDOW LEE J. COBB
KITTY WINN JACK MacGOWRAN JASON MILLER AS FATHER KARRAS
LINDA BLAIR AS REGAN PRODUCED BY WILLIAM PETER BLATTY EXECUTIVE PRODUCER NOEL MARSHALL
SCREENPLAY BY WILLIAM PETER BLATTY BASED ON HIS NOVEL
FROM WARNER BROS. A WARNER COMMUNICATIONS COMPANY
R

Regan is indeed possessed. The two priests and the demon—possibly Satan himself—lock horns in an epic battle of strength and wills that could ultimately lead them all to their demise.

Scariest scene:

The Exorcist is rare in that it's difficult to pinpoint a single most horrific scene. The film itself is filled with frightening scenes, and its final hour-and-twenty-minutes manage to sustain a level of terror that remains unmatched today. Frightening scenes include the possessed Regan stabbing herself in the crotch with a crucifix while spouting vile blasphemous obscenities, Regan's head spinning 360 degrees, her spewing green vomit, and the famed "spider-walk" scene, which finds her contorting her body in a very disturbing manner.

Memorable dialogue:

> **DEMON:** I'm not Regan.
>
> **FATHER KARRAS:** Well, then let's introduce ourselves. I'm Damien Karras.
>
> **DEMON:** And I'm the Devil. Now kindly undo these straps.
>
> **FATHER KARRAS:** If you're the Devil, why not make the straps disappear?
>
> **DEMON:** That's too vulgar a display of power, Karras.

Did you know?

Noted evangelist Billy Graham claimed that an actual demon was living inside the reels of this film.

Cast:

Ellen Burstyn (Chris MacNeil), Max von Sydow (Father Merrin), Lee J. Cobb (Lt. Kinderman), Kitty Winn (Sharon), Jack MacGowran (Burke Dennings), Jason Miller (Father Karras), Linda Blair (Regan), Rev. William O'Malley (Father Dyer), Barton Heyman (Dr. Klein), Peter Masterson (Dr. Barringer).

What the critics say:

Roger Ebert, *Chicago Sun-Times*: "It may be that the times we live in have prepared us for this movie. And Friedkin has admittedly given us a good one. I've always preferred a generic approach to film criticism; I ask myself how good a movie is of its type. *The Exorcist* is one of the best movies of its type ever made; it not only transcends the genre of terror, horror, and the supernatural, but it transcends such serious, ambitious efforts in the same direction as Roman Polanski's *Rosemary's Baby*."

Stanley Kauffmann, *The New Republic*: "This is the scariest film I've seen in years—the only scary film I've seen in years … If you want to be shaken—and I found out, while the picture was going, that that's what I wanted—then *The Exorcist* will scare the hell out of you."

Joe Dante, *Castle of Frankenstein*: "An amazing film, and one destined to become at the very least a horror classic. Director Friedkin's film will be profoundly disturbing to all audiences, especially the more sensitive and those who tend to 'live' the movies they see … Suffice it to say, there has never been anything like this on the screen before."

If you liked this, you might also like:

Abby (1974).

#2 *Psycho* (1960)

A new and altogether different screen excitement!

Why it made the list:

Psycho is one of master filmmaker Alfred Hitchcock's greatest achievements, and that's saying something. A high-brow progenitor of the slasher genre, this Robert Bloch adaptation remains as startling as it was for audiences back in 1960. Hitchcock shocked viewers by doing something they had never seen before—by brutally murdering the film's protagonist halfway into the film, and then switching protagonists to follow the viscous, deranged killer. Ranked as one of the greatest films of all time (any genre) on just about every list of that kind ever fashioned, *Psycho* is more than just a terrifying viewing—it's a genuine work of art that remains one of the finest examples of psychological horror ever captured on film.

Psycho received four Academy Award nominations in 1961, including Best Director, Best Supporting Actress (Janet Leigh), Best Black-and-White Cinematography (John L. Russell), and Best Black-and-White Art Direction-Set Decoration (Joseph Hurley, Robert Clatworthy, George Milo). The film has been listed to the National Film Registry and has spawned countless imitators, three sequels, a remake, a television film spin-off, and a TV series.

Synopsis:

Marion Crane (Leigh) absconds with $40,000 of her boss' money, hoping to run away and start a new life with her married lover, Sam Loomis (John Gavin). Exhausted, she decides to pull over and get a room at the Bates Motel. The motel is operated by Norman Bates (Anthony Perkins), an eccentric young man burdened with taking care of his invalid mother. After having dinner with Norman, Marion decides to go back to her room and take a nice, hot shower. And the rest, as they say, is history.

Scariest scene:

Come on, you know the answer to this. The film's more-than-iconic scene in which unsuspecting protagonist Marion Crane is hacked to pieces in the shower is the film's most frightening offering. The Bernard Herrman score is perfect here with its piercing, punctuating violin. The editing is nothing short of amazing. Close-up on Marion. Close-up on the knife. Marion crumples into the bathtub. The blood swirling down the drain, emptying just as life itself empties from our heroine. Is there any scene in the history of film that's as perfect as this one? I don't think so.

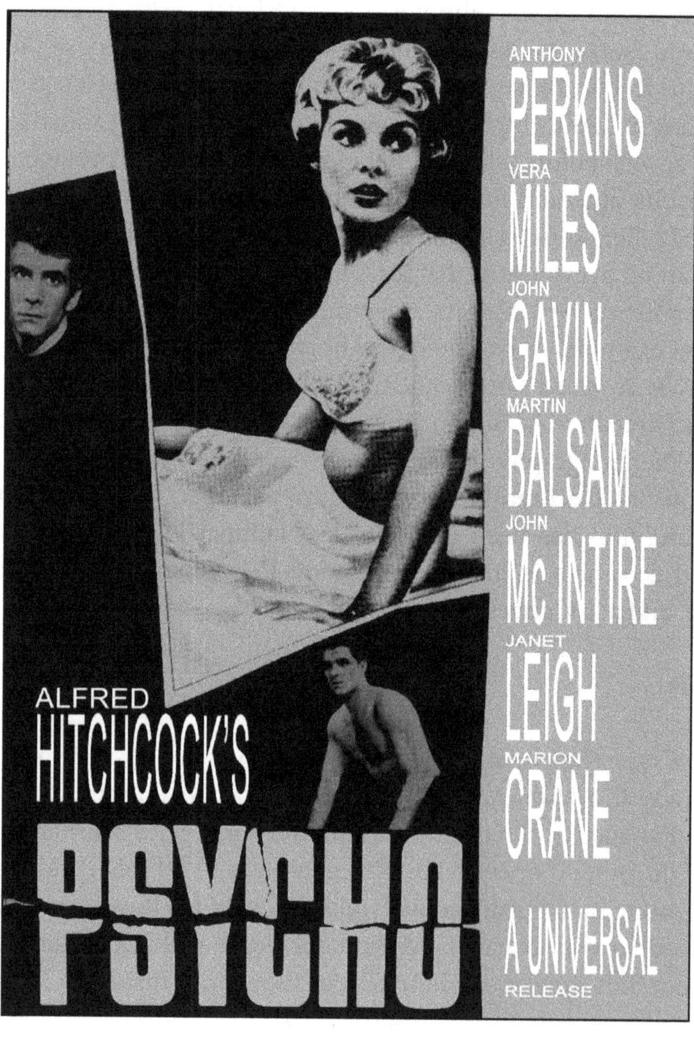

Memorable dialogue:

> **NORMAN BATES:** [Voiceover] It's sad when a mother has to speak the words that condemn her own son. But I couldn't allow them to believe that I would commit murder. They'll put him away now, as I should have years ago. He was always bad, and in the end he intended to tell them I killed those girls and that man … as if I could do anything but just sit and stare, like one of his stuffed birds. They know I can't move a finger, and I won't. I'll just sit here and be quiet, just in case they do … suspect me. They're probably watching me. Well, let them. Let them see what kind of a person I am. I'm not even going to swat that fly. I hope they are watching … They'll see. They'll see and they'll know, and they'll say, "Why, she wouldn't even harm a fly … "

Did you know?

The iconic shower scene in *Psycho* set a new standard for acceptable violence, eventually leading way to gorier films like Herschell Gordon Lewis' *Blood Feast* (1963) and ultimately hundreds of other horror pictures.

Cast:

Anthony Perkins (Norman Bates), Janet Leigh (Marion Crane), Vera Miles (Lila Crane), John Gavin (Sam Loomis), Martin Balsam (Milton

Arbogast), John Mcintire (Al Chambers), Simon Oakland (Dr. Fred Richmond), Frank Albertson (Tom Cassidy), Pat Hitchcock (Caroline), Vaughn Taylor (George Lowery).

What the critics say:

Paine Knickerbocker, *San Francisco Chronicle*: "After his suspense pictures and romantic adventure stories could he come up with a shocker, acceptable to regular American audiences, which still carried the spine-tingling voltage of foreign presentations such as *Diabolique*? The answer is an enthusiastic yes. He has very shrewdly interwoven crime, sex and suspense, blended the real and the unreal in fascinating proportions and punctuated his film with several quick, grisly and unnerving surprises."

Roger Ebert, *Chicago Sun-Times:* "Seeing the shower scene today, several things stand out. Unlike modern horror films, *Psycho* never shows the knife striking flesh. There are no wounds. There is blood, but not gallons of it. Hitchcock shot in black and white because he felt the audience could not stand so much blood in color … The slashing chords of Bernard Herrman's soundtrack substitute for more grisly sound effects. The closing shots are not graphic but symbolic, as blood and water spin down the drain, and the camera cuts to a close-up, the same size, of Marion's unmoving eyeball. This remains the most effective slashing in movie history, suggesting that situation and artistry are more important than graphic details."

Staff Writer, *Classic Film Guide*: "What kind of director kills off his star less than halfway into his film? Only Alfred Hitchcock could (get away with it), of course. And what a killing, too! You won't turn your back on the door to the bathroom when showering for a while after watching this shocker."

If you liked this, you might also like:

Dressed to Kill (1980).

#3 *Alien* (1979)

In space, no one can hear you scream.

Why it made the list:

Alien may be a science-fiction film, but it's got horror in its very DNA. Every element of the movie is designed to disturb and disquiet the viewer. The cramped, dark and dingy hallways of the Nostromo are a claustrophobe's nightmare, and things aren't any nicer down on the planet. Swirling dust storms obscure the landscape, and the utterly alien ship, with its twisted organic construction, is profoundly unsettling. The only warm, inviting space the doomed crew has for respite is the galley, and what happens there shatters the last moments of peace they will have with terrifying suddenness. Finally, H.R. Giger's creature design birthed one of the most iconic and terrifying monsters in movie history.

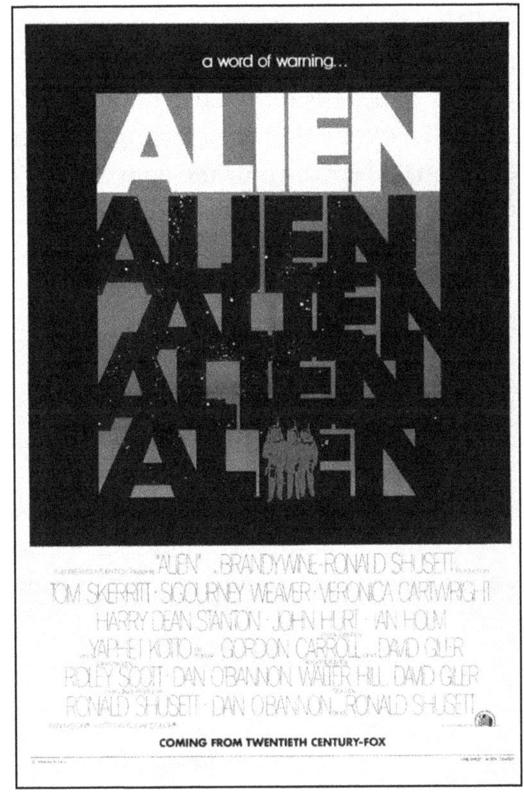

Synopsis:

The commercial mining spacecraft *Nostromo* is returning to Earth with a cargo of mineral ore. The crew is in stasis, but is awakened by the ship's A.I.

when a signal of unknown origin is detected halfway through the journey home. Acting on standing orders, the crew investigates the signal, which is coming from a nearby planet. The *Nostromo* lands, suffering minor damage in the process, and Captain Dallas (Tom Skerritt), Executive Officer Kane (John Hurt), and Navigator Lambert (Veronica Cartwright) head to the planet's surface to find the source of the transmission. As they investigate, Warrant Officer Ripley (Sigourney Weaver) tries to decode the signal, and intuits that it is not an SOS as originally suspected, but a warning. The away team discovers an ancient spacecraft of unknown alien design, and Kane is attacked by some sort of parasite. He is rushed back to the ship, and the parasite eventually detaches itself and seems to die, but it has left behind something much worse. Soon, a monstrous alien killing machine is loose on the ship, and the crew must find a way to defeat the seemingly unstoppable creature.

Scariest scene:

Though *Alien* is stuffed with suspenseful, scary moments, there is no question that the "chestbuster" provoked heights of terror rarely reached in a movie theater. As the crew gathers for a celebratory dinner before returning to stasis for the trip home, Kane begins exhibiting signs of distress. The others fear he's choking, and indeed he is, but it is not on the questionable space chow the crew has been joking about. Lambert's horrified, sickened cry of "Ah! God!" as the creature explodes out in a shower of blood and gore surely reflected the reactions of audiences everywhere.

Memorable dialogue:

> **RIPLEY:** Final report of the commercial starship Nostromo, third officer reporting. The other members of the crew, Kane, Lambert, Parker, Brett, Ash and Captain Dallas, are dead. Cargo and ship destroyed. I should reach the frontier in about six weeks. With a little luck, the network will pick me up. This is Ripley, last survivor of the Nostromo, signing off.
>
> [*to Jonesy the cat*]
>
> **RIPLEY:** Come on, cat.

Did you know?

Actress Veronica Cartwright's did not expect to be sprayed with fake blood during the "chestbuster" scene, and her reaction was completely unrehearsed and authentic.

Cast:

Tom Skerritt (Dallas), Sigourney Weaver (Ripley), John Hurt (Kane), Ian Holm (Ash), Veronica Cartwright (Lambert), Harry Dean Stanton (Brett), Yaphet Kotto (Parker).

What the critics say:

Andrew O'Hehir, *Salon:* "Ridley Scott's original 1979 *Alien* is a film about human loneliness amid the emptiness and amorality of creation. It's a cynical '70s-leftist vision of the future in which none of the problems plaguing 20th century Earth—class divisions, capitalist exploitation, the subjugation of humanity to technology—have been improved in the slightest by mankind's forays into outer space. Although it has often been

described as being a haunted-house movie set in space, *Alien* also has a profoundly existentialist undertow that makes it feel like a film noir—the other genre to feature a slithery, sexualized monster as its classic villain"

Lisa Schwarzbaum, *Entertainment Weekly:* "Those first 45 minutes before the creature drips the first spiral of goo—that eternity in which the camera tracks across a deserted control room and there's nothing for an uneasy audience to do but wait and worry—are more unnerving than the most explosive opening-act stunt in the repertoire today. Even the rib-ripping birth scene, a creationist doozy in which monstrous life is hatched from a man, unfolds at a measured tempo more familiar to a waltz than a rupture."

Erik Lundegaard, *Seattle Times*: "According to the American Film Institute, *Alien* is the sixth greatest American thriller ever made, its villain is the 14th greatest villain, and its hero, Lt. Ripley, is the eighth greatest hero. ... That's one hell of a legacy for one film. Can *Alien* live up to it? It does. And it'll still scare the pants off you."

If you liked this, you might also like:

Scared to Death (1980).

#4 *The Shining* (1973)

A masterpiece of modern horror.

Why it made the list:

In a time when masked slashers were hacking up teenagers like firewood and demonic children were raising hell, *The Shining* (adapted from the best-selling novel by Stephen King) brought forth a new dimension of horror by twisting the expected genre norms. There are no cheap jump scares in *The Shining*. No creaking doors, no ominous shadows in sight. The Overlook Hotel is as disturbing with every light on at three in the afternoon as it is at midnight and it even manages to be more claustrophobic than if darkness prevailed in every corridor. *The Shining* is ponderous and takes its time building steam, giving us a good look at the dynamic of a family heading for inevitable doom. With each frame Stanley Kubrick infuses dread and isolation with long tracking shots, minimalist sound effects, and music that is so fitting and so creepy that it also becomes a character in the story. The acting by Jack Nicholson is dementedly inspired and equally compelling, as is young Danny Lloyd, who puts in a powerful performance as Danny Torrance, a child with incredible psychic abilities.

Synopsis:

Jack Torrance (Nicholson), a writer with a history of alcoholism and abuse, moves his wife and son into an isolated Colorado hotel where he has been employed as the winter caretaker of the hotel in its off-season. There he hopes to write a novel and reconnect with his wife and son. Unfortunately, the powers within the Overlook Hotel have other plans for Jack and his family. As winter mounts and the snow piles up outside, Jack

begins a downward spiral towards madness. Family life for the Torrances just checked into hell. Perhaps permanently.

Scariest scene:

When Jack Torrence goes to investigate his son's claim that someone tried to strangle him in Room 237, he discovers a sensuous and naked woman climbing out of a bathtub. The woman seduces Jack. While Jack is embracing and kissing her he opens his eyes to find that the beautiful young woman has turned into a diseased and decayed mad old hag who chases him from the room.

Memorable dialogue:

> **WENDY:** Please! Don't hurt me!
>
> **JACK:** I'm not gonna hurt you.
>
> **WENDY:** Stay away from me!
>
> **JACK:** Wendy? Darling? Light, of my life. I'm not gonna hurt ya. You didn't let me finish my sentence. I said, I'm not gonna hurt ya. I'm just going to bash your brains in.

Did you know?

The title of the book and subsequent movie was inspired by the refrain ("we all shine on") of the song "Instant Karma" by John Lennon.

Cast:

Jack Nicholson (Jack Torrance), Shelley Duvall (Wendy Torrance), Danny Lloyd (Danny Torrance), Scatman Crothers (Dick Hallorann), Barry Nelson (Stuart Ullman), Philip Stone (Delbert Grady), Joe Turkel (Lloyd the Bartender), Anne Jackson (Doctor), Tony Burton (Larry Durkin), Lia Beldam (Young Woman in Bath).

What the critics say:

Bruce McCabe, *Boston Globe*: "When you sit down to *The Shining*, you sit down with normal expectations of being diverted, perhaps even being gripped, but not being undermined. But the film undermines you in powerful, inchoate ways. It's a horror story even for people who don't like horror stories—maybe especially for them."

Janet Maslin, *The New York Times*: "Meticulously detailed and never less than fascinating, *The Shining* may be the first movie that ever made its audience jump with a title that simply says 'Tuesday.'"

Richard Schickel, *Time*: "Kubrick has made a movie that will have to be reckoned with on the highest level."

If you liked this, you might also like:

The Haunting in Connecticut (2009).

#5 *Halloween* (1978)

The night he came home!

Why it made the list:

John Carpenter's *Halloween* didn't invent the slasher flick, but it set the standard for the massive wave of the genre's movies that would follow in the 1980s. The low-budget film became a box-office hit, thrilling and chilling audiences with its truly creepy, iconic score (composed by Carpenter himself) and terrifying an entire generation with one of horror's most frightening bogeymen, Michael Myers. Surprisingly light on outright gore, *Halloween* relies instead on subtle pacing, escalating dread, and inventive camera angles to keep viewers off balance. Myers is an unstoppable, unknowable force stalking the peaceful streets of a small midwestern city, bringing fear and death to a place that might stand in for any town in America.

Synopsis:

On Halloween night in 1963, six-year-old Michael Myers (Will Sandin) inexplicably murders his own sister with a butcher knife in Haddonfield, Illinois. Confined to an institution, Myers is unresponsive and ignores all questions from his psychiatrist, Dr. Loomis (Donald Pleasence). He remains in this state for years, until he escapes one rainy night on Oct. 30, 1978. Loomis fears the adult Myers (Tony Moran) will return to his hometown and pick up where he left off 15 years earlier. Indeed, Myers does make his way to Haddonfield, where he sees high school student Laurie Strode (Jamie Lee Curtis) and begins to stalk her around town. He has stolen a uniform from a mechanic he murdered on the way from the sanitarium where he was being held, and donned a white rubber mask. Laurie catches glimpses of Myers throughout the day, but initially dis-

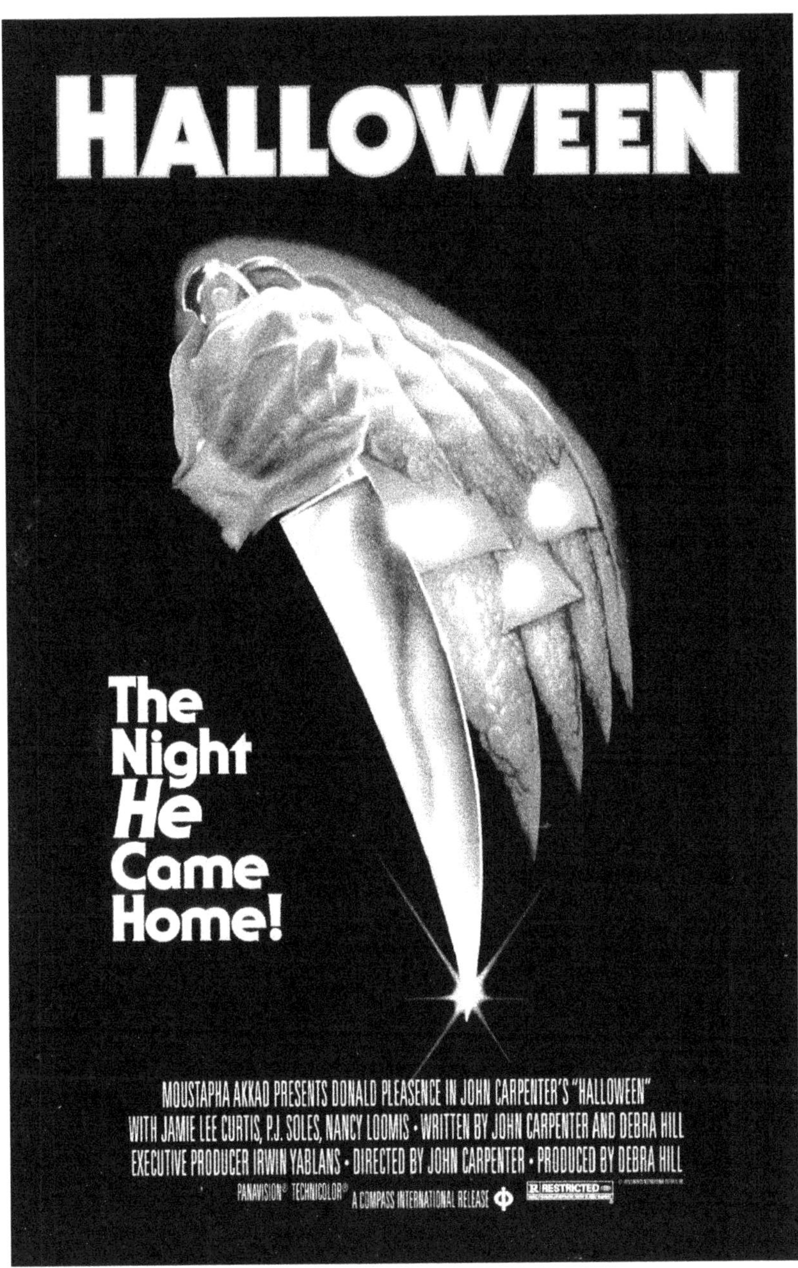

misses him as a creep playing Halloween pranks. That night, Laurie and her friend Annie (Nancy Loomis) have babysitting duties at two houses across the street from each other. Myers follows them, and as darkness falls on Halloween, he begins his killing spree.

Scariest scene:

Laurie has discovered the dead bodies of her friends, and locks herself in the house where she is babysitting. Once she does, she realizes that Myers is inside with her and two children. She sends the children upstairs and fends off several attacks by the seemingly inhuman Myers. Finally, she stabs him with his own knife. The camera watches as Laurie sobs uncontrollably, with the prone body of Myers in the background. Then, without warning, Myers sits up, rises from the ground, and begins his final attack.

Memorable dialogue:

> **SHERIFF BRACKETT**: I have a feeling that you're way off on this.
>
> **DR. LOOMIS**: You have the wrong feeling.
>
> **BRACKETT**: You're not doing very much to prove me wrong!
>
> **LOOMIS**: What more do you need?
>
> **BRACKETT**: Well, it's going to take a lot more than fancy talk to keep me up all night crawling around these bushes.
>
> **LOOMIS**: I- I- I watched him for fifteen years, sitting in a room, staring at a wall, not seeing the wall, looking past the wall – looking at this night, inhumanly patient, waiting for some secret, silent alarm to trigger him off. Death has come to your little town, Sheriff. Now you can either ignore it, or you can help me to stop it.
>
> **BRACKETT**: More fancy talk.

Did you know?

All of the streets in the fictional Haddonfield are named after streets in Bowling Green, Kentucky. John Carpenter attended college there in the early 1970s at Western Kentucky University.

Cast:

Donald Pleasence (Dr. Sam Loomis), Jamie Lee Curtis (Laurie Strode), Nancy Loomis (Annie Brackett), P.J. Soles (Lynda van der Klok), Charles Cyphers (Sheriff Leigh Brackett), Kyle Richards (Lindsey Wallace), Brian Andrews (Tommy Doyle), John Michael Graham (Bob Simms), Nancy Stephens (Marion Chambers). Arthur Malet (Graveyard Keeper), Mickey Yablans (Richie), Brent Le Page (Lonnie Elamb), Adam Hollander (Keith), Robert Phalen (Dr. Terence Wynn), Tony Moran (Michael Myers).

What the critics say:

James Berardinelli, *ReelViews:* "From a shock-and-suspense point-of-view, *Halloween* is the rival of Alfred Hitchcock's *Psycho*. With only a few arguable exceptions (such as *The Exorcist*), there isn't another post-1970 release that comes close to it in terms of scaring the living hell out of a viewer … A modern classic of the most horrific kind."

Staff, *Empire Magazine*: "Turn off the lights. Put on the widescreen version, showcasing Carpenter's masterful framing and chill-inducing, Michael Myers-concealing use of shadows. Crank up the sound, and be scared witless by horror's greatest director."

Staff, *TV Guide*: "There's nary a drop of blood on screen in this rollicking funhouse of a movie but there is enough sheer cinematic ingenuity on display to coax screams out of the most jaded gorehound."

#6 *The Haunting* (1963)

Scream ... no one will hear you! Run ... and the silent footsteps will follow, for in Hill House the dead are restless!

Why it made the list:

This Robert Wise adaptation of Shirley Jackson's *The Haunting of Hill House* is a perfect example of a true horror film. Without the excesses of special effects, CGI and the like, the film maintains a frightening atmosphere by making the most of such subtleties as knocking sounds, creaking floorboards, and piercing screams. There isn't one visible ghost in this film, but it's truly one of the most frightening films ever made. Director Wise learned his craft from scare-master Val Lewton, and it shows here.

Synopsis:

Dr. John Markway (Richard Johnson) is doing a research on the existence of ghosts. In doing so, he gets permission to investigate Hill House, a large, spooky mansion with a dark and troubled history of murder and madness. For this investigation he recruits Luke (Russ Tamblyn), who will one day inherit the house, the psychic Eleanor (Julie Harris), whose insecurities make her susceptible to the forces of the house, and the clairvoyant Theodora (Claire Bloom). As the investigation proceeds, it becomes more and more difficult for anyone to doubt the existence of the supernatural.

Scariest scene:

The most frightening scene in the film is the one in which Eleanor and Theodora are accosted by the ghost in their sleeping chambers. The sounds of knocking become louder and louder, and more and more maddening, until finally the two women (along with the audience) are scared out of their wits.

Memorable dialogue:

> **DR. JOHN MARKWAY:** When people believed the earth was flat, the idea of a round world scared them silly. Then they found out how the round world works. It's the same with the world of the supernatural. Until we know how it works, we'll continue to carry around this unnecessary burden of fear.

Did you know?

Robert Wise cast Julie Harris after seeing her in a play and coming to the conclusion that she was perfect for the lead role.

Cast:

Cast: Julie Harris (Eleanor Lance), Claire Bloom (Theodora), Richard Johnson (Dr. John Markaway), Russ Tamblyn (Luke Sanderson), Fay Compton (Mrs. Sanderson), Rosalie Crutchley (Mrs. Dudley), Lois Maxwell (Grace Markaway), Valentine Dyall (Mr. Dudley), Diane Clare (Carrie Fredericks), Ronald Adam (Eldridge Harper).

What the critics say:

Tyler Foster, *DVD Talk*: "*The Haunting* starts out with dutch angles, muffled noises and anamorphic stretching to build imaginations up to a fever pitch, until striking images like a rickety spiral staircase, ominous chalk writing on the walls, and an extremely unsettling special effect involving a door, leap off the screen and burrow into the viewer's imagination. It's a ghost story without a single ghost, yet people are more than likely to see spooky figures lurking around every corner, and 46 years later, such technique still feels modern."

Bosley Crowther, *The New York Times*: ""Scandal! Murder! Insanity! Suicide! Hill House has everything!" So boasts an off-screen narrator as we pan in to gaze upon a shadowy and gaunt New England mansion that looks for all the world like the old Jefferson Market Courthouse in Greenwich Village at the beginning of the film called *The Haunting*, which came to the Paramount and Cinema I yesterday. And, believe me, before this antique chiller drags to an ectoplasmic end, you'll agree that it does have just about everything in the old-fashioned blood-chilling line except a line of reasoning that makes a degree of sense."

Staff, *TV Guide*: "A bit overrated upon its initial release, *The Haunting* is, nonetheless, an undeniably effective adaptation of the Shirley Jackson novel and remains one of the best haunted-house movies."

If you liked this, you might also like:

The House on Haunted Hill (1959).

#7 Night of the Living Dead (1968)

They keep coming back in a bloodthirsty lust for human flesh!

Why it made the list:

Made in Pittsburgh, Pennsylvania in 1968 on a shoestring budget, *Night of the Living Dead* instantly became something like the zombies it depicts—something that just keeps going and cannot not be stopped. The movie single-handedly reinvented the cinematic zombie and created a whole new subgenre of horror that has spawned (and continues to spawn) countless imitators. Despite the slew of similar films produced since its release, *Night of the Living Dead* remains one of the finest and most effective zombie films ever made. Even though the filmmakers had to use stock music and amateur actors, the film is atmospheric (much of it due to the grainy black-and-white film) and downright scary, holding up even today.

Synopsis:

Two strangers, Ben (Duane Jones) and Barbra (Judith O'Dea), find themselves under siege in a small farmhouse when the recently dead begin to rise and eat the flesh of human beings. Ben and Barbra will later meet others, creating both new possibilities and dangers, and fight through the night just to stay alive.

Scariest scene:

The scariest scene takes place at the beginning of the film. In this iconic scene, Barbra is teased by her brother, Tom (Keith Wayne). Knowing that she is afraid to be in the cemetery as night grows near, Tom chides her with the film's most famous line: "They're coming to get you, Barbra." As he does

this, another man approaches them. Tom jokes that the man may be some sort of living dead creature. These jokes soon come to an abrupt end, however, when Tom discovers (the hard way) that the man really is a member of the living dead. The zombie then chases Barbra to the farmhouse.

Memorable dialogue:

> **REPORTER:** Are they slow moving, chief?
>
> **SHERIFF MCCLELLAND:** Yeah, they're dead. They're all messed up.

Did you know?

Originally titled *Night of the Flesh Eaters,* writers George Romero and John Russo originally envisioned the creatures as aliens. While writing the script, Romero and Russo changed their minds and made them zombies, thus creating a whole new sub-genre of horror.

Cast:

Duane Jones (Ben), Judith O'Dea (Barbra), Karl Hardman (Harry), Marilyn Eastman (Helen), Keith Wayne (Tom), Judith Ridley (Judy), Kyra Schon (Karen), Charles Craig (Newscaster), S. William Hinzman (Zombie), George Kosana (Sheriff McClelland).

What the critics say:

Elliott Stein, *Village Voice*: "George Romero's remarkably assured debut, made on a shoestring, about a group of people barricaded inside a farmhouse while an army of flesh-eating zombies roams the countryside, deflates all genre clichés."

Staff, *Variety*: "Although pic's basic premise is repellent—recently dead bodies are resurrected and begin killing human beings in order to eat their flesh—it is in execution that the film distastefully excels. No brutalizing stone is left unturned: crowbars gash holes in the heads of the living dead, monsters are shown eating entrails, and—in a climax of unparalleled nausea—a little girl kills her mother by stabbing her a dozen times in the chest with a trowel."

Kim Newman, *Empire*: "Many of its plot strands were unprecedented: a heroine who reacts credibly to an appalling situation by become a useless catatonic, a black hero who finally has less to fear from the zombies than from the ghoul-hunting posse combing the countryside as if on a Vietnam search-and-destroy mission, news bulletins that include expert advice from the men on the ground, a relentlessly pessimistic ending. … The original and the best."

If you liked this, you might also like:

Children of the Living Dead (2001).

#8 *The Thing* (1982)

Man is the warmest place to hide.

Why it made the list:

In the late seventies and early eighties, John Carpenter made a slew of notable horror films, but few were as effective as this chiller. A remake of the 1951 Howard Hawks/Christian Nyby film *The Thing from Another World*, Carpenter's bleak picture is as masterful as anything the genre has ever produced. Boasting a superb screenplay by Bill Lancaster, impressive direction by Carpenter, a chilling score by Ennio Morricone, and a wonderful ensemble, *The Thing* is a masterpiece by any standard. The film's sense of isolation, coupled with Morricone's score, lends the film a creeping feeling of dread. Add in some terrific special effects and a few chair-jumper scares, and you have the recipe for a truly frightening cinematic experience.

Despite abysmal box-office receipts and (initially) poor reviews, the film has developed a substantial cult following and is routinely cited as one of the finest horror films ever produced.

Synopsis:

A spaceship has crash landed on the planet earth, and has been buried beneath the Antarctic ice for millions of years. Now it has been uncovered by scientists, who soon learn that the creature on board is still alive. Even more frightening, it's able to adapt and perfectly imitate other living creatures, from sled dogs to human beings. When the alien transforms itself into members of the scientific outpost, things become sticky and no one knows who they can trust. It soon becomes a battle to the death to destroy the creature, as the future of all mankind depends on it.

Scariest scene:

When Dr. Copper (Richard Dysart) reaches into a cavity in the body of a dead man, he gets more than he bargained for. The hole in the body reveals itself to have teeth, which promptly bite Copper's arms off. When this scene played during theatrical screenings, audiences jumped and screamed with fright. Thirty years later, the scene remains as frightening as ever thanks to terrific special effects.

Memorable dialogue:

> **MACREADY:** Someone in this camp ain't what he appears to be. Right now that may be one or two of us. By spring, it could be all of us.

> **CHILDS:** So, how do we know who's human? If I was an imitation, a perfect imitation, how would you know it was really me?

Did you know?

The role of Dr. Blair was originally to have been played by Donald Pleasance, whom Carpenter had worked with on *Halloween*. However, a scheduling conflict interfered and the role was then recast with Wilford Brimley.

Cast:

Kurt Russell (R.J. MacReady), Wilford Brimley (Dr. Blair), T.K. Carter (Nauls), David Clennon (Palmer), Keith David (Childs), Richard Dysart (Dr. Copper), Charles Hallahan (Vance Norris), Peter Maloney (George Bennings), Richard Masur (Clark), Donald Moffat (Gary).

What the critics say:

Scott Foundas, *The Village Voice*: "A flop upon its release (by Universal, two weeks after Spielberg's *E.T.*), this spatial masterpiece of desolate Arctic vistas at odds with close-quarters claustrophobia has since been hailed as a high totem of modern horror-making. There remains something deeply unnerving about Carpenter's ambiguity as to whether the movie's shape-shifting alien is distorting its hosts' personalities or merely revealing something of their primal selves."

Mike Rubino, *DVD Verdict*: "*The Thing*, featuring a Kurt Russell who looks like he just didn't shave after escaping from New York, is a groundbreaking film in terms of practical special effects. While the film is a remake of *The Thing from Another World* (1951), it feels a lot like Ridley Scott's *Alien* in the snow. The film's slow pace is punctuated by intense moments of violence, gore, and pithy comments. Every character in the film is three-dimensional and unique, and like any good ensemble piece, they each have a moment to shine before they're picked off by The Thing."

James Berardinelli, *Reel Views*: "Carpenter's recreation of an Antarctic station is flawless; we never doubt for a moment that these men are trapped and alone in a frozen wilderness. The spartan nature of the lifestyle feeds into the claustrophobia and paranoia that develop when it becomes evident any of them could be standing next to an alien. *The Thing* works on a visceral level, and not just because of the blood and gore. Carpenter's flair for suspense, honed to perfection in *Halloween*, is on display here. Viewers, especially those watching *The Thing* for the first time, will be perched on their seat's edge for a good portion of the movie."

If you liked this, you might also like:

30 Days of Night (2007).

#9 The Texas Chainsaw Massace (1974)

What happened is true. Now the motion picture that's just as real.

Why it made the list:

Based loosely on the true story of Wisconsin serial killer Ed Gein, *The Texas Chainsaw Massacre* is a truly frightening film. Sure, some of the acting is wooden and the characters—particularly Franklin—are annoying as all hell, but director Tobe Hooper utilizes what he has here to craft a near-perfect scare machine. The stationary camera, minimalist lighting, and almost nonexistent score make it feel as though this could actually be some sort of snuff film. As macabre and disturbing as anything that's ever been made, *The Texas Chainsaw Massacre* is a true horror classic.

Synopsis:

Five friends take a road trip through the backroads of Texas to find out if their grandfather's grave has been desecrated. They then make a side trip to their grandfather's now-deserted farm. Along the way they pick up a creepy, half-crazed hitchhiker who cuts himself and one of them. After dropping him off, they proceed to the farm. While there, two of them slip off to a nearby swimming hole. When they hear a generator running nearby, they conclude that maybe they can purchase some gas from the neighbors. However, things quickly go afoul as the neighbors are the ghoulish Leatherface and his clan of crazed, cannibalistic in-breeds, who have more than a few surprises in store for the young travelers.

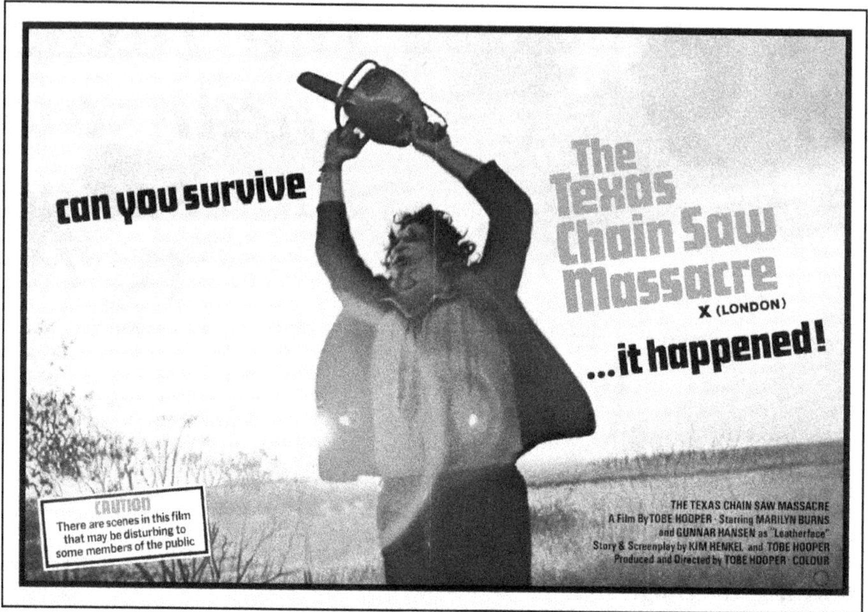

Scariest scene:

This film is filled to the brim with scary moments. Virtually every single scene that takes place inside Leatherface's creepy, bone-covered, dead animal-strewn old shack could be considered a frightening scene. However, two of these scenes stand out as the most disturbing. The first is the gruesome scene in which Pam is hung from a meat hook and forced to watch her boyfriend being chopped up with a chainsaw. The second and perhaps even more effective scene is the famed dinner scene in which Sally is subjected to the family's maddening hoots and hollers, and is then bopped over the head a few times with grandpa's hammer.

Memorable dialogue:

> **NARRATOR:** The film which you are about to see is an account of the tragedy which befell a group of five youths, in particular Sally Hardesty and her invalid brother, Franklin. It is all the more tragic in that they were young. But, had they lived very, very long lives, they could not have expected nor would they have wished to see as much of the mad and macabre as they were to see that day. For them an idyllic summer after-

noon drive became a nightmare. The events of that day were to lead to the discovery of one of the most bizarre crimes in the annals of American history, The Texas Chainsaw Massacre.

Did you know?

After actor John Dugan decided that he would not don the old-man makeup more than once, the cast and crew were forced to shoot out all of his scenes in a single 36-hour block. Most of the time was used to film the dinner table scene. Because the temperature was more than 100 degrees and there was no air conditioning, the actors had to endure the stench of rotting meat and body odor, as well as a lack of sleep. Allegedly a number of crew members passed out during the shoot. Actor Edwin Neal would later say that the experience was even worse than his time in Vietnam as a young soldier.

Cast:

Marilyn Burns (Sally Hardesty), Allen Danzinger (Jerry), Paul A. Partain (Franklin Hardesty), William Vail (Kirk), Teri McMinn (Pam), Edwin Neal (Hitchhiker), Jim Siedow (Old Man), Gunnar Hansen (Leatherface), John Dugan (Grandfather), Robert Courtin (Window Washer).

What the critics say:

Krysten Syxx, *Dread Central*: "Who the hell would have thought that a simple movie about a few kids in a van being murdered one by one could have such an impact on the horror genre? The combination of low budget filmmaking, a terrifying madman with a chainsaw, and the grittiness make the film so much fun. The plot keeps everything basic. There's no back story or explanation as to why there are cannibals eating anyone who wanders into sight. Leatherface is a giant child who likes to wear the skins of his victims, and that's all you need to know, goddammit. This is the sort of domain in which the newer *Chainsaw* films fail. We don't need things laid out for us; we just want to see some craziness with crazy people."

Sam Adams, *The Philadelphia City Paper*: "If you haven't seen it in a while, here's a reminder: It's really fucking scary. Horror movies long ago had the horror taken out of them, but the gritty physicality of *Texas Chainsaw* is all too terrifyingly real. Shot through with Watergate-era malaise, it's a chilling portrait of a nation with nowhere to hide, where selfish hippies are preyed upon by maniac rednecks in a world devoid of order. Hysterical, excessive and, oh yes, a masterpiece."

Michael Dequina, *The Movie Report*: "Hooper is no bloodthirsty hack (or at least he wasn't at this stage of his career); the film's intense final half achieves its unshakable effect through a combination of things (creepy characters; unsettling imagery and editing; a spare, ominous score; star Marilyn Burns' inescapable screams) *aside* from graphic gore. The film's low-budget 16mm look just adds to the grimy atmosphere, creating the illusion of an underground snuff film."

If you liked this, you might also like:

Three on a Meathook (1972).

#10 The Omen (1976)

Good morning. You are one day closer to the end of the world. You have been warned.

Why it made the list:

The Omen is one of the most frightening films ever made because it touches us all, deep down, in that little spot where the butterflies hang out before they attack our stomach. It is dread in its purest form. Although the entire premise of the film is little more than a prequel to the Biblical Revelations, even non-Christian audiences find themselves enthralled and terrified because The Omen is bigger than a devil or a demon, it is the promise of a dystopian future. The big picture, of this picture, is one of secrecy and conspiracy. What happens behind all of our backs has implications on our everyday lives. Secret societies place Earth's future despot in a place of power and protect him using a network of devotees that reach higher than many of us will ever dream? No, what could be terrifying about that? Furthermore, *The Omen* ensures us that it is supernatural, it will be hell on Earth, it is all happening right now and THERE IS NOTHING WE CAN DO ABOUT IT. Nothing. We are lulled into a false sense of justice by the efforts of Robert Thorn, but it is futile. We are doomed.

Synopsis:

The U.S. Ambassador to Great Britain, Robert Thorn (Gregory Peck), and his wife (Lee Remick) live an idyllic life born of old money. He was successful and she was pregnant and on the verge of the perfect family. Katherine's child is stillborn and Thorn is approached by an enigmatic priest who offers a healthy child from a poor family to raise in the stead of his own child. Thorn agrees. As the child, Damien (Harvey Stephens), grows, strange events happen around the youth. With the aid of a photographer and demonologist, Thorn is unconvinced that his child is the Antichrist and must be destroyed at all costs … until the mysterious death of his wife. The fate of the world hangs in the balance.

Scariest scene:

The Omen is one of those films that not only has multiple terrifying scenes, but they build upon one another like a freight train barreling down on you. This results in so much built-up tension that the viewer isn't allowed a cathartic release. It builds and builds, all the way through the moment in the church as Robert Thorn has a knife poised over Damien's body, ready to sacrifice his son, as the police burst in ready to stop Thorn because they just don't know and we… cut to black. Quiet. Nothing. Fade in to a funeral. We don't know whose funeral it is. Thorn? Damien? We realize soon enough that Damien has survived and then we are doomed. The boy turns, stares straight into the camera, and the frame freezes. The Antichrist just stares… at us! Shiver-inducing.

Memorable dialogue:

> **NANNY**: Damien! Damien! Damien, look at me! I'm over here! Damien, I love you.
>
> **DAMIEN**: Look. There's Nanny.
>
> **NANNY**: Look at me, Damien. It's all for you!
>
> *Nanny steps off the ledge and hangs herself.*

Did you know?

Gregory Peck reportedly took the role of an anguished, guilt-ridden father due to the suicide of his son Jonathan in 1975.

Cast:

Gregory Peck (Robert Thorn), Lee Remick (Katherine Thorn), David Warner (Keith Jennings), Billie Whitelaw (Mrs. Baylock), Harvey Spencer Stephens (Damien Thorn), Patrick Troughton (Father Brennan), Martin

Benson (Father Spiletto), Leo McKern (Carl Bugenhagen), Robert Rietti (Monk), Holly Palance (Nanny).

What the critics say:

Roger Ebert, *Chicago Sun-Times*: "What Jesus was to the 1950s movie epic, the devil is to the 1970s, and so all of this material is approached with the greatest solemnity, not only in the performances but also in the photography, the music and the very looks on people's faces."

Allan Bacchus, *Daily Film Dose*: "*The Omen* is my favourite horror film of all time. It scared the hell out of me as a kid, and still gives me the shivers today. At the time *The Omen* was made riding on the success of *The Exorcist* three years earlier… in my mind, hands down, *The Omen* is better."

Bill Gibron, *Pop Matters*: "*The Omen* doesn't need outside signs of malevolence to be a macabre masterwork. As the recent repugnant remake from 2006 proved, a good idea is nothing without expert execution and a cast who can deliver it. By keeping things subtle and serious, as well as allowing Damien to be a little boy, not a telegraphed entity of evil, this director found the right tone for his terribly effective film."

If you liked this, you might also like:

The Bad Seed (1956).

#11 *Rosemary's Baby* (1968)

Pray for Rosemary's baby.

Why it made the list:

Although everyone has their own opinion on director Roman Polanski, one cannot deny the haunting piece of cinema he created in the very quiet, and very creepy, *Rosemary's Baby*. A majority of the film takes place in a gothic high rise in New York populated by seemingly ordinary people... but, like any good scare yarn, therein lies the rub! The 1970s became the decade of the devil with films like *The Exorcist* and *The Omen* ripping through but Polanksi's opus kicked that off in 1968. Even with luminary competition, Rosemary Woodhouse is our girl and her ordeal, paced like a ghost story and building like she really is carrying Satan's child, gets under our skin. Audiences were lulled into being terrified. It crept up on them and built to a harrowing climax ... with inevitable results.

Synopsis:

Rosemary Woodhouse (Mia Farrow) is a young housewife to struggling actor Guy Woodhouse (John Cassavetes) and they have moved into a massive, gothic apartment building in New York. There they meet their neighbors, an older couple, Roman and Minnie Castevet (Ruth Gordon and Sydney Blackmer), that want nothing more than to have young people to dote over. Guy and Rosemary are trying to get pregnant and that becomes the sole guiding force for Ruth Gordon as the nosy, pushy, well-meaning neighbor. Things turn dark quickly. After being given a strange root tea, Rosemary hallucinates her insemination by, ostensibly, the devil as the old couple, Guy, and many others chant around her in robes. She awakes to find that she is pregnant after all. Mysteriously, Guy's acting career takes off after a tragic accident befalls a competitor and the neighbors take great pains to ensure that Rosemary's pregnancy is easy and free of all other concerns as they close her off from the world. Rosemary slowly discovers more and more inconsistencies in the explanations and creepiness of everyone around her. Then the bodies start to pile up. Rosemary comes to the conclusion that these people are after her baby, not even thinking for one moment that maybe she wasn't hallucinating after all.

Scariest scene:

Director Roman Polanksi put together an incredibly unsettling scene as a drugged Rosemary is raped by Satan himself. With the appearance and vibe of a student film, he effectively surrounded Rosemary by the Satanist cult (lead by a naked Ruth Gordon… see, I said it was scary). The scene is quiet, too. It doesn't need to be loud. It doesn't need to be gory… it unsettles. Naked, Rosemary is offered up to the devil and the beast incarnate mounts up and does his deed as Rosemary stares into the blackness. The anguish is in her lack of emotion juxtaposed with the exultation of the elderly Satanists. Creepy.

Memorable dialogue:

> **ROSEMARY:** What have you done to him? What have you done to his eyes, you maniacs!
>
> **ROMAN:** He has his father's eyes!
>
> **ROSEMARY:** What do you mean? Guy's eyes are normal!

Did you know?

In a tragically bizarre life/art conundrum, Roman Polanski was visiting Europe working on a film after the June 12 release of *Rosemary's Baby.* His wife, actress Sharon Tate, stayed in Los Angeles and was visiting with friends on the night of August 8th. She was eight-and-one-half-months pregnant. That evening, members of Charles Manson's infamous Manson Family broke into the Polanski home and slaughtered all of the occupants… including Tate. The crime scene was gruesome; the worst many police officers had ever seen. Some of them even equated it to looking at a horror movie.

Cast:

Mia Farrow (Rosemary Woodhouse), John Cassavetes (Guy Woodhouse), Ruth Gordon (Minnie Castevet), Roman Castevet (Sydney Blackmer), Maurice Evans (Hutch), Ralph Bellamy (Dr. Sapirstein), Victoria Vetri (Terry), Patsy Kelly (Laura-Louise), Elisha Cook Jr. (Mr. Nicklas), Emmaline Henry (Elise Dunstan), Charles Grodin (Dr. Hill).

What the critics say:

Andrew Sarris, *New York Observer*: "Having escaped the horrors of the Nazi Holocaust in Poland by the skin of his teeth, Mr. Polanski was well equipped psychologically to re-imagine what was, before *Rosemary's Baby*, a B-picture genre into an A-picture genre."

Noel Murray, *The AV Club*: "Polanski (who also wrote the screenplay, closely following Levin's novel) is more interested in creating a creeping sense of unease by making everything seem plausible."

Mark Harris, *Entertainment Weekly*: "Polanski worked with an elegant restraint that less talented filmmakers have been trying to mimic ever since."

If you liked this, you might also like:

Incubus (1982).

#12 *Jaws* (1975)

Don't go in the water.

Why it made the list:

Jaws did for swimming what *Psycho* did for showers (while ushering in the era of the blockbuster summer event). A large degree of the film's suspense comes from the fact that *Jaws* isn't revealed until after the first hour of the film! Add to the tension an all-star cast, (including a stand-out performance by Robert Shaw as the grizzled Captain Quint), the amazing directorial abilities of Steven Spielberg at his zenith, and the now legendary score by John Williams, and it combines to make this film one of the greatest horror films ever made.

Synopsis:

As the people of the small summer resort Amity Island prepare its beaches for the fourth of July bash, the police chief, a marine biologist, and a sea captain for hire race against time to kill a great white shark menacing the waters surrounding the island.

Scariest scene:

Brody, Hooper, and Quint come across the wreckage of a fisherman's boat while tangling with Jaws. Hooper goes aboard to see if the fisherman survived. During his search he happens to peer through a glass bottom portion of the boat and is shocked when the fisherman's badly mangled head bumps the glass.

Memorable dialogue:

> **QUINT:** Y'all know me. Know how I earn a livin'. I'll catch this bird for you, but it ain't gonna be easy. Bad fish. Not like going down the pond chasin' bluegills and tommycods. This shark, swallow you whole. Little shakin', little tenderizin', an' down you go. And we gotta do it quick, that'll bring back your tourists, put all your businesses on a payin' basis. But it's not gonna be pleasant. I value my neck a lot more than three thousand bucks, chief. I'll find him for three, but I'll catch him, and kill him, for ten. But you've gotta make up your minds. If you want to stay alive, then ante up. If you want to play it cheap, be on welfare the whole winter. I don't want no volunteers, I don't want no mates, there's just too many captains on this island. Ten thousand dollars for me by myself. For that you get the head, the tail, the whole damn thing.

Did you know?

The mechanical shark spent most of the movie broken-down, and was unavailable for certain shots. This led Spielberg to use the camera as the "shark," and film from the shark's point of view. Many think this added to the "chilling/haunting" quality in the final release saying that it would have made it too "cheesy" had they shown the shark as much as originally planned.

Cast:

Roy Scheider (Chief Martin Brody), Robert Shaw (Sam Quint), Richard Dreyfuss (Matt Hooper), Lorraine Gary (Ellen Brody), Murray Hamilton (Mayor Larry Vaughn), Carl Gottlieb (Meadows), Jeffrey Kramer (Hendricks), Susan Backlinie (Christine 'Chrissie' Watkins), Jonathan Filley (Cassidy), Chris Rebello (Michael Brody).

What the critics say:

A.D. Murphy, *Variety*: "Getting right to the point, *Jaws* is an artistic and commercial smash. Producers Richard D. Zanuck and David Brown, and director Steven Spielberg, have the satisfaction of a production problem-plagued film turning out beautifully. Peter Benchley's bestseller about a killer shark and a tourist beach town has become a film of consummate suspense, tension, and terror. The Universal release looks like a torrid moneymaker everywhere."

Staff, *TV Guide*: "From the outrageously frightening opening—in which a beautiful young woman skinny-dipping in the moonlight is devoured by the unseen shark—to the claustrophobic climax aboard Quint's fishing boat, Spielberg has us in his grip and rarely lets go. "

Richard Corliss, *Time*: "Spielberg works self-effacingly, with subtly correct camera placement and meticulous editing. He twists our guts with false alarms, giving us the real thing with heart-stopping suddenness."

If you liked this, you might also like:

Alligator (1980).

#13 Carnival of Souls (1962)

This is the shocking story of a girl who crawled from a river to race to a nightmare. Walking the tightrope between heaven and hell. From the unreal she crashes through to reality.

Why it made the list:

Industrial and educational film director Herk Harvey made *Carnival of Souls* his one and only theatrical release. For reasons largely unknown, Harvey stepped away from his normal routine to create a low-rent but awfully stylish horror film. It's a shame that Harvey didn't continue on this path, as *Carnival of Souls* shows him to be a talented director with a flair for the grim and the offbeat.

For audiences in 1962 (primarily the raucous drive-in crowd), *Carnival of Souls* delivered a creepy and crawly story full of dark and dank atmosphere. The film was the antithesis of standard teen date fare, which might have included such cheapie potboilers as *13 Ghosts*, *The Brainiac*, or *Atom Age Vampire*. As it stands, Herk Harvey's lone voyage into feature filmmaking resulted in a minor masterpiece of well-constructed spooks and scares.

Synopsis:

Pretty but shy, Mary Henry (Candace Hilligoss) takes a car ride with two of her girl friends. Along the way, they are coaxed into a drag race that ends with the girl's car plunging into a river. The three are presumed dead, but days later Mary emerges from the car and the river.

Undaunted by her near-death experience, Mary carries on with life and takes a job in Utah as a church organist. In route to her new home, she passes a vacant amusement park that holds an alarming lure for her. While driving that same night, a grisly-looking apparition (Herk Harvey) appears in her windshield. Once settled in Utah, Mary will be visited time and time again by this odd and persistent phantom.

Things are very peculiar in Utah, and ultimately not to Mary's liking. Her landlady (Frances Feist) is too nosey. Her employer (Art Ellison) is insistent that she attend church when not on the clock. Then lastly, her male neighbor (Sidney Berger), the classic slobbering letch, puts the moves on her. All the while Mary seems to be slipping in and out of reality. It's enough to send a girl over the edge, and it does.

Desperately searching for anything more palatable than her new surroundings and its inhabitants, Mary takes to the highway in her car. She finds herself at the neglected theme park she'd felt strangely drawn to only days earlier. Here, Mary finds her destiny amongst a group of the dancing dead. They are the carnival of souls and they've been waiting for Mary to accept her place with them.

Scariest scene:

Mary Henry's journey into the deserted amusement park exposing a room filled with pasty-faced zombies dancing in the night takes the prize. It's hardly a shocking moment, but a rather weird and sinister sequence that begins as an ethereal POV shot. Mary slowly walks towards the festivities revealing the film's true horror; Mary is very much a part of this ghoulish shindig, the carnival of souls.

Memorable dialogue:

> **MARY:** It's funny … the world is so different in the daylight. In the dark, your fantasies get so out of hand, but in the daylight everything falls back into place again.

Did you know?

The film's centerpiece, the abandoned fun park, was actually the Saltair Amusement Park in Salt Lake City, Utah. This particular version of the park burned down in the 1970's and was reconstructed in the 80's, only to be flooded out and rebuilt again in 1993.

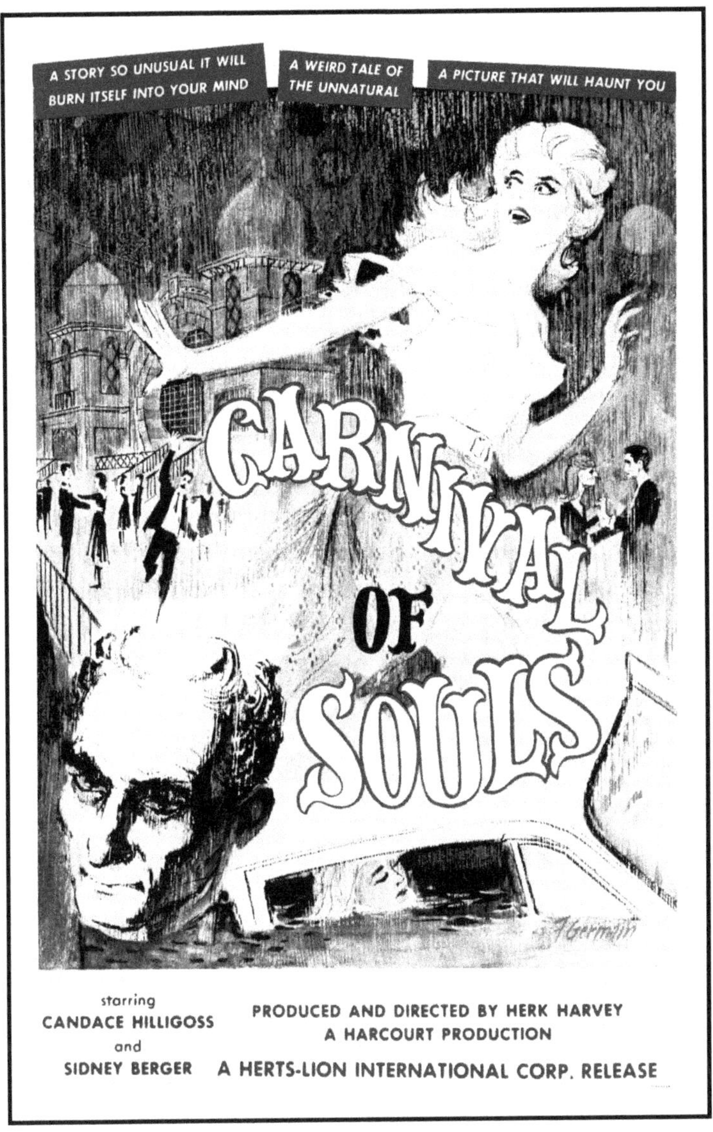

A STORY SO UNUSUAL IT WILL BURN ITSELF INTO YOUR MIND
A WEIRD TALE OF THE UNNATURAL
A PICTURE THAT WILL HAUNT YOU
CARNIVAL OF SOULS
starring
CANDACE HILLIGOSS
and
SIDNEY BERGER
PRODUCED AND DIRECTED BY HERK HARVEY
A HARCOURT PRODUCTION
A HERTS-LION INTERNATIONAL CORP. RELEASE

Cast:

Candace Hilligoss (Mary Henry), Frances Feist (Mrs. Thomas, Landlady), Sidney Berger (John Linden), Art Ellison (Minister), Herk Harvey (Zombie Man), Stan Levitt (Dr. Samuels), Larry Sneegas (Drag Racer), Cari Conboy (Lake Zombie), T.C. Adams (Dancing Zombie), Sharon Scoville (Mary's Girlfriend), Mary Ann Harris (Mary's Girlfriend), Peter Schnitzler (A Walking Corpse), Bill Sollner (Lake Zombie).

What the critics say:

Jonathan Ross, *The Incredibly Strange Film Book*: "Strange to think that a little film, written around a couple of key locations and with a first time cast, writer, and director should be one of the most lyrical and memorable horror films ever. But it is."

Roger Ebert, *Chicago Sun-Times*: "Unlike most of today's horror movies, *Carnival of Souls* has few special effects—some wavy lines as we pass through various levels of existence, and that's it. Instead, it depends on crisp black-and-white photography, atmosphere and surprisingly effective acting."

Joe Bob Briggs, *The Joe Bob Report*: "It's a zombie movie. In fact, the star of the movie, Candace Hilligoss, is the most beautiful zombie ever to appear in a zombie movie. The fun of the movie is that you're never really sure when she's being a zombie and when she's just being a ditzy stuffed-shirt church organist."

If you liked this, you might also like:

Cat People (1942).

#14 *Evil Dead II* (1987)

The sequel to the ultimate experience in grueling terror.

Why it made the list:

Sam Raimi's high-octane sequel to his cult classic *The Evil Dead* is the exception to the rule in that it's a sequel that's actually better than the original film. Credit Raimi's hyperkinetic swooping cameras, goofy but effective special effects, quick editing, a bravura slapstick performance by lead actor Bruce Campbell, and a wacky screenplay (co-written with Scott Spiegel) for the film's success. Raimi takes a no-holds barred approach to storytelling here, presenting us with a film in which literally *anything* can happen. *Evil Dead 2* accomplishes an even more spectacular feat in that it manages to be both comedic and frightening. It's as if Raimi took *The Texas Chainsaw Massacre* and mixed it in a pot with a few Three Stooges shorts; the result of this cinematic gumbo is a wildly-entertaining romp the likes of which horror has rarely seen.

Synopsis:

The film imagines that Ash (Bruce Campbell) never went to that creepy old cabin in the woods in the first film. Here Ash and his new gal pal Linda (Denice Bixler) stop off at the same seemingly-deserted cabin in search of a good time. Ash once again discovers a reel-to-reel tape player and makes the mistake of pressing "play." The voice of now-dead archaeology Professor Raymond Knowby starts to recite an incantation from *Necronomicon Ex-Mortis* (the "Book of the Dead") on the tape, which once again causes evil spirits to emerge from the forest and descend upon the unsuspecting couple.

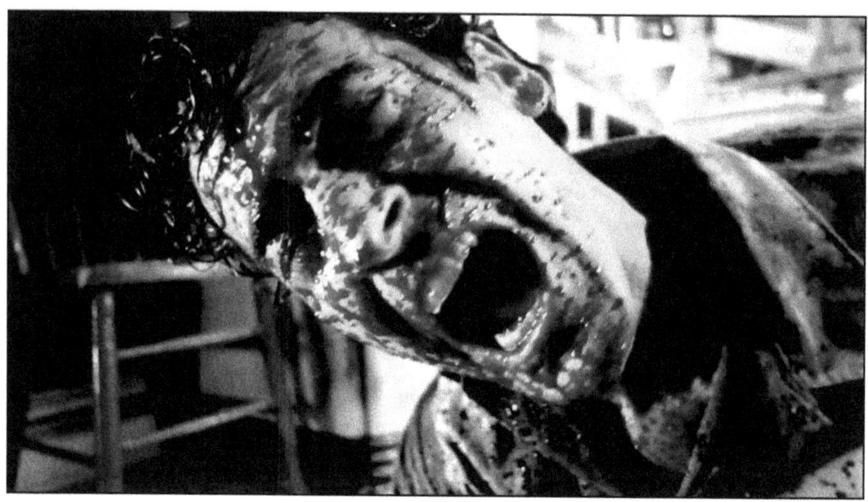

Scariest scene:

Evil Dead 2 is a film that's brimming with cinematic creepiness from start to finish. Its consistency in delivering jolts and horrific atmospherics makes selecting a single most frightening scene somewhat of a chore. However, if we were pressed to select one and only one, we'd have to go with the possessed Henrietta's attack on Ash in the fruit cellar. "I'll swallow your soul!" she threatens. "I'll swallow your soul!" And who can forget her promise that Ash and company will be "dead by dawn" later in the movie?

Memorable dialogue:

> **ANNIE:** In 1300 A.D. they called this man the "hero from the sky." He was prophesied to have destroyed the evil.
>
> **ASH:** He didn't do a very good job.

Did you know?

After Ash chops off his possessed hand, he traps it inside a canister and places a stack of books on top of it to weigh it down. The book on the top is Ernest Hemingway's *A Farewell to Arms.* This is, of course, a wink to the audience regarding Ash's now-severed appendage.

Cast:

Bruce Campbell (Ash), Sarah Berry (Annie Knowby), Dan Hicks (Jake), Kassie Wesley DePaiva (Bobby Joe), Ted Raimi (Posessed Henrietta), Denise Bixler (Linda), Richard Domeier (Ed Getley), John Peakes (Professor Raymond Knowby), Lou Hancock (Henrietta Knowby), Snowy Winters (Dancer).

What the critics say:

Richard Harrington, *Washington Post*: "Sam Raimi's *Evil Dead 2* is a scream of consciousness, a goremonger's nightmare, and so what if it's an almost exact replica of its predecessor, one of the most successful (and, believe it or not, critically acclaimed) films in the horror-gore genre. With their virtually nonstop geysers of blood, dismemberments and ghastly ugliness, (the Evil Dead are not high on personal hygiene), these films are not for the faint-hearted or lily-livered—and definitely not for children."

Caryn Jaymes, *New York Times*: "*Evil Dead 2* is genuine, if bizarre, proof of Sam Raimi's talent and developing skill. But it is definitely not for the squeamish; its ideal audience would be full of Three Stooges fans with streaks of grotesque humor."

Staff, *TV Guide*: "A deliriously cinematic experience for those with a taste for Grand Guignol, this is a relentlessly energetic nightmare world where quite literally anything can happen—and does. By pushing the events to an absurd extreme, the film frequently leaves the realm of horror and becomes a cartoon gone mad. Animation director Tex Avery is a stronger influence here than the German Expressionists or modern masters of horror. Campbell's admirably straight-faced performance suggests a modern-day Harold Lloyd trapped in a splatter film spinning madly out of control."

If you liked this, you might also like:

Army of Darkness (1992).

#15 Nosferatu (1922)

A symphony of horror!

Why it made the list:

F.W. Murnau's 1922 *Dracula* rip-off is as creepy as anything ever filmed and remains one of the premier German Expressionist films. Anyone who doubts the effectiveness of silent films would be encouraged to watch this brooding atmospheric gem. Almost a century later, *Nosferatu* remains one of the finest *Dracula* adaptations, even if Bram Stoker wasn't properly credited. Note the dramatic effect of the shadows and low angles utilized by cinematographer Fritz Arno Wagner, which make the vampire appear to loom large over his surroundings. *Nosferatu* is easily one of the greatest silent horror films ever produced, and, depending on which version of the film you watch—different versions have different scores—the film can be as effective today as it was in 1922.

Synopsis:

A German real estate agent dispatches an associate to Count Orlok's (Max Schreck) castle in Transylvania to discuss an isolated home the count wishes to purchase. Hutter (Gustav von Wangenheim), the associate, sells the home to the count, but then begins to experience several strange occurrences. Hutter soon comes to the realization that Orlok is a vampire, but it may be too late. Soon Orlok, hiding in a shipment of coffins, will make his way to Germany, leaving a trail of dead bodies in his wake.

Scariest scene:

When the captain of the ship goes below deck to where Count Orlok's body is being stored, the skipper gets more than he bargained for when

the vampire raises up stiffly and dramatically in the film's most memorably creepy scene. In fact, the captain is so frightened that he jumps overboard to certain death.

Memorable dialogue:

> **KNOCK:** It will cost you sweat and tears, and perhaps… a little blood.

Did you know?

The 2000 film *Shadow of the Vampire*, directed by E. Elias Merhige, provided a fanciful account of the making of *Nosferatu*. The film, which stars John Malkovich and Willem Dafoe, contends that actor Max Schreck was a real-life vampire who was convinced to appear as an actor.

Cast:

Max Schreck (Count Graf Orlok), Gustav von Wangenheim (Hutter), Greta Schroder (Ellen Hutter), Alexander Granach (Knock), Georg H. Schnell (Westenra), Ruth Landshoff (Lucy), John Gottowt (Professor Bulwer), Gustav Botz (Professor Sievers), Max Nemetz (Ship Captain), Wolfgang Heinz (Matrose 1).

What the critics say:

Staff, *TV Guide*: "It's a truly horrifying and scary film, but it's also frequently poetic and beautiful, using real locations and a naturalistic style to create an overpowering atmosphere of evil. Unlike Murnau's later films, which employed a sensually moving camera and extremely stylized expressionistic sets, *Nosferatu* relies mostly on stark, static compositions, and cinematic tricks, such as jump cuts, sped-up action, stop-motion, negative images, and double-exposures, to show such things as carriages speeding through the night, doors and caskets opening and closing by themselves, and Orlok magically appearing and disappearing, or rising straight up out of his coffin. Murnau creates a visceral sense of fear and menace through the accumulation of subtle details…"

Roger Ebert, *Chicago Sun-Times*: "In a sense, Murnau's film is about all of the things we worry about at three in the morning—cancer, war, disease, madness. It suggests these dark fears in the very style of its visuals. Much of the film is shot in shadow. The corners of the screen are used more than is ordinary; characters lurk or cower there, and it's a rule of composition that tension is created when the subject of a shot is removed from the center of the frame. Murnau's special effects add to the disquieting atmosphere: the fast motion of Orlok's servant, the disappearance of the phantom coach, the manifestation of the count out of thin air, the use of a photographic negative to give us white trees against a black sky."

Dave Kehr, *Chicago Reader*: "A masterpiece of the German silent cinema and easily the most effective version of *Dracula* on record."

If you liked this, you might also like:

Shadow of the Vampire (2000).

#16 Poltergeist (1982)

They're here.

Why it made the list:

Poltergeist is hard at work on several levels, exploring familiar tropes like the banal horrors of suburbia, the child in peril, and the haunted house built on an old graveyard. From drawn out, quiet moments of building tension to explicit gore and finally huge, chaotic set pieces, the film's director, Tobe Hooper, uses every tool in the box to elicit scares, and the script, co-written by Steven Spielberg, provides moments of levity to give the audience a breather before the next shock comes. A perfectly normal family's life is utterly upended by forces beyond their control, and when the beatifically innocent youngest child calmly intones, "They're here," the formerly cheerful, nurturing family home is turned into a house of horrors.

Synopsis:

The Freeling family—parents Steven (Craig T. Nelson) and Diane (JoBeth Williams) and children Dana (Dominique Dunne), Robbie (Oliver Robins), and Carol Anne (Heather O'Rourke)—live a perfectly normal life in the perfectly normal planned community of Cuesta Verde. Steven works for the developer of the community that built the suburb, and Diane is a stay-at-home mom. One night, after Steven falls asleep in front of the television after sign-off, Carol Anne wakes and comes downstairs, drawn to the static on the screen. She begins speaking to the television, causing her parents some concern. The next night, a large storm rolls in, and both Carol Anne and Robbie go to spend the night in their parents' bedroom. Again, Carol Anne is drawn to the static on the television after the rest of the family is asleep. This time, an apparition appears, shooting from the television and striking the wall of the bedroom. What feels like a minor earthquake then shakes the house, waking the family. Carol Anne then tells them, simply, that, "They're here." Soon the family is dealing with furniture that moves on its own, twisted silverware, and perfectly good drinking glasses suddenly breaking. For the Freeling family, the nightmare has only just begun.

Scariest scene:

The scares build and build throughout *Poltergeist*, culminating in a fantastic, thrilling final confrontation between the family and the powerful forces that inhabit their home. As the unquiet dead burst from the ground, the being known only as "The Beast" makes its presence fully known in a memorable, masterful sequence.

Memorable dialogue:

> **DIANE:** Sweetheart, last night, when you said, "They're here ..."
>
> **CAROL ANNE:** Can I take my goldfish to school?
>
> **DIANE:** Sweetheart, do you remember last night when you woke up, and you said, "They're here"?
>
> **CAROL ANNE:** Uh huh.
>
> **DIANE:** Who did you mean?
>
> **ROBBIE:** She's stoned.
>
> **DANA:** Oh yeah? What do you know about it?
>
> **ROBBIE:** More than you. Ask Dad.

Did you know?

The production crew used real human skeletons in the final scenes because they were cheaper to procure than producing fake ones.

Cast:

Craig T. Nelson (Steven Freeling), JoBeth Williams (Diane Freeling), Beatrice Straight (Dr. Lesh), Dominique Dunne (Dana Freeling), Oliver Robins (Robbie Freeling), Heather O'Rourke (Carol Anne Freeling), Michael McManus (Ben Tuthill), Martin Casella (Marty), Richard Lawson (Ryan), Zelda Rubenstein (Tangina Barrons).

What the critics say:

Vincent Canby, *New York Times*: "*Poltergeist* is like a thoroughly enjoyable nightmare, one that you know that you can always wake up from, and one in which, at the end, no one has permanently been damaged. It's also witty in a fashion that Alfred Hitchcock might have appreciated."

Roger Ebert, *Chicago Sun Times*: "Hooper and Spielberg hold our interest by observing the everyday rituals of this family so closely that, since the family seems real, the weird events take on a certain credibility by association."

Dave Kehr, *Chicago Reader*: "Though the shocks are well conveyed, it's the sweetness that lingers, making this the first cute and cuddly entry in the genre."

If you liked this, you might also like:

Poltergeist II: The Other Side (1986).

#17 *Aliens* (1986)

Somewhere in deepest space all hell is breaking loose.
This time it's war.

Why it made the list:

Nearly 30 years after its initial release, *Aliens* still clocks in as one of the greatest cinematic thrill rides of the science fiction genre. James Cameron's sequel to Ridley Scott's surprise success *Alien* ups the ante in nearly every conceivable manner. There's more action, suspense, high-tech gadgetry, slime, goo and glop and with the additional slime, goo and glop comes more and more aliens.

Synopsis:

Years later, after narrowly surviving her first alien ordeal on the planet LV-426, Ellen Ripley (Sigourney Weaver) and her ship the *Nostromo* are intercepted. Ripley is awakened from her hypersleep only to be appalled by the amount of skepticism leveled at her and her tale of slime-oozing, murdering extra-terrestrials. Ripley is also appalled to discover that, while in her deep space slumber, the planet she barely escaped has been colonized.

Ripley's employer, the Weyland-Yutani Corporation, had seized the opportunity to inhabit and exploit her old stomping ground and war zone, Planet LV-426. The planet was, for some time, successfully undergoing modifications to mirror the Earth's atmosphere, temperature, and surface topography. Sadly, things have taken a turn for the worst and all communication with the altered planet and its colony have currently been lost.

Lieutenant Gorman (William Hope) of the Colonial Marines implores Ripley to accompany Weland-Yutani representative Carter Burke (Paul Reiser) on an investigation of the wayward planet. The two will be

ALIENS

flanked by a unit of space marines lead by Sergeant Apone (Al Matthews) and Corporal Dwayne Hicks (Michael Biehn). Also in tow is an android called Bishop (Lance Henriksen).

Still mortified by her previous rendezvous with the disagreeable space assailants, Ripley swiftly declines the offer. Later, she accepts their proposal when convinced and assured that any remaining aliens will be destroyed rather than brought back to Earth for studies and examinations. To the good ship *Sulaco*, and into outer space the team goes. Once upon the surface of LV-426, the expedition begins and uncovers the colony has been abandoned, except for one young girl nicknamed "Newt" (Carrie Henn). Upon further inspection of the planet, a large alien nest is found. This nest is home to cocoons of some sort or another, and contain the remainder of the lost colonists.

The aliens are not the least bit impressed by what they consider space invaders and begin a violent attack upon the human intruders. More and more aliens pop up and more and more humans die. In the end, Ripley is forced to use her prowess as an airlock operator to rid herself of yet another pesky space critter.

Scariest scene:

The last hour of *Aliens* is a full-blown cinematic attack on the viewer. However, when the queen alien impales and eviscerates Bishop, all bets are off. We have a winner.

Memorable dialogue:

> **RIPLEY:** Bishop, how much time?
>
> **BISHOP:** Plenty. Twenty-six minutes!
>
> **RIPLEY:** We're not leaving!
>
> **BISHOP:** We're not?

Did you know?

The producers of *Aliens* apparently found the $18 million budget so crippling that only six hypersleep chambers could be constructed at $4,300 each. The remaining six chambers would have to be created by the use of mirrors and clever editing. So the assumption is that if another $26,000 had been spent on these props, the production would have been brought to a grinding halt. Meanwhile, Sigourney Weaver was paid a cool one million dollars for her efforts.

Cast:

Sigourney Weaver (Ellen Ripley), Carrie Henn (Rebecca 'Newt' Jorden), Michael Biehn (Cpl. Dwayne Hicks), Paul Reiser (Carter Burke), Lance Henriksen (Bishop), Bill Paxton (Pvt. Hudson), Jenette Goldstein (Pvt. Vasquez), William Hope (Lt. Gorman), Al Matthews (Sgt. Apone), Mark Rolston (Pvt. Drake).

What the critics say:

Roger Ebert, *Chicago Sun-Times*: "The ads for *Aliens* claim that this movie will frighten you as few movies have, and, for once, the ads don't lie."

Anthony Lane, *The New Yorker*: "[T]he result is a formidable acceleration of all the fears that lurked in the first film: the frigidity of [Ridley] Scott's detached and spooky manner is replaced by the relentlessness of a racing heart. Action thrillers assail but rarely test us; this is the tautest, most provoking, and altogether most draining example ever made."

Jay Boyar, *Orlando Sentinel*: "*Aliens* is one of the most intensely shocking films to open in ages. Even if you think you've got the stamina for cinematic suspense, you may find yourself out in the lobby, midway, catching your breath. This film is also the best monster movie of the year and the best picture of any kind to open so far this summer. Put it another way: *Aliens* is the *Jaws* of the '80s."

If you liked this, you might also like:

Screamers (1995).

#18 The Fog (1980)

Lock your doors. Bolt your windows. There's something in The Fog!

Why it made the list:

John Carpenter, the mastermind behind *Halloween*, followed up his slasher-opus with this creepy ghost story set in coastal California. This film oozes not only fog, but phantasm as Carpenter sets us up again with a heroine we love and sticks her all by herself right at the epicenter of danger. We are greeted with some wide, expansive shots that should make the viewer feel free and safe… but not for long. As that fog rolls in, and something rolls in with it, that freedom is choked off. John Carpenter is the only director alive that can make the California coast feel as closed in as a tomb. Claustrophobia and the inability to escape pervade this film, visually and thematically.

Synopsis:

Antonio Bay, California, is celebrating the town's 100th anniversary. This centenary celebration is met with a mix of skepticism and happiness by the residents. Local DJ, Stevie Wayne (Adrienne Barbeau), views the proceedings as nothing more than small town hijinks… but the truth is about to be revealed. The town was founded on the backs and blood of others and a deep dark secret from the past is making its way to Antonio Bay 100 years later. The iconic lighthouse, the historical marker of the town, is the target of a supernatural attack, as are the citizens of Antonio Bay. As the descendants of the town's founders, and everyone else who dares get in the way, are slaughtered gruesomely by vengeful spirits. The priest (Hal Holbrook), historian (John Houseman) and other townfolk (including Charles Cyphers, Nancy Loomis and Carpenter Girl, Jamie Lee Curtis) are all menaced by the ghosts of the crew of the 100-year-old ship "The Elizabeth Dane." Apparently, the Dane was purposefully run aground and the ship's treasure taken by the city forefathers. The crew members have returned as a thick fog during the celebration to exact vengeance and only Stevie, her young son, and a small band of citizens stand in the way of complete annihilation.

Scariest scene:

Father Malone and others trapped in the church are finally facing the full onslaught of Blake, the captain of the Elizabeth Dane, and his ghostly crew. The fog spills in from underneath the doors, the smallest cracks in the windows, everywhere! Stevie is cornered in the lighthouse at this very moment, menaced by the crew of the Dane as the fog spills around her. As Malone and Elizabeth hide, they discover some of the lost gold from the shipwreck that has been melted into a large crucifix in the church. Led by Blake, the ghosts converge upon the cross as Malone holds it aloft, offering it and himself as sacrifice to the vengeful spirits.

Memorable dialogue:

> **KATHY WILLIAMS:** Sandy, you're the only person I know who can make "Yes, Ma'am" sound like "screw you".
>
> **SANDY FADEL:** Yes, Ma'am.

Did you know?

Many of the character names are those of people that writers Carpenter and Debra Hill worked closely with in the past. Charles Cyphers plays Dan O'Bannon, the name of the co-writer of *Dark Star*. Tom Atkins plays Nick Castle, the name of the young actor who played The Shape (one of many) in *Halloween*. George Flowers plays Tommy Wallace, a long-time collaborator of Carpenter and the director of *Halloween III*.

Cast:
Adrienne Barbeau (Stevie Wayne), Jamie Lee Curtis (Elizabeth Solley), Janet Leigh (Kathy Williams), John Houseman (Machen), Tom Atkins (Nick Castle), James Canning (Dick Baxter), Charles Cyphers (Dan

Bolt Your Doors.
Lock Your Windows.
There's Something
in The Fog!
JOHN CARPENTER'S
THE FOG
JOHN CARPENTER, who startled the world with "Halloween,"
now brings you the ultimate experience in terror.
JOHN CARPENTER'S "THE FOG" A DEBRA HILL PRODUCTION
Starring ADRIENNE BARBEAU, JAMIE LEE CURTIS, JOHN HOUSEMAN and JANET LEIGH as Kathy Williams
and starring HAL HOLBROOK as Father Malone
Produced by DEBRA HILL Written by JOHN CARPENTER and DEBRA HILL Directed by JOHN CARPENTER
Executive Producer CHARLES B. BLOCH an ENTERTAINMENT DISCOVERIES, INC. PRESENTATION
Read the BANTAM Book AVCO EMBASSY PICTURES Release

O'Bannon), Nancy Kyes (Sandy Fadel), Ty Mitchell (Andy), Hal Holbrook (Father Malone).

What the critics say:

Roger Ebert, *Chicago Sun-Times*: "*The Fog* is encouraging… because it contains another demonstration of Carpenter's considerable directing talents. He picked the wrong story, I think, but he directs it with a flourish. "

Clint Morris, *Film Threat*: "Ten remakes wouldn't even surpass this creepy classic's greatness. The definitive horror film."

Noel Murray, *A. V. Club*: "*The Fog* lingers as a crafty and loving assemblage of pulp gimmicks, played out in a location that rivals Hitchcock locales for pure eye-vacation appeal. Then there's the fog itself, which rolls over the cliffs and down the streets of Antonio Bay with inexorable menace, every bit as chilling as it was two decades ago."

If you liked this, you might also like:

Prince of Darkness (1987).

#19 A Nightmare on Elm Street (1984)

If Nancy doesn't wake up screaming, she won't wake up at all.

Why it made the list:

Wes Craven's *A Nightmare on Elm Street* delivers plenty of blood and guts to go along with its disquieting mingling of the characters' dreaming lives and the real world. The iconic Freddy Krueger is all burned flesh and razor fingers, a truly demonic figure taunting and torturing his innocent victims. Craven plays with the audience's perceptions, so we're never quite sure if the characters are awake or asleep, and whether Krueger may be lurking around the next corner, or hiding somewhere in the shadows.

Synopsis:

A group of high school friends begins experiencing vivid, terrifying nightmares. At first, they are written off as merely bad dreams, but the dreams turn real one horrifying night. Tina (Amanda Wyss) is home alone for the night and her best friend Nancy (Heather Langenkamp) is visiting for a sleepover. Tina's boyfriend Rod (Nick Corri) and Nancy's boyfriend Glen (Johnny Depp) also show up. Rod and Tina retire to the bedroom, where Tina, after falling asleep, is once again thrust into a nightmare. This time, however, the nightmare becomes real. As a terrified Rod watches, Tina is murdered in her sleep by some invisible force, gutted and brutalized. Rod escapes through the window and becomes the subject of a citywide manhunt. Nancy doubts Rod's guilt, but her father, the police chief, uses her friendship with Rod to bring him in. Nancy also begins to experience bad dreams, where she is chased by a scarred figure with razor sharp blades on his hand. Nancy, convinced that the adults in town know more about what's happening than they are letting on, confronts her mother, who finally breaks down and tells Nancy the story of Fred Krueger, a child killer who escaped justice only to be burned alive in a boiler room in an act of vigilante justice carried out by the town's parents. Nancy is now certain that Krueger has somehow found a way to return, in dreams, and sets her plan to capture him and drag him into the real world into motion.

Scariest scene:

Tina's death scene is depicted in a gory, surreal manner. Her descent into sleep and dreaming build tension, as she finds herself wandering the streets, stalked by Krueger before he corners her in the dream and attacks. Tina's screams wake Rod, and he can only watch in horror as Tina is thrown about the room and sliced up, though he cannot see who or what is killing her.

Memorable dialogue:

> **NANCY:** The killer's still loose, you know.
>
> **DONALD:** You're saying somebody else killed Tina? Who?

NANCY: I don't know who he is, but he's burned and he wears a weird hat and a red and green sweater, really dirty. And he uses these knives, like giant fingernails …

Did you know?

A Nightmare on Elm Street was Johnny Depp's first film.

Cast:

John Saxon (Lt. Donald Thompson), Ronee Blakely (Marge Thompson), Heather Langenkamp (Nancy Thompson), Amanda Wyss (Tina Gray), Nick Corri (Rod Lane), Johnny Depp (Glen Lantz), Charles Fleischer (Dr. King), Joseph Whip (Sgt. Parker), Robert Englund (Freddy Krueger), Lin Shaye (Teacher).

What the critics say:

Staff, *Variety:* "A highly imaginative horror film that provides the requisite shocks to keep fans of the genre happy."

Staff, *Time Out:* "Hard though it is to divorce the image of Fred Krueger from the farrago of a franchise that we now know was to follow, there are some genuinely frightening dream sequences—and some throwaway black humour … it's all good scary fun."

Staff, *TV Guide:* "This movie intelligently probes into the audience's terror of nightmares and combines it with another horrific element—the very real fear of killers in one's own neighborhood. The teenagers in the film, who are paying for the sins of their parents, are not simply fodder for the special-effects crew but have distinct personalities and are independent and intelligent."

If you liked this, you might also like:

Wes Craven's New Nightmare (1994).

#20 *Suspiria* (1977)

The most frightening film you'll ever see!

Why it made the list:

Few films match the level of creepy atmospherics that Dario Argento's masterpiece *Suspiria* achieves. Master filmmaker Argento makes it all seem effortless, squeezing out frame after frame of gooey, evil horror film goodness. Assisted by a haunting score by rock band The Goblins, *Suspiria* looks amazing on the screen, as well. Its vivid blues, reds, and greens dance right off the picture. This is like candy for your eyeballs. The compositions are artful and look like something that should be hanging in the Louvre. This is a film that's low on plot (to say it's thin would be somewhat of an understatement), but it manages to achieve so much on a visceral level. This is that rare horror film that deserves to be shown to up-and-coming filmmakers in Film School 101. There's not much of a story here, but if you're going to tell it, this is the way you go about it.

Synopsis:

American dancer Suzy Bannion (Jessica Harper) arrives in Germany to attend a prestigious ballet academy. When a student is murdered in a grisly fashion on a dark, rainy night, it sets the stage for all that is about to come. As students continue to be murdered nastily, it becomes immediately apparent that something is wrong at the academy. Suzy and her compatriots soon learn the dark truth—that the academy is actually a front for an age-old coven of witches.

Scariest scene:

Although the film is filled with gore-ific scenes of young women being hacked to pieces, its most frightening scene comes from a rather unex-

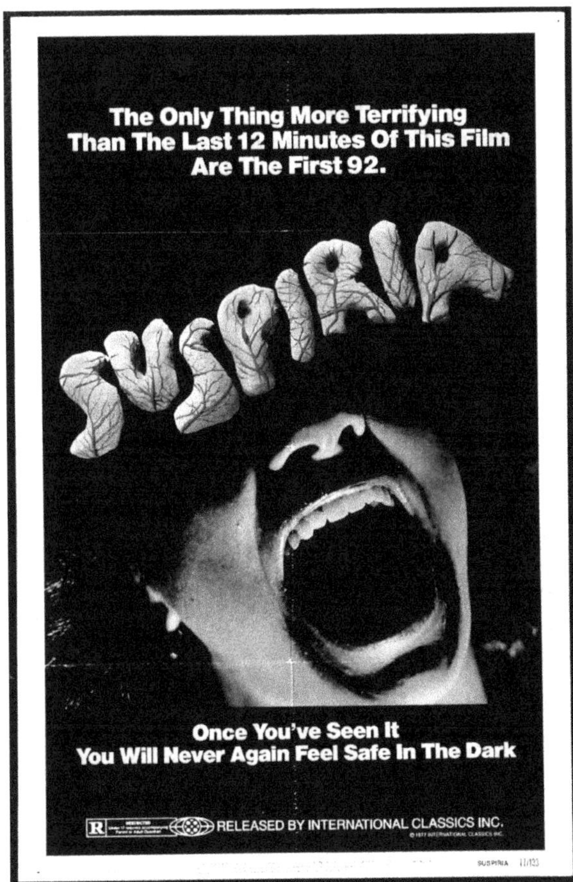

pected source. When Daniel (Flavio Bucci), a blind man, walks through the empty courtyard at night with his dog, the music builds a creepy tension that is almost maddening. The dog continues to bark at God knows what, and Daniel weakly asks, "Who's there?" And all of this tension ultimately pays off when Daniel's dog unexpectedly mauls him and eats him.

Memorable dialogue:

> **HELENA MARKOS:** I've been expecting you! The American girl! I knew you'd come. You want to kill me! You want to kill Helena Markos! You to kill me! You wanted to kill me! What are you gonna do now? Now death is coming for you! You wanted to kill Helena Markos! Hell is behind that door! You're going to meet death now—the living dead!

Did you know?

Dario Argento originally conceived the film to be about a ballet school for pre-teens. However, both the studio and the film's producers refused to make such a picture, knowing that such a film about young children would be banned in many places. When Dario cast the girls as older actresses, he opted to leave the dialogue the way it was originally. This is why the girls in the film act so naïve and childlike.

Cast:

Jessica Harper (Suzy Bannion), Stefania Casini (Sara), Flavio Bucci (Daniel), Miguel Bose (Mark), Barbara Magnolfi (Olga), Susanna Javicoli (Sonia), Eva Axen (Pat Hingle), Rudolph Schundler (Professor Milius), Udo Kier (Dr. Frank Mandel), Alida Valli (Miss Tanner), Joan Bennett (Madame Blanc), Margherita Horowitz (Teacher), Jacopo Mariani (Albert), Fulvio Mingozzi (Taxi Driver), Franca Scagnetti (Cook).

What the critics say:

J. Hoberman, *The Village Voice*: "A movie that makes sense only to the eye (and even then …)."

Dave Kehr, *Chicago Reader*: "Argento works so hard for his effects—throwing around shock cuts, colored lights, and peculiar camera angles—that it would be impolite to not be a little frightened."

Michael McKenzie, *DVD Times*: "A lot of criticism can be leveled against the films of Dario Argento. Superficially, his characters are underdeveloped, actors wooden, plots inane and dialogue unbelievable. Yet for some reason all that is thrown to one side when watching one of his films. His near-perfect combination of audio and visual elements works so well that it can transport you to a world completely detached from reality, if you let it."

If you liked this, you might also like:

Tenabrae (1982)

#21 The Bride of Frankenstein (1935)

More frightful than the monster himself!

Why it made the list:

James Whale's *Frankenstein* terrified a nation in 1931… but, there was much more in store! In a prologue to the film, Elsa Lanchester plays Mary Shelley and explains that the story continued in her original novel, and did it ever! Many critics believe this to be Whale's true masterpiece, outdoing his original film in camp value and chills. The concept here is much darker: Not only did Frankenstein create a monster, but he is blackmailed into creating a mate for the monster. The process of this unholy wedding sent chills up and down the spine of audiences everywhere. Desire, danger and murder were again the norm, but the sequel was injected with an even more depraved undertone… the wedding night of two inhuman creatures.

Synopsis:

After the aforementioned introduction by Mary Shelley (Elsa Lanchester), we find out that Dr. Frankenstein (Colin Clive) and his monster (Boris Karloff) both survived the windmill fire of the first film. Frankenstein believes himself out of the monster business, but the evil Dr. Pretorius (Ernest Thesiger) kidnaps Elizabeth (Valerie Hobson), the beautiful wife of Frankenstein and forces the good doctor back into business to create a mate for the creature. To save his wife, Frankenstein does just that. The local population is thinned out a bit by the creature just trying to fit in and the quest for perfect source material for the bride. Our monster is humanized in this sequel but it is the acts of man that truly terrify us.

Frankenstein is successful in creating a bride for his creature, but when she awakens nothing can prepare them for what she has in store.

Scariest scene:

Frankenstein and Pretorius stand, excited and in anticipation, as the bride they have labored on for so long has awakened. She makes her debut, entering the room. Pretorius claims she is "The Bride of Frankenstein." The bride staggers and is caught, unused to the new body. Her movements are jagged and abrupt. The Monster enters and is entranced by her beauty. She finds him ugly, loathsome and terrifying. She tries to say something, anything, as the Monster beckons to her. Finally, she releases a blood curdling scream still effective to this day. She moves into the arms of Frankenstein and he sits her down, but the Monster follows. He takes her hand and she screams again, scared of the thing before her. The Monster growls, "She hate me." Spurned, the Monster pushes Pretorius away and grabs the lever for the electrical system. As Frankenstein escapes, the Monster looks at his bride one last time. She hisses at him and he pulls the lever, destroying them all.

Memorable dialogue:

ELIZABETH: Open the door, Henry! Henry!

FRANKENSTEIN: Get back! Get back!

ELIZABETH: I won't unless you come!

FRANKENSTEIN: But I can't leave them, I can't!

MONSTER: Yes, go! You live! Go! (To Pretorius) You stay. We belong dead.

BRIDE: *hisses*

MONSTER: *moans*

CASTLE: *explodes*

Did you know?

Based on the popularity of Boris Karloff as a thriller actor, he was billed only as "Karloff." Elsa Lanchester was credited for her part as Mary Shelley, but the on-screen credit for the titular bride was "?".

Cast:

Colin Clive (Dr. Henry Frankenstein), Elizabeth (Valerie Hobson), The Monster (Boris Karloff), Dr. Pretorius (Ernest Thesiger), Mary Shelley/The Bride (Elsa Lanchester), Gavin Gordon (Lord Byron), Douglas Walton (Percy Shelley), Una O'Connor (Minnie), E. E. Clive (Burgomaster), Lucien Prival (Butler).

What the critics say:

Frank Nugent, *The New York Times*: "Mr. Karloff is so splendid in the rôle that all one can say is 'he is the Monster.' Mr. Clive, Valerie Hobson, Elsa Lanchester, O. P. Heggie, Ernest Thesiger, E. E. Clive and Una O'Connor

fit snugly into the human background before which Karloff moves. James Whale, who directed the earlier picture, has done another excellent job; the settings, photography and the make-up (contributed by Universal's expert, Jack Pierce) contribute their important elements to a first-rate horror film."

Don Durker, *The Chicago Reader:* "James Whale's quirky, ironic 1935 self-parody is, by common consent, superior to his earlier *Frankenstein.* Whale added an element of playful sexuality to this version, casting the proceedings in a bizarre visual framework that makes this film a good deal more surreal than the original. Elsa Lanchester is the reluctant bride; Boris Karloff returns as the love-starved monster. Weird and funny."

Variety Magazine (1934): "Karloff manages to invest the character with some subtleties of emotion that are surprisingly real and touching. Especially is this true in the scene where he meets a blind man who, not knowing that he's talking to a monster, makes a friend of him."

If you liked this, you might also like:

Frankenstein (1931).

#22 *Funny Games* (1997)

You must admit, you brought this on yourself.

Why it made the list:

There are no undead ghouls fresh from the grave in this sophisticated horror offering. There are no intricate traps designed to force victims to chop off their own limbs. There are no boogie monsters hiding in the closet, ready to pop out at any moment. No, the power of this dark, chilling picture lies in the fact that its boogie monsters are real people, presumably just like the people we pass on the street every day. There is a harsh brutality to *Funny Games* that makes it seem painfully realistic, as though these events could actually happen (and they can!). Sure, zombies and hockey-mask-wearing murderers probably won't have you looking under your bed at night, but *Funny Games*' seemingly-neighborly young gentlemen with a psycho's taste for blood just might. If you don't find this film disturbing, there's something very wrong with you.

Synopsis:

Georg (Ulrich Muhe) and his wife, Anna (Susanne Lothar), along with their young son, travel to their beautiful summer home. When they arrive, they are immediately greeted by two seemingly intelligent, educated young men named Peter (Frank Glering) and Paul (Arno Frisch). The two men claim to be friends of the neighbors and use this claim to gain entrance into the family's home. Once inside, it becomes apparent that they are playing a dangerous, not-so-funny game in which the family's lives hang in the balance.

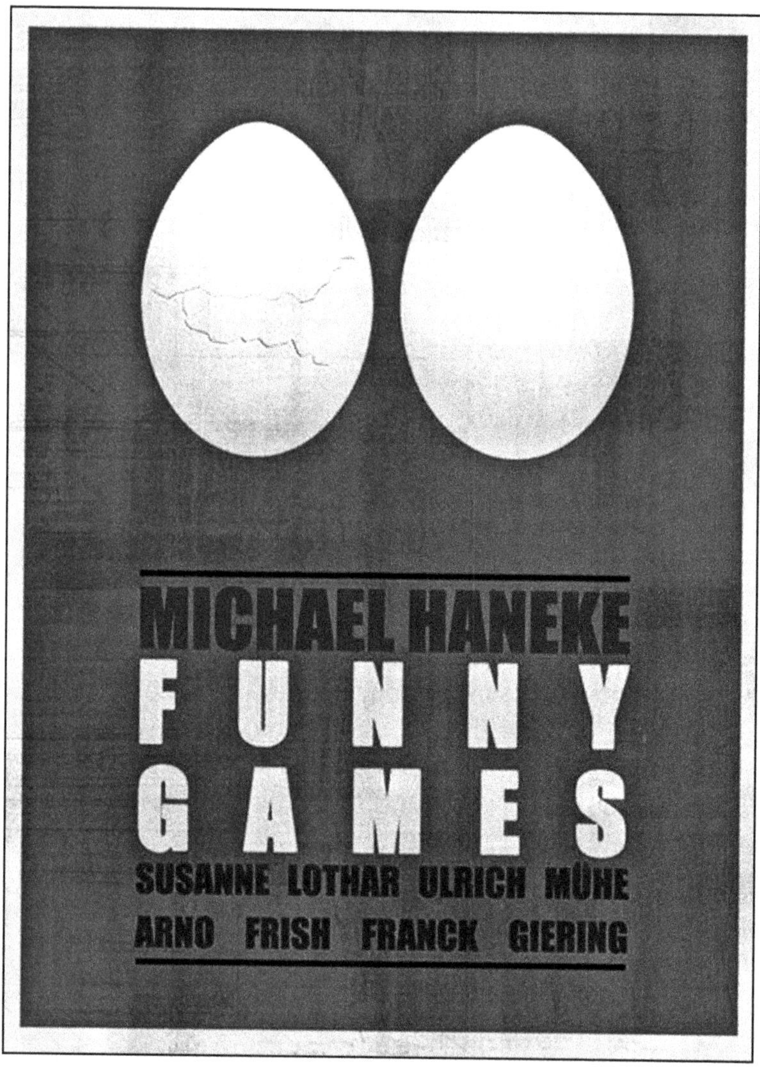

Scariest scene:

The film's most frightening scene comes with the psychos' brutal murder of the couple's young son. At this point, the audience is jarred into a reality in which literally anything can happen, no matter how dark and disturbing it might be. Up until this scene, the two men were just screwing around, torturing the couple and playing some sort of sick game. But once the little boy dies, all bets are off. Can the couple possibly survive until sunrise?

Memorable dialogue:

> **GEORG:** Why are you doing this to us?
>
> **PAUL:** Why not?

Did you know?

During a screening at the Cannes film festival in 1997, many viewers—and critics—were so repulsed by what they were seeing onscreen that they walked out of the theater.

Cast:

Ulrich Muhe (Georg), Susanne Lothar (Anna), Arno Frisch (Paul), Frank Glering (Peter), Stefan Clapczynski (Schorschi), Doris Kunstmann (Gerda), Christoph Bantzer (Fred), Wolfgang Gluck (Robert), Monika Zallinger (Eva), Susanne Meneghel (Gerdas Schwester).

What the critics say:

Geoff Andrew, *Time Out*: "Brilliant, radical, provocative; it's a masterpiece that is at times barely watchable."

Lisa Alspector, *Chicago Reader*: "The emotions of the victims are clear and complex—their conflicts dominate our experience of the narrative as powerfully as all the devices telling us to look elsewhere for the movie's themes."

Stephen Holden, *New York Times*: "*Funny Games* observes the family's excruciating terror and suffering with the patient delight of a cat luxuriantly toying with a mouse that it is in the process of slowly killing. Posing as a morally challenging work of art, the movie is really a sophisticated act of cinematic sadism. You go to it at your own risk."

If you liked this, you might also like:

The Strangers (2008).

#23 *Audition* (1999)

She always gets a part.

Why it made the list:

Takashi Miike directs *Audition* with a deft and careful hand, layering slow-burning moments of seeming normality atop odd, surreal encounters until the film takes a sudden, savage turn. The brutal climactic torture scene has, in itself, become something of legend.

Synopsis:

Widower Shigeharu Aoyama (Ryo Ishibashi) lives a quiet, lonely life in the home he shares with his teenaged son, Shigehiko (Tetsu Sawaki). Shigehiko wants his father to start dating again, but Aoyama is unsure. Then, Aoyama's friend, a film producer, comes up with a plan to stage a mock audition to screen potential dating partners for Aoyama. He agrees, and quickly becomes fixated on one of the women, Asami Yamazaki (Eihi Shiina) based on her application and audition. He decides to call her, and she agrees to meet him for lunch. The pair begin dating, and eventually take a trip together to a seaside hotel. Asami reveals painful information about her childhood, and asks Aoyama to love only her. He agrees, and they make love. The next morning, however, Asami is gone, and Aoyama can find no trace of her. He searches the city for clues, unaware that Asami's past holds even darker secrets, and that the future is about to become very painful.

Scariest scene:

Asami, having drugged Aoyama's drink, begins to slowly torture him, believing that he has not lived up to his promise to love only her. After plunging needles into his abdomen and under his eyes, she uses a long wire saw to begin cutting off his left foot in a deliberate, horrifically matter-of-fact manner.

Memorable dialogue:

> **ASAMI:** I've paralyzed your body but your nerves are still awake. You can enjoy the pain and suffer incredibly.
> You guys collect many girls from auditions. Make them fail.
> You contact them later. Just wanting to have sex. Everybody is the same. Deeper, deeper … Deeper, deeper … Painful?
> Words create lies. Pain can be trusted.

Did you know?

When the film was screened at the Rotterdam Film Festival 2000 it had a record number of walkouts. At the Swiss premiere someone passed out and needed emergency room attention.

Cast:

Ryo Ishibashi (Shigeharu Aoyama), Eihi Shiina (Asami Yamazaki), Tetsu Sawaki (Shigehiko Aoyama), Jun Kunimura (Yasuhisa Yoshikawa), Renji Ishibashi (Old Man in Wheelchair), Miyuki Matsuda (Ryoko Aoyama), Toshie Negishi (Rie), Ren Ohsugi (Shimada), Shigeru Saiki (Toastmaster), Ken Mitsuishi (Director).

What the critics say:

Patrick Z. McGavin, *Chicago Tribune*: "Miike is brilliant at transforming the mundane and familiar - like the sounds of sheets snapping or a telephone ringing - into something sinister and eerie. What had been discretely suggested turns terrifyingly concrete after Asami disappears and Aoyama discovers some startling information about her: Asami is either an emotionally scarred woman seeking refuge from a traumatic past, or a vengeful sadomasochist exacting revenge for past grievances. The final confrontation is both a formal tour de force and emotionally riveting, as *Audition* creates an atmosphere of frenzy that is both powerful and unforgettable, providing neither solace nor comfort."

Kevin Thomas *L.A. Times*: "Miike is such a compelling filmmaker that he makes it hard to turn away from the unspeakable. While he packs a major jolt for horror fans, *Audition* is actually carrying a critique of the lingering subordinate status of women in Asian society to its horrendous, hideous extreme. It also makes the larger point that 'nice' people in the unconscious clutch of archaic attitudes make those living in the less privileged and powerful strata of society vulnerable to a living hell."

Elvis Mitchell, *New York Times*: "Mr. Miike's skill comes in the accretion of emotional details and in his knack for dropping information in at just the right instant. Aoyama can't help but evoke ambivalence; though we're sympathetic to his plight, he has done the wrong thing. It would be easier if he were mean, or crazy. It's worse—at heart, he's a desperate romantic who has fallen for a mirage. When his vision clears and he sees what's really there, it's much too late."

If you liked this, you might also like:

Ichi the Killer (2001).

#24 *The Evil Dead* (1981)

Can they be stopped? The ultimate experience in grueling terror.

Why it made the list:

Sam Raimi's directorial debut *The Evil Dead* delivers a seemingly unending succession of scares augmented by demonic possession, gallons of blood, gore and screaming. There's an urgency in Raimi's style that radiates from the screen with an ironclad determination seldom seen within the horror genre. Raimi's volatile compounding of horror, comedy and the absurd worked tremendously well; subsequently he's repeated his recipe two more times. Even with its peppering of slapstick humor *The Evil Dead* still comes across as a harrowing nightmare of vicious proportions.

Synopsis:

Five friends make their way to a remote cabin in the woods for a weekend of partying. Upon examination of their temporary digs, a reel-to-reel tape machine is found. The five gather around to listen and learn what the previous occupants had unfortunately found. The voice on the tape recorder tells of excavating the ruins of Kandar. It also tells of locating a book on Sumerian burial practices entitled *Noturan Demonto*, or *The Book of the Dead*. The book, bound in human flesh and inked in human blood, " … deals with demons, demon resurrection and those forces which roam the forests and dark bowers of man's domain."

The taped voice continues by reciting an incantation to the evil in the woods. Cheryl (Ellen Sandweiss), obviously shaken, switches off the machine, but it's far too late. Scott (Hal Delrich) makes a joke of it, fast forwards the tape and they continue listening. Unfortunately for the listeners, the evil forces have heard aplenty and have been summarily released.

One by one the teenagers are possessed. They begin to turn against one another. They mutate, deform and contort into screaming, squirming, sacrilegious human hosts to unadulterated evil. Only one will survive the demonic bloodbath.

Scariest scene:

The Evil Dead is host to many a scary scene, but the rape of Cheryl by the literally frenetic and apparently lecherous backwoods sends audiences into a tizzy every time.

Honorable mention: A newly possessed Cheryl levitating, jerking and growling "Why have you disturbed our sleep? Awakened us from our Ancient slumber? You will die like the others before you. One by one we will take you!"

Memorable dialogue:

> **VOICE ON TAPE RECORDER:** I have seen the dark shadows moving in the woods and I have no doubt that whatever I have resurrected through this book is sure to come calling for me … I fear that the only way to stop those possessed by the spirits of the book is through the act of bodily dismemberment.

Did you know?

The Evil Dead was one of the first films to be labeled as a "Video Nasty" in the U.K.

Cast:

Bruce Campbell (Ash), Ellen Sandweiss (Cheryl), Richard Demanincor (Scott), Betsy Baker (Linda), Theresa Tilly (Shelly), Bob Dorian (Voice on Tape Recorder).

What the critics say:

Pat Graham, *The Chicago Reader*: "Sam Raimi directed this horror feature fresh out of film school, and his anything-for-an-effect enthusiasm pays off in lots of formally inventive bits. The film is ferociously kinetic and full

"… The most ferociously original horror film of the year …"
—Stephen King
author of Carrie and The Shining
THE EVIL DEAD
Starring BRUCE CAMPBELL ELLEN SANDWEISS HAL DELRICH BETSY BAKER SARAH YORK
Make-up Effects by TOM SULLIVAN Photographic Effects by BART PIERCE Photography by TIM PHILO
Music by JOE LoDUCA Produced by ROBERT G. TAPERT Written and Directed by SAM RAIMI
Color by TECHNICOLOR® Renaissance Pictures Ltd. From NEW LINE CINEMA All Rights Reserved
THE PRODUCERS RECOMMEND THAT NO ONE UNDER 17 BE ALLOWED TO SEE THE EVIL DEAD

of visual surprises, though its gut-churning reputation doesn't seem fully deserved: if anything the gore is too picturesque and studied, an abstract decorator's mix of oozing, slimy color, like some exotic species of new-wave interior design."

James Blake Ewing, *Cinema Sights*: "The true star of the film is Sam Rami's smart direction. His vision for many of the shots, a good handful of which are compelling and complex long takes, shows a vision and a smart eye that some of the most lauded directors tend to lack. The camera is just as important as what is being shown as it becomes an active participant in the film on many occasions."

Joe Bob Briggs, *The Joe Bob Briggs Report*: "I'll give you an idea of what I'm talking about: This one may make *Chainsaw* look eligible for the Disney Channel. We're talking 19 gallons of blood. One breast. Four beasts, unless you include the raping forest. No kung fu. No motor vehicle chases. No question about it: grisly, nasty, disgusting…four stars."

If you liked this, you might also like:

Within the Woods (1978).

#25 *High Tension* (2003)

Hearts will bleed.

Why it made the list:

In 2003, French helmer Alexandre Aja made quite a splash with this deliciously violent brutality fest. Although it's known for having one of the stupidest, most contrived, groan-inducing endings the genre has ever produced, *High Tension* has plenty of good things going for it to make it a memorable entry in the horror genre. For one, it's literally overflowing with chilling moments from start to finish. Aja's direction is sleek and stylish (he proves himself a master of the genre), and he produces gritty, disturbing, ultra-violent death scenes as well as anyone in horror. If you haven't seen this little gem, you are urged ... and warned ... to do so at your own peril.

Synopsis:

Marie (Cecile De France) and her friend Alexia (Maiwenn) are on holiday, visiting Alexia's family at her isolated childhood home. That night, a vulgar, grotesque monstrosity of a man invades the home and chops the family all to hell with a straight razor. Marie and Alexia are then taken hostage by the man, who padlocks them into the back of his rusty, broken down old truck. Marie eventually escapes, and things begin to get really interesting (and intense) as she first flees the killer, and later attempts to turn the tables on him. But as the film progresses, the viewer begins to question what he/she knows to be true.

Scariest scene:

Trapped inside the house, Marie can do nothing but listen to her girlfriend's family being hacked to pieces. The most frightening moment in this fifteen-minute gore extravaganza finds Marie inside a shuttered closet, watching Alexia's mother die one of the most unforgettably brutal scenes ever filmed. Arterial blood spews forth, body parts are ripped apart and dismembered, and neither Marie nor Alexia's mother will ever be the same after this, the grisliest of attacks.

Memorable dialogue:

> **MARIE:** I won't let anyone come between us anymore.

Did you know?

The scene in which Marie hides from the killer inside a gas station was intended as a homage to William Lustig's 1980 film *Maniac*.

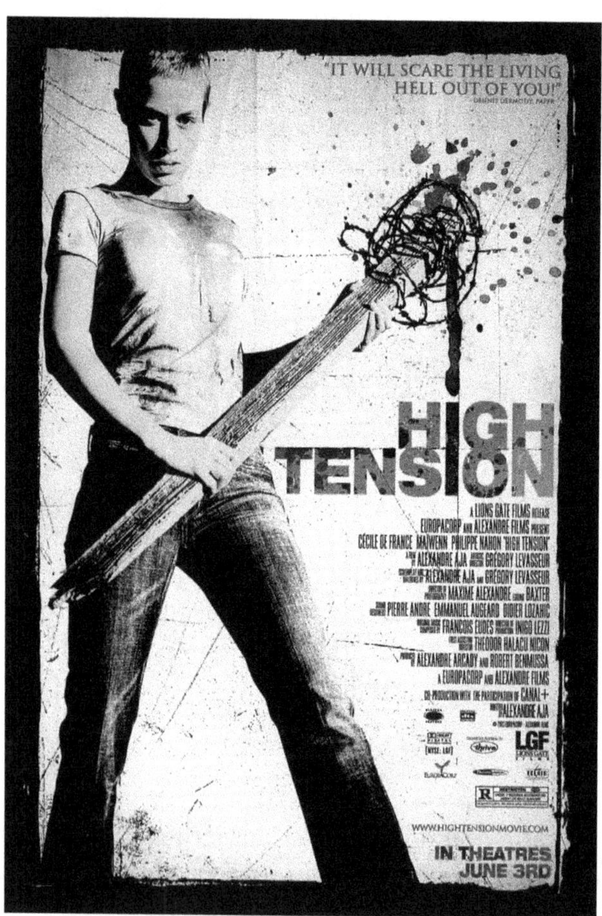

Cast:

Cecille De France (Marie), Maiwenn (Alexia), Vera Miles (Lila Crane), John Gavin (Sam Loomis), Martin Balsam (Milton Arbogast), Phillippe Nahon (Le tueur), Frank Khalfoun (Jimmy), Andrei Finti (Pere Alex), Oana Pellea (Mere Alex), Marco Claudiu Pascu (Tom).

What the critics say:

Mark Holcomb, *Village Voice*: "The truth of the situation is exposed shortly afterward in a twist that lets the air out of the movie, but the revelation is both inevitable and exceedingly clever—if also backhandedly puritanical. Such deficits are easy to overlook thanks to *High Tension*'s knowing performances and unnerving combination of ambient sound, fluidly jittery cutting, and sly widescreen setups. It's enough to give horror fans reason to anticipate Aja's next project … "

Mark Savlov, *The Austin Chronicle*: "*The Last House on the Left* meets *Psycho* in this stylistically thrilling but ultimately tedious French import, dubbed and recut for an Americanized R-rating. Aja has recently been tagged to helm the remake of Wes Craven's giddy take on the Sawney Bean cannibal family, *The Hills Have Eyes*, and watching *High Tension* it's easy to see why. He directs from the gut, in more ways than the obvious, and this gruesome, hyper-violent tale of rural stalkings and nameless dread plays like early Craven minus the warped social commentary."

Maitland McDonagh, *TV Guide*: "The first two thirds of the screenplay by Aja and cowriter Gregory Levasseur is a relentless exercise in bare-bones nastiness, even if it is so indebted to veteran horror novelist Dean Koontz's *Intensity* that it verges on the actionable. Unfortunately, they squander their white-knuckle goodwill on an 11th-hour about-face so preposterous it undermines everything that preceded it (though in its defense, it also sets up a stunning final shot). "

If you liked this, you might also like:

Inside (2007).

#26 *Salo, or The 120 Days of Sodom* (1975)

We Fascists are the only true anarchists.

Why it made the list:

Pier Pasolini was, and is, Italy's most controversial director, novelist, and poet. He was a great intellectual and social critic who utilized his artistic voice and visions to make his stances, popular or not, very well known. It stands to some reason that his 1975 feature film *Salo, or The 120 Days of Sodom* would become an object of heated (and hated) debate. Ultimately, it is something of a legend.

Pasolini based his cinematic swansong on the 1785 writings of the Marquis De Sade's *120 Days of Sodom*. He built and managed his film in four separate parts, not at all unlike Dante's *Inferno*. The director's inspirations were dubious at best and, in the company of one another, unsettling to say the least. Still, the politically vocal Pasolini felt the need to push the envelope one step further, and put his homeland under the microscope. He took De Sade's storyline and placed it in post-Mussolini and Fascist-occupied Italy in 1944.

The only things remotely pleasant about Salo are the photography, the sets, the editing, and the acting. Yet, with each of these positives comes a cavalcade of unthinkable and unspeakable deviances. As vile and gratuitous as the film is on the surface, there is a heavy-handed anti-establishment theme surging (or in Pasolini's case hemorrhaging) through the heart of the story. It's not a morality play (unless, of course, immorality is your game), but rather an attack on the bourgeoisie and their obscene predilection towards complacency.

Synopsis:

Mussolini's head is about to be kicked in and four wealthy Italian dignitaries are bored. One is a Duke (Paolo Bonacelli), one a Magistrate (Umberto Paolo Quintavalle), another is a Bishop (Giorgio Cataldi), and rounding out this group of silver-spoon-fed boys is the President (Aldo Valletti). All the money and the power just isn't enough. A weekend getaway is in order, or rather 16 consecutive weekend getaways is in order.

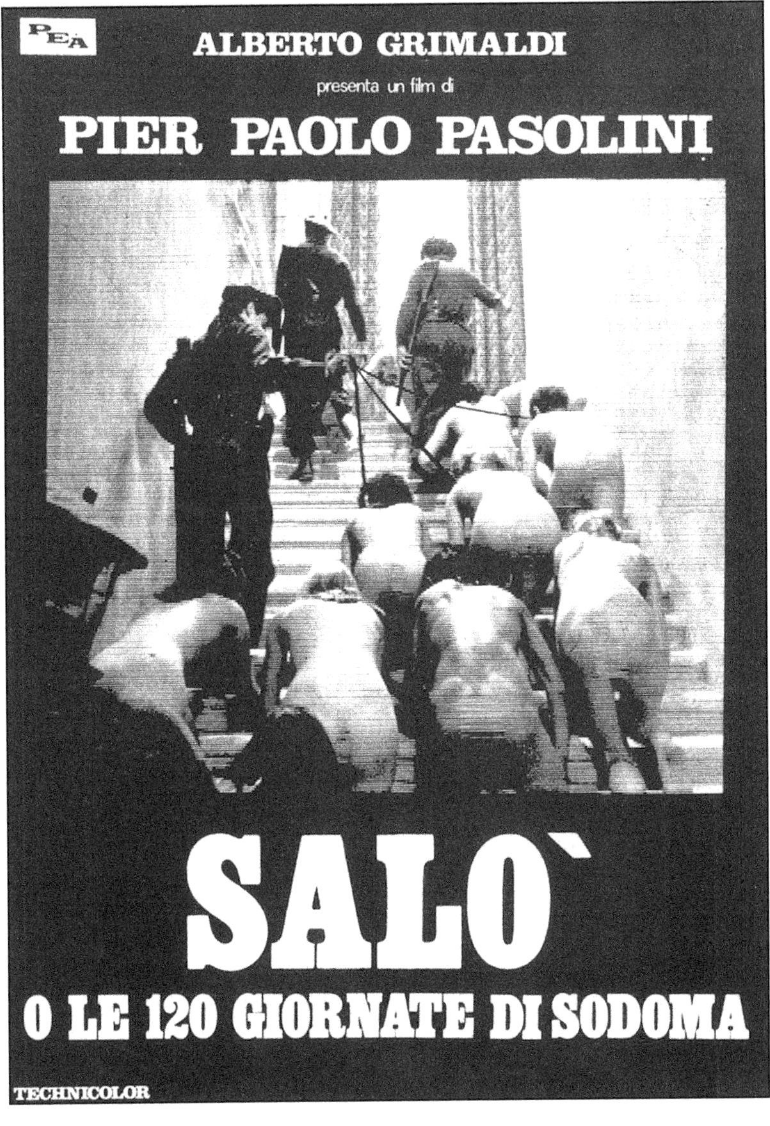

To start things off proper, these four degenerates marry each other's teen-aged daughters. Then four males are appointed as guards and four more are appointed as "studs" or "cocksmen." These eight teenage boys and four men go about hunting the finest young flesh Italy has to offer, nine males and females. Because of the immense influence and wealth these luminaries possess, obtaining the finest human specimens proves to be a non-issue.

Once the subjects are collected, they are whisked away to a glamorous rural retreat near Salo. This ornate palace will be these captives house of hell. None of them possibly could, or would ever be able to imagine the horrors and indignities that await them. It will be their final stop, and with 120 days to go it most assuredly will not stop soon enough. The agenda for these hapless and hopeless victims can, and do, include being naked around the clock, being force fed-dog food laced with razor blades, mental abuse, verbal abuse, physical abuse, emotional abuse and sexual abuse (homosexual and heterosexual). The sickening abominations continue with a feast of human excrement that is heartily partaken by the antagonist men and regrettably forced upon the teen aged protagonists.

Dignitaries or not, it's painfully evident that these human defectives aren't in possession of even the most malfunctioning of moral compasses. Their fervor and excitement over the past four months' proceedings is culminated in an absolute blood bath of inconceivable proportions. These four men, indefensible excuses of humankind, cannot be easily contented. Every last one of those broken-down teenage bodies must be mutilated, scalped, branded and dismembered before their eyes.

Scariest Scene:

Salo is a near two-hour long grab bag of cinematic torture and terror. Singling out one scene that is more horrifying than another is impossible. The sheer act of working oneself up to enduring this piece of viciously graphic social commentary is more than most can handle. However, once strapped in, it's sink or swim.

Memorable Dialogue:

> **THE DUKE:** They've no idea the bourgeoisie has never hesitated to kill its children.

Did You Know?

Pier Paolo Pasolini was murdered days before editing was complete on *Salo.*

Cast:

Paolo Bonacelli (The Duke), Giorgio Cataldi (The Bishop), Umberto Paolo Quintavalle (The Magistrate), Aldo Valletti (The President), Caterina Boratto (Signora Castelli), Elsa De Giorgi (Signora Maggi), Hélène Surgère (Signora Vaccari), Sonia Saviange (The Pianist).

What the Critics Say:

Michael Weldon, *The Psychotronic Video Guide*: "Scenes of the torture of naked teenagers helped make it one of the most controversial features of all time."

Carol Schwartz, *Video Hound's Cult Flicks & Trash Pics*: "Those who watched this film and aren't disturbed and sickened by the goings on, should probably be put away where they can't hurt anybody."

Ken Hanke, *Mountain Xpress*: "There's a sense of pure evil clinging to the film like nothing I've ever experienced. I do not believe this is unintentional, nor do I believe it is pointless."

If you liked this, you might also like:

Caligula (1979)

#27 Deathdream (1972)

Andy's coming home ...

Why it made the list:

A sterling example of 1970's atmospheric horror films, this underrated gem is as creepy as all hell. Shot almost entirely at night, *Deathdream* is sure to give even the most hardcore of horror fans the willies. Although the screenwriting and direction are top-notch, as is the acting, led by *The Godfather's* John Marley, the real star here is Carl Zittrer's chillingly effective score. As walking corpse Andy Brooks (Richard Backus) leaves a trail of dead bodies in his bloody wake, the scares add up almost as quickly.

Synopsis:

Andy Brooks is shown being killed in Vietnam. Then we see his father and mother, played to perfection by John Marley and Lynn Carlin, being presented with the news that their only son is dead. But this will not be the end of Andy's story. The living dead soldier soon returns from the battlefield, killing people willy-nilly. After Andy murders the family dog, Butch, Dad starts to suspect that something's wrong here. Andy won't eat or drink, and rarely ever speaks. There is something strange about his demeanor. When Dad's pal, Dr. Allman (Henderson Forsythe), suggests that Andy may be responsible for the recent murder of a truck driver, all hell breaks loose.

Scariest scene:

When Doc Allman decides to telephone the police to tell them he believes Andy Brooks is the murderer, he sees a silhouette in the darkness. Then the line goes dead. Predictably, but nonetheless creepy, Andy soon steps out of the shadows. "I came for my check up," he says. He then instructs the doctor to check his pulse and heartbeat, but the doctor can find neither. At this point, both Doc Allman and the audience know that Doc is screwed. Andy then picks up a hypodermic needle and proceeds to stab the doctor to death.

Memorable dialogue:

> **MOTHER:** Do you know they sent us a telegram tonight? I mean, they actually sent us a telegram telling us that you were killed!
>
> **FATHER:** They actually said that my son was dead.
>
> **ANDY:** I was.

Did you know?

This was make-up wizard Tom Savini's first film. He provided the make-up for Andy's rotting flesh and the sliced-open throat of the dead man's first victim.

Cast:
John Marley (Charles Brooks), Lynn Carlin (Christine Brooks), Richard Backus (Andy Brooks), Henderson Forsythe (Doc Allman), Anya Ormsby (Cathy Brooks), Jane Daly (Joanne), Michael Mazes (Bob), Arthur Anderson (Postman), Arthur Bradley (Army Captain), David Gawlikowski (Truck Driver).

What the critics say:

Paul Corrupe, *DVD Verdict*: "Boasting first-rate performances and a rarely-equaled sense of dread, *Deathdream* has earned its reputation as an undiscovered gem of 1970s drive-in horror … Part of the reason that *Deathdream* has captivated audiences throughout the last thirty years is the understated and creepy way in which it unfolds. Although evident from the first few scenes, the film never explicitly reveals that Andy is actually dead until more than halfway through, adding a level of ambiguity to his sinister actions. This charges the film with a sense of mystery and encourages the audience to piece together the plot themselves."

Staff, *TV Guide*: "*Deathdream* is a powerful, creepy film that reworks the classic tale 'The Monkey's Paw,' relying on mood and tension to convey the terror. It uses the horror genre quite successfully to explore the difficulty of post-Vietnam adjustment (stretched to a horrible, exaggerated limit) and the disintegration of the American family in the 1970s."

Staff, *Time Out*: "Modest and reasonably intriguing horror film. Andy is reportedly killed in action, but returns from the grave to seek retribution from family and small-town society that drove him to enlist in the first place. The film's novelty lies in its observation of Andy's home life; notably the tensions between Mom (impressively played by Carlin) and Dad which degenerate from minor squalls to major sores."

If you liked this, you might also like:

Children Shouldn't Play with Dead Things (1972).

#28 Dawn of the Dead (1978)

When there's no more room in hell ... the dead will walk the earth.

Why it made the list:

The dead coming to life to feast on the flesh of the living is a scary enough prospect as it is. But the sheer magnitude of George A. Romero's apocalyptic parable is overwhelming and in the end, exhausting. There is no escape in Romero's world, and the living are forced to always be alert, on guard and ready to kill what has already been killed.

Synopsis:

A godforsaken plague, likely from heavy radiation fallout, has caused the reanimation of the dead who subsist on the flesh of the living. The entire planet is seemingly affected by this outbreak and sheer chaos has stricken all of humankind. A group of four take up refuge in a shopping mall recently abandoned due to this catastrophe.

Stephen (David Emge) and Francine (Gaylen Ross) are reporters and the balance of the quartet is made up of two SWAT team members, Peter (Ken Foree) and Roger (Scott H. Reiniger). These survivors decide that a mall is as good a place as any to set up shop and try to carry on as best they can. There are supplies aplenty, but there are flesh-eating zombies aplenty too.

For a while things go along as well as expected, but then a marauding, violent and living motorcycle gang show up to spoil the fun. The outlaws revel in the bloody and gruesome destruction of the zombies, but then turn their sights on the film's protagonists. Now, the foursome have to defend themselves from the alive and the dead.

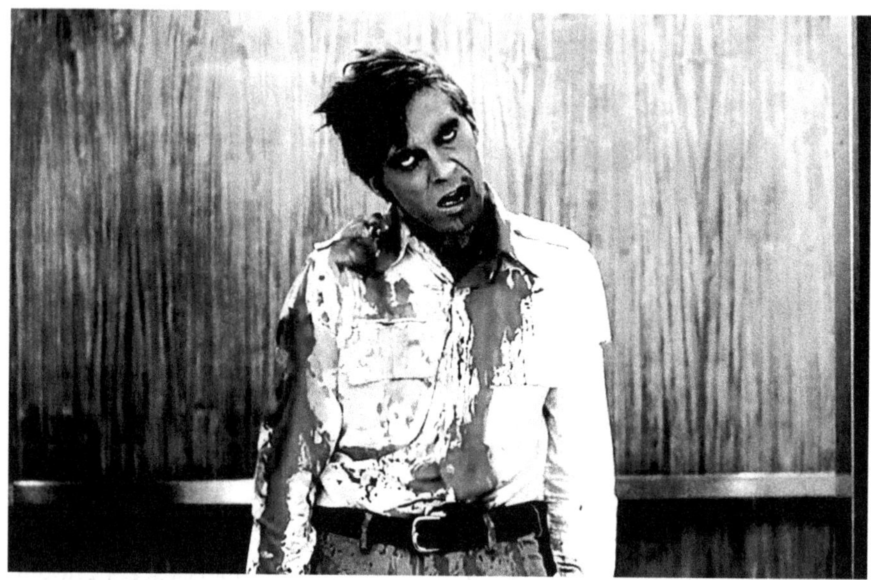

Scariest scene:

Dawn Of The Dead is overflowing with enough blood and gore to nauseate and disgust the most hardened of horror hounds, but the film's bleak ending is where the real scare resides. There is seemingly no escape from these man-eating creatures who are multiplying at a startling rate and all appears hopeless.

Memorable dialogue:

> **DR. FOSTER:** Every dead body that is not exterminated becomes one of them. It gets up and kills! The people it kills get up and kill!

Did you know?

The film's main set-piece, the Monroeville Mall located on the outskirts of Pittsburgh, Pennsylvania, is still standing and in full operation.

Cast:

David Emge (Stephen), Ken Foree (Peter), Scott H. Reiniger (Roger), Gaylen Ross (Francine), David Crawford (Dr. Foster), David Early (Mr.

Berman), Richard France (Scientist), Howard Smith (TV Commentator), Daniel Dietrich (Givens), Fred Baker (Commander).

What the critics say:

Dave Kehr, *Chicago Reader*: "George Romero's 1979 sequel to *Night of the Living Dead* is a more accomplished and more knowing film, tapping into two dark and dirty fantasies—wholesale slaughter and wholesale shopping—to create a grisly extravaganza with an acute moral intelligence. The graphic special effects (which sometimes suggest a shotgun Jackson Pollock) are less upsetting than Romero's way of drawing the audience into the violence. As four survivors of the zombie war barricade themselves inside a suburban shopping mall, our loyalties and human sympathies are made to shift with frightening ease. Romero's sensibility approaches the Swiftian in its wit, accuracy, excess, and profound misanthropy."

Staff, *TV Guide*: "One of the key horror films of the 1970s (a particularly fecund period for the genre), George Romero's apocalyptic follow-up to his classic *Night of the Living Dead* abandons easy scare tactics in favor of a darkly satirical assault on bourgeois culture, traditional notions of masculinity, and rampant consumerism. Zesty contributions from cinematographer Michael Gornick and special makeup effects mastermind Tom Savini help make this feel like a brightly colored action comic book peppered with gruesome (but not gratuitous) violence."

Roger Ebert, *Chicago Sun-Times*: "*Dawn of the Dead* is one of the best horror films ever made—and, as an inescapable result, one of the most horrifying. It is gruesome, sickening, disgusting, violent, brutal and appalling. It is also (excuse me for a second while I find my other list) brilliantly crafted, funny, droll, and savagely merciless in its satiric view of the American consumer society. Nobody ever said art had to be in good taste."

If you liked this, you might also like:

City of the Living Dead (1980).

#29 The Silence of the Lambs (1991)

Prepare yourself for the most exciting, mesmerizing and terrifying two hours of your life!

Why it made the list:

Few horror films are so widely respected and revered as Jonathan Demme's 1991 masterpiece of terror, *Silence of the Lambs.* Adapted from Thomas Harris' bestselling novel of the same title, this masterful film keeps audiences on the edge of their seats. Particularly effective (and frightening) is Anthony Hopkins' simultaneously intense and restrained performance as the brilliant cannibal Dr. Hannibal Lecter. While Hopkins has a habit of sometimes chewing through scenery like a ravenous T-Rex (see any of the *Silence of the Lambs* sequels for examples), here he gives the performance of a lifetime. If Hopkins' Lecter doesn't get under your skin, then nothing will. Demme, screenwriter Ted Tally, cinematographer Tak Fujimoto, and actors Jodie Foster and the aforementioned Hopkins are all working at the peak of their powers here, and together they crafted one of the most frightening and suspenseful films ever made.

Synopsis:

A promising young FBI trainee named Clarice Starling (Jodie Foster) is sent to a psychiatric facility to interview notorious serial killer Hannibal "the Cannibal" Lecter (Anthony Hopkins). The renowned psychiatrist-turned-murderer agrees to assist Starling in tracking down a serial killer known as Buffalo Bill. Clarice, still somewhat unsure of herself, must match wits with the brilliant Lecter, whose morbid sense of curiosity forces her to confront her own inner demons. Lecter never provides clear-cut answers regarding Buffalo Bill, but instead delivers veiled clues which must be analyzed and decoded. As a result of his interactions with Clarice, Lecter eventually escapes his restraints and goes into hiding. Now Clarice must deal with two serial killers on the loose instead of just one.

Scariest scene:

There are a number of frightening scenes in the film, including each and every one of Clarice's interactions with Hannibal Lecter. However, the scariest scene in the film comes near the end when we see Clarice through Buffalo Bill's night vision goggles. As Clarice stumbles around blindly in the darkness, Bill reaches out as if to touch her face, and then raises his pistol to shoot her.

Memorable dialogue:

> **HANNIBAL LECTER:** You know what you look like to me, with your good bag and your cheap shoes? You look like a rube. A well-scrubbed, hustling rube with a little taste. Good nutrition's given you some length of bone, but you're not more than one generation from poor white trash, are you, Agent Starling? And that accent you've tried so desperately to shed: Pure West Virginia. What is your father, dear? Is he a coal miner? Does he stink of the lamp? You know how quickly the boys found you—all those tedious sticky fumblings in the back seats of cars—while you could only dream of getting out...getting anywhere ... getting all the way to the FBI.

> **CLARICE STARLING:** You see a lot, Doctor. But are you strong enough to point that high-powered perception at yourself? What about it? Why don't you—why don't you look at yourself and write down what you see? Or maybe you're afraid to.

Did you know?

Three real-life serial killers served as the inspiration for the character Buffalo Bill. These were Ed Gein, who skinned his victims, Ted Bundy, who used a cast to trick unsuspecting victims into his van, and Gary Heidnick, who kept his kidnap victims inside a pit in his basement.

Cast:

Jodie Foster (Clarice Starling), Scott Glenn (Jack Crawford), Anthony Hopkins (Dr. Hannibal Lecter), Ted Levine (Jame Gumm), Anthony Heald (Dr. Frederick Chilton), Brooke Smith (Catherine Martin), Kasi Lemmons (Ardelia Mapp), Diane Baker (Senator Ruth Martin), Frankie Faison (Barney Matthews), Dan Butler (Roden).

What the critics say:

Todd McCarthy, *Variety*: "The juiciest part is Hopkins,' and he makes the most of it. Helped by some highly dramatic lighting, actor makes the role the personification of brilliant, hypnotic evil, and the screen jolts with electricity whenever he is on."

Roger Ebert, *Chicago Sun-Times*: "It has been a good long while since I have felt the presence of Evil so manifestly demonstrated as in the first appearance of Anthony Hopkins in *The Silence of the Lambs*."

Rita Kempley, *Washington Post*: "*The Silence of the Lambs* is just plain scary—from its doomed and woozy camera angles to its creepy Freudian subtext. It scares like some Poevian raven croaking a warning, perched in the night over the chamber door."

If you liked this, you might also like:

Manhunter (1986).

#30 *Invasion of the Body Snatchers* (1956)

Walter Wanger creates the ultimate in science fiction!

Why it made the list:

Don Seigel has directed a taut, frightening science fiction film that many people declare is *the* political metaphor of the mid-1950s. On its face, the film is a nice, mid-budget thriller but as political allegory, *Invasion of the Body Snatchers* is absolutely chilling. The rise of McCarthy-ism in the United States, the Red Scare and the fear of Communism crash headfirst into one another and, suddenly, we are all afraid of being replaced by alien pod people… all afraid of having our ideologies replaced and becoming part of the hive mind. That is the true terror of the film. How closely it mirrors the fallibility of humanity. It is horrifying to know that we are just minutes away, possibly, from becoming something of an "other." Falling asleep in the film is dangerous; we can never let our guard down. That mirrors our own reality so closely there isn't enough separation to feel comfortable.

Synopsis:

Dr. Miles Bennell (Kevin McCarthy) returns home to California from a conference. Something is strange in his small town. His friends have reports of odd behavior, patients calling and a distinct uptick in new ailments. Miles investigates only to find that something sinister is in this small town, something that is changing the residents of Santa Mira. Bennell discovers that strange plants have been seen around town and, much to his chagrin, these plants are taking over. When a human falls asleep, that human's body is replicated and the mind replaced. The bodies are grown in the pods. Horrified, Bennell goes to ground and attempts to escape the invasion, but it just keeps growing and growing.

Scariest scene:

An evening in with friends sees Dr. Bennell mixing a drink and entering his pal Danny's greenhouse looking for lighter fluid. What he finds are four pods, for the four dinner guests, popping open and dumping half-formed creatures onto the floor. The pods ooze whatever passes for alien embryonic fluid and the almost-things flop to the ground. Horrified, the four barbecue enthusiasts realize that there is something amiss and that this is proof of something invading and replacing human beings.

Memorable dialogue:

> **MILES:** In my practice, I've seen how people have allowed their humanity to drain away. Only it happened slowly instead

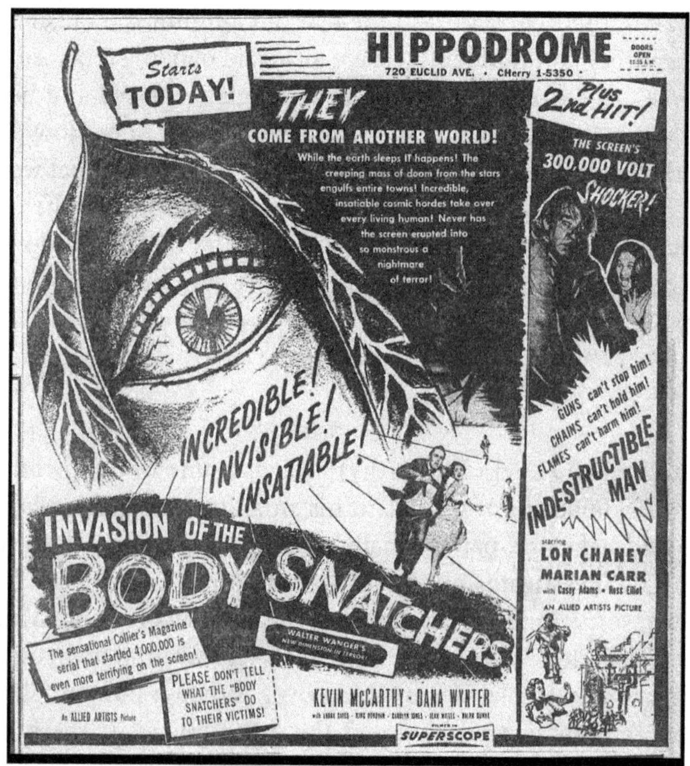

> of all at once. They didn't seem to mind … All of us—a little bit—we harden our hearts, grow callous. Only when we have to fight to stay human do we realize how precious it is to us, how dear.

Did you know?

Kevin McCarthy reprised the role of Dr. Miles J. Bennell in the 1978 remake of *Invasion of the Body Snatchers* starring Donald Sutherland and in 2003's *Looney Tunes: Back in Action.*

Cast:

Kevin McCarthy (Dr. Miles J. Bennell), Dana Wynter (Becky Driscoll), Larry Gates (Dr. Dan Kauffman), King Donovan (Jack Belicec), Carolyn Jones (Theodora Belicec), Jean Wiles (Sally Withers), Ralph Dumke (Police Chief Nick Grivett), Virginia Christine (Wilma Lentz), Tom Fadden (Ira Lentz), Kenneth Patterson (Stanley Driscoll).

What the critics say:

Tom Huddleston, *Time Out*: "This modest, sci-fi-inflected 1956 horror movie may come to be seen as the defining metaphorical work of the twentieth century."

Alan Jones, *Radio Times*: "Although expertly remade twice - in 1978 and 1993 - and rather less successfully in 2007, the original is still the most striking, with a justly famous scalp-freezing ending."

Don Drucker, *Chicago Reader*: "Don Siegel's superb little effort, with its matter-of-fact isolation of hero Kevin McCarthy (ironic, no?) from the smarmy complacency of a small town gone to hell -- and way beyond -- points the way to his gripping action films of the 60s and 70s."

If you liked this, you might also like:

THEM! (1954).

#31 *Diabolique* (1955)

Don't Reveal The Ending!

Why it made the list:

Widely acclaimed as one of the finest mystery thrillers ever made, Henri-Georges Clouzot's *Diabolique* delighted and shocked audiences with a wild twist ending. For the rest of its two-hour running time, the film is a masterpiece of tension as the camera dispassionately observes the ever tightening web of suspense. The mystery heightens moment by moment until suddenly, shockingly unspooling in the brilliant climactic scene.

Synopsis:

The cruel, spendthrift headmaster of a French boarding school, Michel Delassalle (Paul Meurisse) is despised by both his wife, Christina (Vera Clouzot), who actually owns the school, and his mistress, Nicole (Simone Signornet), who teaches there. The two commiserate over their harsh treatment at the hands of Michele, and conspire in a complicated plot to murder him. The pair lure him away from the school during a vacation, drowning him in the tub at Nicole's apartment in her hometown. They stuff the body in a wicker trunk and return to the school in the dead of night and dump it into the swimming pool, where they hope it will be found and the death ruled accidental. The corpse disappears from the pool, however, causing the women to panic. Further strange events follow, including the return of the suit Michel was wearing when he was drowned, and the discovery of a key to an empty hotel room rented in Michel's name in town.

Scariest scene:

Christina, who has been ordered to stay on bed rest by her doctor because of her heart condition, wakes in the middle of the night to find a light

shining into her room from an adjoining building. She moves to investigate, and a shadowy figure follows her through the darkened halls of the school as she becomes more and more terrified.

Memorable dialogue:

> **CHRISTINA:** So it's a coincidence?
>
> **NICOLE:** A coincidence, yes.
>
> **CHRISTINA:** And Fichet. Was his being at the morgue a coincidence? And the suit. And the hotel. And now the children! Is it a coincidence that it's getting… closer and closer?

Did you know?

When director Henri-Georges Clouzot bought the film rights to the original novel, he reportedly beat Alfred Hitchcock by only a matter of hours.

Cast:

Simone Sigornet (Nicole Horner), Vera Clouzot (Christina Delassalle), Paul Meurisse (Michele Delassalle), Charles Vanel (Alfred Fichet, le commissaire), Jean Brochard (Plantiveau, le concierge), Therese Dorny (Mme. Herboux), Michel Suerrault (M. Raymond, le surveillant), George Chamarat (Dr. Loisy), Robert Dalban (Le garagiste), Camille Guerini (Le photographe).

What the critics say:

Sukhdev Sandhu, *The Telegraph*: "Plot-wise and shock-wise, it's a bridge between Buñuel's *Un Chien Andalou* and contemporary Korean cinema. Sonically, it creates a compelling tension between the straight-out-of-Zéro De Conduite uproar of its anarchic schoolboys and the silent terror that a guilt-stricken Christina endures. *Les Diaboliques* is not only a black comedy about the limits of sisterhood; it's an exhilaratingly cold film that treats all its characters as flawed or self-interested. It's a diabolical masterpiece."

Neal Smith, *Total Film*: "There's more than a corpse missing in Henri-Georges Clouzot's 1955 masterpiece. So is any sense of human warmth and compassion, the *Wages Of Fear* man instead presenting a bleak world full of suspicion, manipulation, fear and loathing. The ending, much copied, is justly famous. But it's the implacable build-up that seals its classic status, a rundown school providing a suitably ominous backdrop for a finely crafted mystery with a diabolical twist."

Staff, *Time Out London*: "In this black world (where, ironically, only the dead comes to life) everyone is in the end a victim, and their actions operate like snares setting traps that leave them grasping for survival. The camera watches these clammy proceedings with a cold precision that relishes its neutrality. At least one source claims that all Clouzot's films were shot in an atmosphere of bitterness and recrimination. It shows. But in this case it makes for a great piece of Guignol misanthropy."

If you liked this, you might also like:

Rear Window (1954)

#32 *Dracula* (1931)

The story of the strangest person the world has ever known!

Why it made the list:

Regardless of the age of this film. Regardless of the lack of color, or gore or screeching sound effects. Regardless of the lack of hi-definitionisiosity or incredibly beautiful people waging a war of words against the Prince of Darkness, Tod Browning's *Dracula* is still creepy, still effective and still scary. Due in large part to the performance of Bela Lugosi as the Count, Dwight Frye as Renfield and those terrifyingly sultry vampire brides. Following his harrowing *Freaks*, Browning was given the nod to, in all reality, kick off the Universal Monster craze that has lasted nearly 100 years. Bela Lugosi is the iconic version of Dracula. Suave, elegant… deadly. This is a departure, of course, from the epistolary novel on which it is based, but the mood evoked from the film is downright spine-chilling even 80-plus years later.

Synopsis:

Renfield (Dwight Frye) travels to the Carpathian Mountains to solidify a business deal with the mysterious Count Dracula (Bela Lugosi). The Count wishes to travel to London and reside there in Carfax Abbey as an ex-pat from Transylvania. Renfield slowly realizes that the Count is a vampire and falls under his spell and joins the bloodsucker on his sea voyage. Upon arrival, the Count vamps the beautiful Lucy Weston and turns her into a creature of the night. He then sets his sights on Lucy's friend, Mina Seward. Unlucky for the Count, Mina's dad is Dr. Seward who just happens to know one Abraham Van Helsing. With the help of Mina's friends, Van Helsing takes the fight to the exotic, foreign dignitary and mayhem ensues.

Scariest scene:

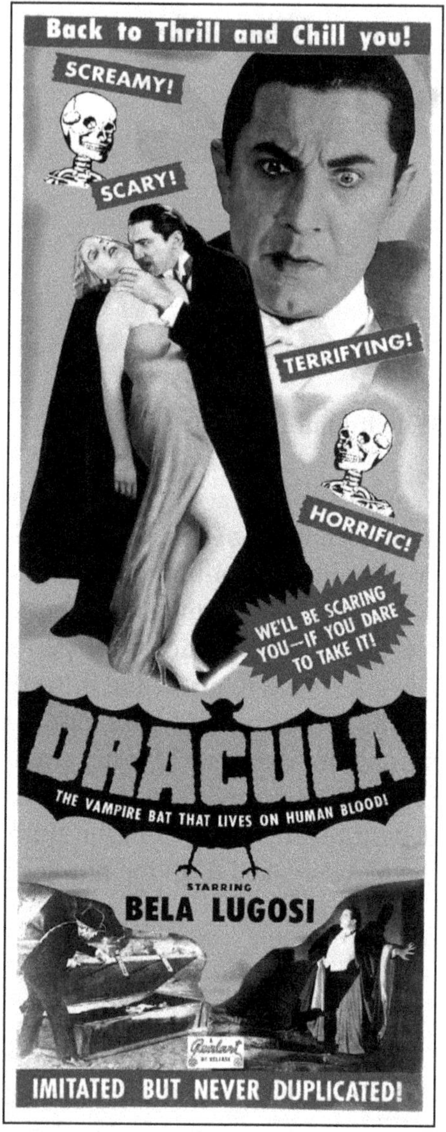

Debate rages, but Renfield's first glimpse of Dracula is harrowing, even today. The young real estate mogul takes a treacherous carriage ride, without a driver, through the Carpathian Mountains only to find a large, crumbling and creepy castle. Alone he enters (don't mind the random armadillos) and spies bats hovering, watching him. As he backs toward a large staircase, a lone figure holding a single candle descends. Renfield has no clue until he turns. The poor guy can only stand and stare up at the embodiment of all evil as it says, "I am Dracula." AAAH! The creepy vampire brides (three, just like the bats) make their appearance and add even another layer of goosebumps.

Memorable dialogue:

WOLF (off screen): AWOOOOO!

DRACULA: Listen to them… children of the night. What music they make!

Renfield follows Dracula through cobwebs.

DRACULA: A spider spinning a web for the unwary fly. The blood is the life Mr. Renfield.

RENFIELD: Why, yes.

Did you know?

After the cast and crew of *Dracula* left for the day at Universal, the sets were taken over by the Spanish-language cast and crew and a version (in Spanish of course) was shot at night.

Cast:

Bela Lugosi (Count Dracula), Helen Chandler (Mina), David Manners (Jonathan Harker), Dwight Frye (Renfield), Edward Van Sloane (Van Helsing), Herbert Bunston (Dr. Seward), Frances Dade (Lucy Weston)

What the critics say:

Roger Ebert, *Chicago Sun-Times*: "Lugosi was by all accounts a strange, deliberately theatrical man, who drew attention to himself with stylized behavior. He made his foreignness an asset, and in Hollywood and New York used his sinister, self-mocking accent to advantage."

Alan Jones, *Radio Times*: "It remains the most subtly romantic and highly atmospheric rendition of Bram Stoker's tale about the Transylvanian count, with Browning orchestrating the opening scenes to macabre perfection."

Mourdant Hall, *New York Times*: "With Mr. Browning's imaginative direction and Mr. Lugosi's makeup and weird gestures, this picture succeeds to some extent in its grand guignol intentions."

If you liked this, you might also like:

Dracula: Prince of Darkness (1966)

#33 *Re-Animator* (1985)

Death is just the beginning …

Why it made the list:

There really is no other horror film quite like Stuart Gordon's *Re-Animator*. It's a modern genre classic filled with buckets and buckets of blood and gore, and offers shocks and surprises at every turn. It's a modern-day retooling of the classic *Frankenstein* premise (with a little H.P. Lovecraft thrown in for good measure). Equal parts funny, frightening, and appalling, *Re-Animator* is the real deal. It's not simply some dumb rehash like ninety-percent of horror films made now; it's innovative and exciting, and it holds up today despite having special effects that are nearly 30 years old. Where else can you find twitching severed arms galore, a headless body with a fake head pretending to be a doctor and sneaking around the hospital at night, or a body-less head attempting to perform oral sex on a beautiful woman? Nowhere. Quite simply, *Re-Animator* is incomparable. It's the undisputed work of a sick genius (the aforementioned Gordon), and I say that with nothing but respect.

Synopsis:

Medical student Herbert West (Jeffrey Combs) returns from abroad after studying with a famous scientist who died working on an experiment. Herbert has now taken those studies a step further, perfecting a serum which will bring back the dead. He will soon enlist the aid of another medical student, Dan Cain (Bruce Abbott). Once the dead start coming back to life, all hell breaks loose and Herbert finds himself having to use the serum again and again to cover his tracks.

Scariest scene:

This movie is disturbing as all hell. The scene in which the severed head of Dr. Carl Hill (David Gale) licks Megan's (Barbara Crampton) naked, strapped-down body is as disturbing as anything this side of a *Faces of Death* video. First the Hill head tongues at her ear, then her breasts, and then makes his way down toward her nether regions, making this the first time a severed head has performed oral sex in the history of film. (It is unlikely we will ever see such a thing again, barring a remake.) But that's not necessarily the scariest scene. Also competing for this title is a scene which occurs only minutes later; just as it looks like the beheaded Hill is about to get his comeuppance, he somehow makes a room filled with cadavers come to life in gruesome fashion. The bodies then attack Dan, Megan, and Herbert with everything from blunt instruments to strangulation by intestines.

Memorable dialogue:

> **HERBERT:** Hill took my serum, my notes, everything!
>
> **DAN:** Herbert, you're insane! Now what happened here?
>
> **HERBERT:** I had to kill him!
>
> **DAN:** What? He's dead?
>
> **HERBERT:** [Pauses.] Not anymore.

Did you know?

If you look closely, a poster of the band the Talking Heads is visible on the wall in Dan's bedroom. Considering the outcome of the story involving Dr. Hill and his severed head, this was likely an inside joke by the filmmakers.

Cast:

Jeffrey Combs (Dr. Herbert West), Bruce Abbott (Dan Cain), Barbara Crampton (Megan Halsey), David Gale (Dr. Carl Hill), Robert Sampson

(Dean Halsey), Gerry Black (Mace), Carolyn Purdy-Gordon (Dr. Harrod), Peter Kent (Melvin), Barbara Pieters (Nurse), Ian Patrick Williams (Swiss Professor).

What the critics say:

Gregory P. Dorr, *DVD Journal*: "This is a qualified superlative: *Re-Animator* is the best horror film of the 1980s."

Janet Maslin, *New York Times*: "All of this, ingenious as it may be and much as it will redound to Mr. Gordon's credit in hardcore horror circles, is absolutely to be avoided by anyone not in the mood for a major bloodbath."

Keith Phipps, *The Onion A.V. Club*: "Loosely adapting a series of H.P. Lovecraft stories, in 1985 director Stuart Gordon made what might best be described as a comedic look at body horror. A first-time director with roots in avant-garde theater, Gordon gleefully pushes the edges with *Re-Animator*, courting infamy with one scene after another."

If you liked this, you might also like:

Basket Case (1982).

#34 *The Fly* (1986)

Be afraid. Be very afraid.

Why it made the list:

Although a loose remake of Vincent Price's classic from the 1950s, Cronenberg's *The Fly* holds its own as a member of the splatterpunk generation's frontline of cinematic fare. Like Price's version, this is a demented version of Beauty and the Beast, expertly managing to thrill the audience with an almost Mary Shelley-esque version of science run amok, the dangers of genius, and just how far love can go - all wrapped up in cutting edge gore and effects that flipped the stomachs of the most jaded fright fans. Best of all, though, this isn't gore for gore's sake. Cronenberg uses spilled entrails and puking man-flies and armpit-injector prostitutes to make statements. Horror, in general, and splatter, specifically, have been useful tools for filmmakers and fictioneers alike to communicate what REALLY scares us. Wrapping it up in an oozing or exploding gore-soaked metaphor makes the kids forget that they are learning something or getting a message and that, dear friends, is where Cronenberg succeeds like very few before him and even less after.

Synopsis:

Seth Brundle (Jeff Goldblum) is a genius scientist working for Bartok Industries and stumbled upon teleportation between two 'pods' as a means of matter transmittal. He is seduced by investigative reporter Veronica 'Ronnie' Quaife (Geena Davis) in order for her to find out what the secretive scientist is working on. Ronnie, eventually, does fall in love with Seth as he gets closer and closer to teleporting a living being. In a moment of scientific fervor, Brundle tests the pod on himself, transporting from one to the other. Little does he know, a common house fly was trapped in the pod with him and they have now melded DNA. Seth slowly starts to exhibit fly tendencies, becoming a hybrid creature. He documents the change, with Ronnie,

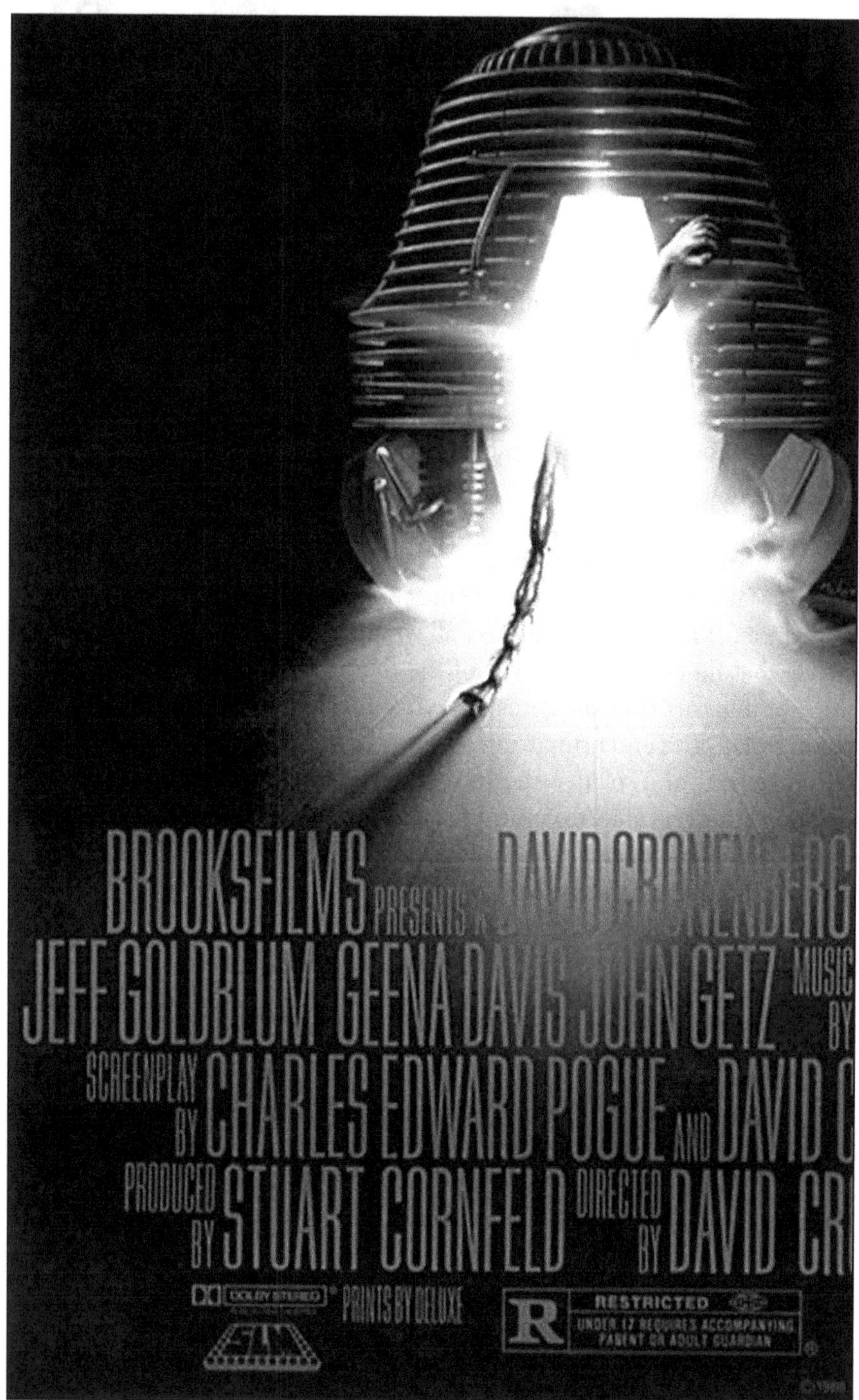
BROOKSFILMS PRESENTS
JEFF GOLDBLUM GEENA DAVIS JOHN GETZ
MUSIC BY
SCREENPLAY BY CHARLES EDWARD POGUE AND DAVID
PRODUCED BY STUART CORNFELD
DIRECTED BY DAVID
DOLBY STEREO
PRINTS BY DELUXE
R
RESTRICTED
UNDER 17 REQUIRES ACCOMPANYING PARENT OR ADULT GUARDIAN

but as his body changes, so does his mind. He becomes more insect-like, his consciousness being subsumed by the instincts of the fly. He regresses to a disgusting, half-human, half-insect monstrosity and not even Ronnie is safe from his new desires. He is Brundlefly now and he will not be stopped.

Scariest scene:
As Brundle changes, he attempts to document it all in pursuit of science. With Ronnie's help, he videotapes his new process of digestion. Brundle vomits an acidic, bile-like digestive fluid onto some food (much like a fly) with the intent of sucking it back up as a nutritious bio-shake. Ronnie is horrified at what she sees and knows that the Seth she loved is disappearing. As she realizes, so does the audience. That danger that her proximity to Brundlefly puts Ronnie in is palpable. As one, we know that this creature is just that… no longer a man but some terrible thing. The crawling on the ceiling just punctuates the sentiment. Chills.

Memorable dialogue:

> **SETH BRUNDLE:** What's there to take? The disease has just revealed its purpose. We don't have to worry about contagion anymore … I know what the disease wants.
>
> **RONNIE:** What does the disease want?
>
> **SETH BRUNDLE:** It wants to … turn me into something else. That's not too terrible is it? Most people would give anything to be turned into something else.
>
> **RONNIE:** Turned into what?
>
> **SETH BRUNDLE:** Whaddaya think? A fly. Am I becoming a hundred-and-eighty-five-pound fly? No, I'm becoming something that never existed before. I'm becoming … Brundlefly. Don't you think that's worth a Nobel Prize or two?

Did you know?

Rarely credited, Mel Brooks served as a producer on this film. He opted to keep his name off of it in an effort to NOT have *The Fly* taken as a comedy. At the premiere, though, Brooks was in attendance and did hand out deely boppers (large insect antennae hooked to a headband).

Cast:

Jeff Goldblum (Seth Brundle), Geena Davis (Veronica Quaife), John Getz (Stathis Borans), Jay Boushel (Tawny), Leslie Carlson (Dr. Brent Cheevers), George Chuvalo (Marky), Michael Copeman (Second Man in Bar), David Cronenberg (Gynecologist), Carol Lazare (Nurse), Shawn Hewitt (Clerk).

What the critics say:

Carrie Rickey, *Philadelphia Inquirer*: "Wildly imaginative, gut-wrenchingly scarifying and profoundly primal (not to mention funny), David Cronenberg's *The Fly* is a movie that whacks you in the solar plexus and leaves you gasping."

Richard Corliss, *Time Magazine*: "A gross-your-eyes-out horror movie that is also the year's most poignant romance."

Dave Kehr, *The Chicago Tribune*, "*The Fly* seizes on our ingrained, instinctive horror of sexuality, the sense of shame that our fundamentally puritanical society can't help but teach us, and by confirming our worst fears, helps us, for a moment, to move beyond them."

If you liked this, you might also like:

Slither (2006).

#35 *It Follows* (2014)

It doesn't think. It doesn't give up. It doesn't feel.

Why it made the list:

Screenwriter/director David Robert Mitchell's film *It Follows* debuted at the Cannes Film Festival in 2014, and quickly became the most talked about American horror film in decades. And for good reason, too! *It Follows* is a moody, tense, unique little gem that will have audiences on the edges of their chairs for years to come. This is easily the finest American horror films since … well, shit, since when? *A Nightmare on Elm Street*? *Halloween*? Only classic films come to mind, which is appropriate because *It Follows* is sure to become a tried-and-true classic, as well.

Synopsis:

After having what seems like a harmless bout of backseat sex with her crush-of-the-moment, Jay (Maika Monroe) finds herself burdened with more than she bargained for. An apparition that only she can see begins to follow her. If it catches her, she'll die. It can only walk, and very slowly at that, but it never stops coming. It just keeps on following. That's all it does. That's all it knows how to do—follow and kill.

There is some small glimmer of hope, though; by having sex with someone—*anyone*—she makes them the creature's new target. But once that person is dead, the deadly apparition will return to stalk her to the ends of the earth.

Scariest scene:

Jay has locked herself in her upstairs room, hiding from something only she can see. Finally the door is opened and her friends start pouring in—

with "It" filing in amongst them, in the personification of a large, hulking man. The audience I shared my first screening of this film with jumped a good three feet into the air when the creature emerged.

Memorable dialogue:

> **HUGH:** It could look like someone you know or it could be a stranger in a crowd. Whatever helps it get close to you.

Did you know?

The movie house shown at the beginning of the film is The Redford Theater, a historic theater where Sam Raimi's *The Evil Dead* once premiered.

Cast:

Keir Gilchrist (Paul), Carrollette Phillips (Woman with Groceries), Loren Bass (Annie's Father), Olivia Luccardi (Yara), Lili Sepe (Kelly Height), Maika Monroe (Jay Height), Jake Weary (Hugh/Jeff), Daniel Zovatto (Greg Hannigan), Charles Gertner (Neighbor Boy), Bailey Spry (Annie).

What the critics say:

Linda Cook, *Quad City Times*: "A kind of art-house horror movie, an allegory about AIDS and, believe it or not, a love story, *It Follows* is one of a kind."

Steve Persall, *Tampa Bay Times*: "*It Follows* has an impressively sustained sense of dread, less explicit gore than measured tension. Mitchell slyly inverts the conventions of dead-meat teenager flicks, although not with wink-wink comedy like the *Scream* series."

James Berardinelli, *ReelViews*: "Good horror films rely on suspense and tension, and this one has both elements aplenty."

If you liked this, you might also like:

Contracted (2013).

#36 Ringu (1998)

The original movie that inspired The Ring.

Why it made the list:

Why did *Ringu* made the list? Because it's scary as all hell, that's why. Also, the makers of the cursed video within the film threatened to pay us a visit in a few days if we didn't list it here. And we didn't want any part of that nonsense. But all joking aside, this is a truly horrific film and stands as one of the finest horror films ever produced in Japan—or anywhere else for that matter. If this one doesn't give you the heeby-jeebies, then why the hell are you reading this book? You're obviously immune to the fear-inducing charms of a good horror film.

Synopsis:

Reiko Asakawa (Nanako Matsushima) is researching a supposedly "cursed video" and interviewing people about its possible existence. When her niece falls dead of sudden heart failure with a horrified expression on her face, Reiko starts to investigate deeper. She soon learns that some of her niece's friends had died on the same night in exactly the same manner. In researching the deaths, Reiko finds an unmarked tape. She watches it and soon learns the truth of the "cursed video."

Scariest scene:

The scariest scene, without a doubt, is that damned video that plays again and again in the film. A montage of truly frightening images, the tape manages to make us squirm in our seats. It's that montage we remember vividly late at night as we lie down to try and sleep in our dark, quiet homes.

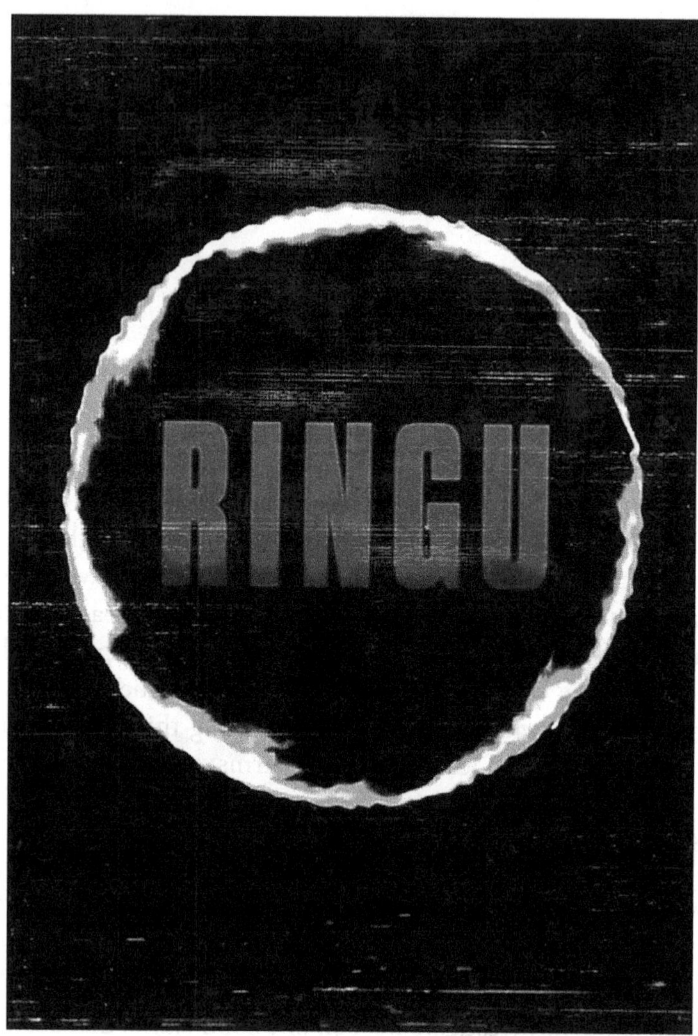

Memorable dialogue:

REIKO ASAKAWA: How did the rumors about the video even start in the first place?

RYUJI TAKAYAMA: This kind of thing … it doesn't start by one person telling a story. It's more like everyone's fear just takes on a life of its own.

REIKO ASAKAWA: Fear …

> **RYUJI TAKAYAMA:** Or maybe it isn't our fear, maybe it's what we secretly hope is true.

Did you know?

This is the highest-grossing horror film in Japanese history.

Cast:

Nanako Matsushima (Reiko Asakawa), Miki Nakatani (Mai Takano), Yuko Takeuchi (Tomoko Oishi), Hitomi Sato (Masami), Yoichi Numata (Takashi Yamamura), Yukata Matsushige (Yoshino), Katsumi Muramatsu (Koichi Asakawa), Rikiya Otaka (Yoichi Asakawa), Masako (Shizuko Yamamura), Daisuke Ban (Heihachiro Ikuma).

What the critics say:

Staff, *Variety*: "Classically shot, with effective use of stereo sound effects, the movie is almost entirely free of visual horror and the usual Eastern ghost clichés, managing to suspend auds' disbelief in the hokey story through pure atmosphere."

Daniel Fierman, *Entertainment Weekly*: "*The Ring* scared the bejesus out of me in theaters last year, so it was with some trepidation that I screened the widely-hailed-as-superior 1998 Japanese original, *Ringu*, about that cursed video that kills all unlucky enough to watch it. (And no, it doesn't star Eddie Murphy.) … The plots differ only slightly, but the scares are more or less the same. So now, if you don't mind, I'm off to the corner of my office to curl into a fetal position and rock slowly."

Peter Travers, *Rolling Stone*: "As good as *The Ring* is, it can't top the original for sheer, shivering terror. The 1998 film from director Hideo Nakata broke box-office records in Japan … It's not so much the gore that interests Nakata as the reporter digs into the case, it's the subtle dread that keeps you up at night in a cold, clammy sweat."

If you liked this, you might also like:

Ju-On: The Grudge (2000).

#37 *The Cabinet of Dr. Caligari* (1920)

The most amazing story ever screened.

Why it made the list:

The Cabinet of Dr. Caligari is universally considered the very first feature-length horror film ever produced. Prior to *Caligari*, moviegoers were treated to the macabre only in movie shorts (many of which were directed by Georges Méliès). While the film would hardly scare an audience today, its distorted set pieces, abstract lighting, unique jerking physical acting and the overall surreal tone would still leave most viewers disconcerted and uncomfortable. For filmgoers in 1920, the film, an exceptional piece of German Expressionism, successfully worked its magic and was simply terrifying.

Synopsis:

In a series of flashbacks, Francis (Friedrich Fehér) recounts a ghastly tale involving himself and his fiancée Jane (Lil Dagover). Francis attends the local annual fair with his friend Alan (Hans Heinrich von Twardowski). The two decide to take in the Dr. Caligari show.

Here the quirky Caligari (Werner Krauss) exhibits the equally strange Cesare (Conrad Veidt). Cesare is a somnambulist, who appears to be in a death-like trance. While in these hypnotic states, Caligari pitches that Cesare can predict the future. Alan takes the bait and Cesare informs him that he will be dead before dawn.

The prophecy becomes a reality and Francis assumes Cesare has killed his friend. Francis begins an investigation of the odd carnival attraction and its purveyors. In the meantime, Cesare is sent to murder Jane, but with a change of heart he kidnaps her. With Jane's father and his servants on his tail, Cesare eventually tires and relents, leaving Jane behind. He slips

away into the night and dies from exhaustion. Francis turns his sights on Caligari and pursues him straight into an insane asylum. The film returns to the present, revealing that Francis, Jane and Cesare are all inmates of the bedlam and that Dr. Caligari is just that, a doctor—their doctor.

Scariest scene:

It would be difficult to pinpoint one particular scene that could be considered the scariest. *Caligari* is one of those films that is greater than the sum of its parts. There is absolutely nothing that can comfortably be taken out of its context. The entire movie is infused with a bewildering and claustrophobic atmosphere that can feed directly into the anxieties of the viewer whether rational or irrational.

Memorable dialogue:

> **ALAN:** How long shall I live?
>
> **CESARE:** The time is short. You die at dawn!

Did you know?

Robert Wiene was not the producers' first choice as director. They initially approached Fritz Lang who was still seven years away from directing his master work, *Metropolis*.

Cast:

Werner Krauss (Dr. Caligari), Conrad Veidt (Cesare), Friedrich Fehér (Francis), Lil Dagover (Jane Olsen), Hans Heinrich von Twardowski (Alan), Rudolf Lettinger (Dr. Olsen), Rudolf Klein-Rogge (Criminal), Hans Lanser-Rudolf (Old man), Henri Peters-Arnolds (Young doctor), Ludwig Rex (Murderer), Elsa Wagner (Landlady).

What the critics say:

Carl Sandburg, *Chicago Daily News*: "It is a healthy thing for Hollywood, Culver City, Universal City, and all other places where movie film is being produced, that this photoplay has come along at this time. It is sure to have healthy hunches and show new possibilities in style and method to our American Producers."

Jonathan Rosenbaum, *Chicago Reader*: "Robert Wiene's groundbreaking 1919 silent, the most famous and influential work of the German expressionist cinema, involves a mad doctor (Werner Krauss) and the somnambulist who does his bidding (Conrad Veidt). Aided and abetted by one of Carl Mayer's best scripts and remarkable, distorted sets painted by Hermann Warm, Walter Röehrig, and Walter Reimann, this is more than just a textbook classic; the narrative frame creates ambiguities that hold certain elements of the story in disturbing suspension. A one-of-a-kind masterpiece."

Roger Ebert, *Chicago Sun-Times*: "A case can be made that *Caligari* was the first true horror film. There had been earlier ghost stories and the eerie serial *Fantomas* made in 1913-14, but their characters were inhabiting a recognizable world. *Caligari* creates a mindscape, a subjective psychological fantasy. In this world, unspeakable horror becomes possible."

If you liked this, you might also like:

From Morning to Midnight (1920).

#38 *Let the Right One In* (2008)

Eli is 12 years old. She's been 12 for over 200 years, and she just moved in next door.

Why it made the list:

A grim and brittle film that matches its frozen Stockholm setting, *Let The Right One In* builds suspense and scares atop more mundane childhood traumas like bullying and isolation. The understated yet powerful performances of the young lead actors provide pathos and, eventually, horror, in equal measures.

Synopsis:

A 12-year-old boy named Oskar (Kåre Hedebrant) lives in an apartment building in suburban Stockholm with his mother. He makes monthly trips to the country to visit his father on a farm. These escapes are important for Oskar, because he is bullied and ostracized at school. He is obsessed with crime and violence, and keeps a hunting knife hidden under his mattress. Oskar spends most of his free time alone until he meets a strange girl named Eli (Lena Leandersson) who has just moved into his building. At first, Eli tells Oskar that they cannot be friends, but the pair becomes closer as they spend time together in the courtyard of the apartment building. Eli encourages Oskar to stand up to the bullies at school, and Oskar accepts Eli despite her many quirks. As they bond more closely, Oskar discovers Eli's true nature. She is a vampire, and she encourages Oskar's vengeful tendencies, telling him to be like her. But until a fateful showdown with the bullies one night, Oskar cannot understand what that truly means.

Scariest scene:

Eli, desperately hungry for blood, attacks a local woman and bites her before being driven off. The woman becomes very ill and is taken to the hospital, and realizes she has somehow become infected. When a desire for blood makes clear the nature of her situation, the woman wants to die, and does so by having a nurse open the blinds to her room, exposing her to the sun and setting her body aflame.

Memorable dialogue:

> **OSKAR:** Are you a vampire?
>
> **ELI:** I live off blood … Yes.
>
> **OSKAR:** Are you … dead?
>
> **ELI:** No. Can't you tell?
>
> **OSKAR:** But … are you old?
>
> **ELI:** I'm 12. But I've been 12 for a long time.

Did you know?

In the film's final scene, Oskar and Eli use Morse code to communicate. They are tapping out the letters P-U-S-S, which is Swedish for "small kiss."

Cast:

Kåre Hedebrant (Oskar), Lina Leandersson (Eli), Per Ragnar (Håkan), Henrik Dahl (Erik), Karin Bergquist (Yvonne), Peter Carlberg (Lacke), Ika Nord (Virginia), Mikael Rahm (Jocke), Karl-Robert Lindgren (Gösta), Anders T. Peedu (Morgan).

What the critics say:

Carina Chicano, *Los Angeles Times*: "Oskar and Eli might look like two innocent children in love, but one of them is neither innocent nor a child.

The double-edged title—which refers to a bloodsucking technicality that says vampires must be invited into a victim's home before they can attack—raises the question of who we allow into our lives when our options are limited. Eli's and Oskar's story is literally one of a lonely boy saved by love, but the movie's title sounds an alarm."

Alissa Simon, *Variety*: "Otherworldly child actors Hedebrant and Leandersson perfectly embody their roles. Their opposite looks are used as elements of production design by Eva Noren, who brilliantly contrasts darkness and light. Exquisitely detailed lensing by Dutch-Swedish DP Hoyte van Hoytema adds dimensions to the multilayered story while using snow-white and blood-red as leitmotifs."

Colin Covert, *Minneapolis Star Tribune*: "*Let the Right One In* is one of the essential horror films of the decade. It's also one of the most enthralling romances and one of the best films about children. While it contains spurts of violence that are as shocking as a splash of blood on snow, it is a touching, moody romance. Imagine a Venn diagram where preadolescent innocence, budding sexuality and escalating dread overlap, and you have located the strange territory this Swedish exercise in Northern Gothic occupies."

If you liked this, you might also like:

Martin (1977).

#39 *The Entity* (1982)

Something evil is after Carla Moran and it will stop at nothing to get her.

Why it made the list:

This film, directed by journeyman helmer Sidney J. Furie, is an amazing film. Released the same year as *Poltergeist,* it covers much of the same ground. However, *The Entity* is a much darker film. The special effects aren't as good here as *Poltergeist*, but the film packs a wallop—particularly in its scenes involving the raping of Barbara Hershey's character. The film is frightening because it goes well beyond what we usually see supernatural forces do in films, going so far as to actually rape the film's protagonist in front of her small children. This film isn't for the weak-hearted. And we haven't even touched on Barbara Hershey's Avoriaz Fantastic Film Festival-winning performance, which is one of the all-time great turns in American horror.

Synopsis:

At the beginning of the film Carla Moran (Barbara Hershey) is forcefully awakened from slumber when she is beaten violently and raped by an unseen supernatural force. She and everyone around her believe she's having a breakdown. No one in the film is particularly nice or supportive to the character (they all think she's full of shit), and she continues to be terrorized by the entity throughout the duration of the film. Eventually Carla meets up with a team of paranormal investigators who hope to free her of the entity, but the poltergeist does not relent.

Scariest scene:

Any one of the multiple supernatural rape scenes could be considered a "scariest scene," but we have to go hands down here with the scene in which Carla is forcibly raped in front of her helpless children. This is truly horrifying stuff. When her teenage son, Bill, tries to stop the poltergeist from ravaging his mother, he's electrocuted and suffers a broken wrist for the effort.

Memorable dialogue:

> **CARLA:** All right. All right, bastard. I've finished running. So do what you want. Take your time, buddy. Take your time. Really, I'm thankful for the, uh, rest. I'm so … tired of being scared. So it's all right, it really is, it's all right. You can do anything you want to me, you can, uh, torture me, kill me, anything. But you can't have me. You cannot touch me. … That's mine.

Did you know?

Co-stars George Coe (Dr. Weber) and Alex Rocco (Jerry Anderson) both died on the same day—July 18, 2015.

Cast:

Barbara Hershey (Carla Moran), Ron Silver (Phil Sneiderman), David Labiosa (Bill), George Coe (Dr. Weber), Margaret Blye (Cindy Nash), Jacqueline Brookes (Dr. Cooley), Richard Brestoff (Gene Kraft), Michael Alldredge (George Nash), Raymond Singer (Joe Mehan), Natasha Ryan (Julie).

What the critics say:

Glenn Erickson, *DVD Savant*: "Barbara Hershey makes the hocus-pocus plot work like gangbusters. Her terror during the attacks is as credible as her trepidation when trying to describe them to doubting doctors, and she keeps Carla Moran's experience on a plane much higher than the voyeuristic peep-show around her. Movies may have become much more crude, but gratuitous nudity has all but disappeared from mainstream films these days, and modern actresses would never do these scenes. That makes Ms. Hershey all the more exceptional as an actress-daredevil."

Staff, *Arrow in the Head*: "*The Entity* is a nerve-wracking film to sit through. The performances make it happen, the effects weaken it and it's not really a 'fun' movie to watch. It accomplishes the basic goals it sets out to do: create credible drama and scare you. I had trouble sleeping after watching this one … "

Jeffrey M. Anderson, *Combustible Celluloid*: "Veteran director Sidney J. Furie films in an appealingly inky widescreen frame, employing a very intense hammering score to underline the terror. The A-list cast and very good dialogue by Frank De Felitta—who adapted his own book—helps a great deal."

If you liked this, you might also like:

Burnt Offerings (1976).

#40 *The Innocents* (1961)

A strange new experience in shock.

Why it made the list:

The Innocents has quite the pedigree. Adapted from the classic novella "The Turn of the Screw" by Henry James and co-written for the screen by the legendary Truman Capote, *The Innocents* paints a grim psychological portrait of the effects of haunting and possession. It greatly benefits from the striking lighting effects of cinematographer Freddie Francis and artful direction from Jack Clayton. Deborah Kerr's performance is considered among her finest, and the work of the child actors is especially effective.

Synopsis:

An inexperienced young woman named Miss Giddens (Deborah Kerr) is hired to be the governess to two young children living at the country estate of their uncle (Michael Redgrave). When she arrives at the estate, Miss Giddens is taken with the sister of the pair, Flora (Pamela Franklin). Things begin to take a turn for the strange when Flora's brother Miles (Martin Stephens) returns from boarding school. Unexplained voices and strange visions begin to trouble Miss Giddens, and she is soon convinced that the children are in mortal danger and she must do whatever it takes to save their souls from the corruption that has seized them.

Scariest scene:

After Flora has a terrible fit, Miss Giddens sends her away from the estate, sure that if the girl remains she is in terrible danger. She then attempts to tackle the possession of Miles head on, resulting in a scene of escalating

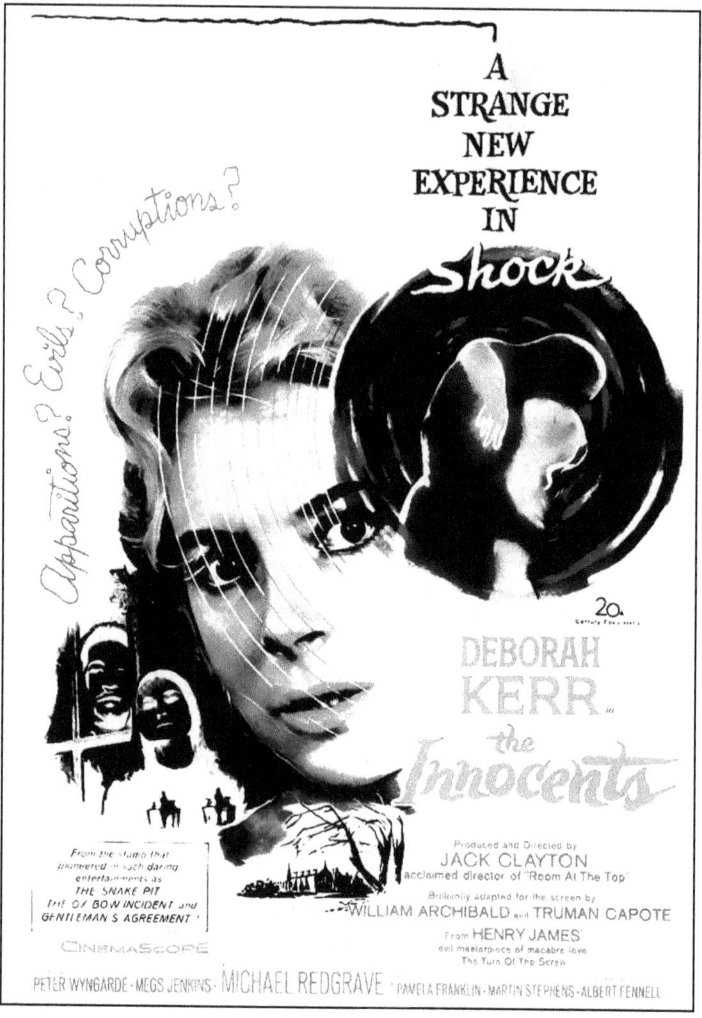

tension and terror as the ghost that haunts Miles appears at the window to taunt Miss Giddens before unleashing its ultimate revenge.

Memorable dialogue:

> **MILES**: What shall I sing to my lord from my window? What shall I sing for my lord will not stay? What shall I sing for my lord will not listen? Where shall I go when my lord is away? Whom shall I love when the moon is arisen? Gone is my lord and the grave is his prison. What shall I say when my lord comes a calling? What shall I say when he knocks on my door? What

> shall I say when his feet enter softly? Leaving the marks of his grave on my floor. Enter my lord. Come from your prison. Come from your grave, for the moon is a risen. Welcome, my lord.

Did you know?

Director Jack Clayton didn't want the children to be exposed to the darker themes of the story, so they never saw the screenplay in its entirety. The children were given their pages the day before they were to be filmed.

Cast:

Deborah Kerr (Miss Giddens), Peter Wyngarde (Peter Quint), Megs Jenkins (Mrs. Grose), Michael Redgrave (The Uncle), Martin Stephens (Miles), Pamela Franklin (Flora), Clytie Jessop (Miss Jessel), Isla Cameron (Anna).

What the critics say:

Michael Atkinson, *The Village Voice:* "Is it the finest, smartest, most visually savvy horror film ever made by a big studio? Deborah Kerr is the sexually straitjacketed governess subject to either the ghastly duplicity of her dead-eyed charges or the threatening ghosts of the estate's previous servants—or both—and it might be the most unforgettable performance by a British actress in its decade. Clayton's filmmaking, mustering frisson by both candle and blazing daylight, could serve as an object lesson in its genre."

Geoff Andrew, *Time Out:* "No shock tactics here, just the careful creation of sinister atmosphere through decor, Freddie Francis' haunting camerawork, and evocative acting. Kerr, especially, is excellent."

Staff, *Variety:* "This catches an eerie, spine-chilling mood right at the start and never lets up on its grim, evil theme. Director Jack Clayton makes full use of camera angles, sharp cutting, shadows, ghost effects and a sinister soundtrack."

If you liked this, you might also like:

The Uninvited (1944).

#41 *The Conjuring* (2013)

Based on the true case files of the Warrens.

Why it made the list:

Director James Wan (*The Saw*) isn't exactly the name that pops into your head when you think of subtle, psychological horror. At least it wasn't until he crafted 2013's *The Conjuring*, a film that plays like one of the 1970s haunted house films it pays homage to. In an era when horror is rarely effective and more often than not nothing more than a string of jump-scares and gross outs, this film stands out as perhaps the finest American horror film produced in more than a decade. *The Conjuring* is well crafted, well-acted, and both startlingly effective and deliciously fun. It was also the first film the Motion Picture Association of America slapped with an R rating based only on its being "too frightening." A book about the scariest horror films of all time just wouldn't be complete without its inclusion.

Synopsis:

Years before the famed "haunting" in Amityville, Carolyn (Lili Taylor) and Roger Perron (Ron Livingston) experienced similar happenings at their Harrisville, Rhode Island, farmhouse. As the supernatural occurrences escalated and the family learned of the grisly deaths which had taken place inside their home, they decided to seek expert assistance. They then contacted noted paranormal investigators Ed (Patrick Wilson) and Lorraine Warren (Vera Farmiga) to take a look at the house. The Warrens immediately recognized a strong satanic force within the house. In what will become the case of their lives, the Warrens must utilize every trick they've learned and lean heavily on spiritual faith to defeat the menacing demonic presence.

Scariest scene:

The most frightening scene in *The Conjuring* is an easy one to pinpoint. Despite its being revealed in trailers for the film (don't you hate that?), the scene in which a pair of ghostly hands emerge from the darkness behind Carolyn Perron and clap twice still made audiences jump a foot into the air. It's also one of the most iconic scenes in the history of horror cinema. Clap twice in quick succession and virtually every horror buff will instantly know exactly what you are referring to.

Memorable dialogue:

> **ED WARREN:** We've been called ghost hunters. Paranormal researchers. Wackos.
>
> **LORRAINE WARREN:** But we prefer to be known simply as Ed and Lorraine Warren.

Did you know?

Filmmaker James Wan carefully modeled *The Conjuring's* cinematography and atmospherics after classic horror films of the 1970s—the era in which the Perron haunting actually took place.

Cast:

Vera Farmiga (Lorraine Warren), Patrick Wilson (Ed Warren), Lili Taylor (Carolyn Perron), Ron Livingston (Roger Perron), Shanley Caswell (Andrea), Hayley McFarland (Nancy), Joey King (Christine), Mackenzie Foy (Cindy), Kyla Deaver (April), Shannon Kook (Drew).

What the critics say:

Bruce Diones, *The New Yorker*: "Wan … builds the many bumps in the night into a small Hitchcockian symphony of terror by way of long, eerie tracking shots, dramatic silences, and sudden scares that are frighteningly immersive."

Ian Buckwalter, *The Atlantic*: "Here's what took place at the screening I attended last week for *The Conjuring*. Things started out with the usual chatter, but then something curious started to develop, gradually, as the movie went on. People largely kept quiet. There were startled screams, collective jumps and armrest-grabbing, and laughter at the needed comic relief that Wan provides throughout the film. But as the director slowly wound up the tension in preparation for the film's chaotic climax, there were moments where it seemed the entire theater was holding its breath. We were united in one feeling: Terror."

Peter Howell, *Toronto Star*: "This is a horror film where a pair of suddenly clapping hands gives you the heebie-jeebies, and Wan doesn't cheat with his jump scares."

If you liked this, you might also like:

The Amityville Horror (1979).

#42 *Frankenstein* (1931)

A monster science created—but could not destroy!

Why it made the list:

Frankenstein is one of the true, original templates for horror films for many generations that followed. All of the tropes are here—isolated laboratories, scientists trying to play god, horrifying ramifications for taking moral and ethical liberties with nature, and so on. People often credit Boris Karloff's humane interpretation of the Monster for the success of this movie, and rightly so. However, Colin Clive's inspired performance as the tortured Henry Frankenstein, a scientist on the verge of insanity, is sadly overlooked. Clive's performance is the glue that holds this horror fairy tale together.

Synopsis:

Henry Frankenstein is an extremely bright med student who decides to drop out of college to fully pursue his mad dream of bringing new life to the dead. As the film opens, Frankenstein and his deformed assistant Fritz (Dwight Frye) rob a fresh grave, giving no thought or respect to the dearly departed. A short time later, Fritz is sent to the university to steal a better brain for the patchwork corpse Frankenstein has assembled. Unfortunately, there's an accident; Fritz destroys the good brain and is forced to take the brain of a criminal. Meanwhile, Frankenstein's fiancée Elizabeth (Mae Clarke), troubled over a rambling letter the good doctor has sent her (and haunted by chilling premonitions of doom), enlists the aid of Frankenstein's best friend Victor (John Boles) along with a Frankenstein's former college professor Dr. Waldman (Edward Van Sloan), to find Frankenstein and bring him safely home. The trio discover Frankenstein on the very night that he successfully reanimates a corpse (Boris Karloff). Horrified by his own creation and jarred back to sanity, Frankenstein leaves the destruction of his monster to Dr. Waldman and flees with Elizabeth and Victor. Frankenstein quickly recovers from his madness and moves forward with his wedding plans. Unbeknownst to him, however, the monster has escaped destruction and is now free to roam the countryside …

Scariest scene:

If you want to scare the most people possible you don't need fancy digital effects or annoying jump cuts or blaring music or even gore. No, you simply threaten to kill innocence. That's right. If you want a sure-fire horror moment just put a child in danger. That's exactly what happens in *Frankenstein* once the Monster has escaped his lab prison. He roams the countryside until he stumbles onto a child playing by the water. At first the little girl Maria (Marilyn Harris) is unsure what to make of the Monster (just as the audience is giving a collective "Oh no!") but she warms to the bizarre stranger and even gets him to play with her quite merrily as she tosses flower heads into the pond and watches them float around. Things go well until the Monster runs out of petals and decides to throw the little girl in to see if she floats around too.

Memorable dialogue:

> **HENRY FRANKENSTEIN:** Look! It's moving. It's alive …
> It's alive, it's moving, it's alive, it's alive, it's alive, it's alive,
> IT'S ALIVE!
>
> **VICTOR MORITZ:** Henry, in the name of God!
>
> **HENRY FRANKENSTEIN:** Oh, in the name of God! Now
> I know what it feels like to be God!

Did you know?

According to *The People's Almanac*, at one point the movie was to have included a line of dialogue giving the Monster the name Adam. The Almanac indicates that an early print of the film may have indeed been released with just such a scene, but that it was cut when audiences began referring to the Monster by the name Frankenstein.

Cast:

Colin Clive (Henry Frankenstein), Mae Clarke (Elizabeth), John Boles (Victor Moritz), Boris Karloff (The Monster), Doctor Waldman (Edward Van Sloan), Baron Frankenstein (Frederick Kerr), Dwight Frye (Fritz), The Burgomaster (Lionel Belmore), Little Maria (Marilyn Harris).

What the critics say:

Mordaunt Hall, *The New York Times*: "Out of John L. Balderston's stage conception of the Mary Shelley classic, *Frankenstein*, James Whale, producer of *Journey's End* as a play and as a film, has wrought a stirring grand-guignol type of picture, one that aroused so much excitement at the Mayfair yesterday that many in the audience laughed to cover their true feelings. "

Tom Milne, *Time Out* : "A stark, solid, impressively stylish film, overshadowed (a little unfairly) by the later explosion of Whale's wit in the delirious *Bride of Frankenstein*. Karloff gives one of the great performances of

all time as the monster whose mutation from candour to chill savagery is mirrored only through his limpid eyes. The film's great imaginative coup is to show the monster 'growing up' in all too human terms. First he is the innocent baby, reaching up to grasp the sunlight that filters through the skylight. Then the joyous child, playing at throwing flowers into the lake with a little girl whom he delightedly imagines to be another flower. And finally, as he finds himself progressively misjudged by the society that created him, the savage killer as whom he has been typecast. The film is unique in Whale's work in that the horror is played absolutely straight, and it has a weird fairytale beauty not matched until Cocteau."

Alfred Rushford Greason, *Variety*: "Playing is perfectly paced. Colin Clive, the cadaverous hero of *Journey's End*, is a happy choice for the scientist driven by a frenzy for knowledge. He plays it with force, but innocent of ranting. Boris Karloff enacts the monster and makes a memorable figure of the bizarre figure with its indescribably terrifying face of demoniacal calm, a fascinating acting bit of mesmerism"

If you liked this, you might also like:

The Curse of Frankenstein (1957).

#43 The Babadook (2014)

If it's in a word, or in a book, you can't get rid of ...
The Babadook.

Why it made the list:

The Babadook establishes from the beginning a grim and oppressive tone, employing a muted color palette, visuals of dead gray skies and skeletal trees, and dark, claustrophobic interiors. As the titular bogeyman grows in influence and power, unease transmutes into dread and then into outright terror. The Babadook is not the only thing haunting the mother and child in this brilliantly scripted tale, however. The death of the woman's husband and boy's father seven years prior hangs over the proceedings throughout, giving extra weight and power to the supernatural forces that have come to torment them. Grief and terror co-mingle to produce something much more horrible than either might by itself, and as the mother slips along the razor's edge of sanity, she must overcome both or lose everything she is and everything she has.

Synopsis:

Amelia (Essie Davis), the widowed mother of Samuel (Noah Wiseman), struggles to care for her son as his behavior grows increasingly out of control both at home and at school. She also still mourns the death of her husband, Oskar (Benjamin Winspear), who was killed in an accident while driving her to the hospital to deliver Samuel. The boy's behavior worsens after Amelia reads him a bedtime story from a pop-up book called *Mister Babadook*, about a sinister figure with long, sharp fingers and teeth and a top hat that promises to torment those who become aware of its existence. Samuel is convinced that the creature is real, and sinister events begin to plague both mother and son. Amelia at first believes the events to be a product of Samuel's overactive imagination, but is soon forced to face the truth: The Babadook is real.

Scariest scene:

Amelia is confronted by the Babadook in the guise of her dead husband, Oskar. She is overcome with love at first, but realizes the terrible truth when Oskar tells her repeatedly that she must bring him the boy. She flees to her bedroom and bars the door, but The Babadook enters through the fireplace, attacking her and taking possession of her body. She is then seen twitching and shaking as she sits in front of the television, before chasing down and killing the family dog.

Memorable dialogue:

> **AMELIA:** (Reading from *Mister Babadook)* His name is Mister Babadook, and this is his book. A rumbling sound, then three sharp knocks Ba-ba-ba Dook Dook DOOK. That's when you'll know that he's around. You'll see him if you look.
>
> **SAMUEL:** Ba-ba-ba Dook Dook Dook.
>
> **AMELIA:** We might read another one tonight, hey?
>
> **SAMUEL:** But you said I could choose.
>
> **AMELIA:** (continues reading) This is what he wears on top. He's funny, don't you think? See him in your room at night …
>
> **SAMUEL:** Mom? Does it hurt the boy? Mom? Does it live under the bed? Mom? Mommy!

Did you know?

Director Jennifer Kent originally planned to film the movie in black and white.

Cast:

Essie Davis (Amelia), Daniel Henshall (Robbie) Noah Wiseman (Samuel). Tiffany Lyndal-Knight (Supermarket Mom), Tim Purcell (The Babadook), Michelle Nightingale (Eastern Suburbs Mom 3), Benjamin Winspear (Oskar), Peta Shannon (Eastern Suburbs Mom 2), Hayley McElhinney (Claire), Cathy Adamek (Prue).

What the critics say:

Joshua Rothkopf, *Time Out New York*: "On purely formal grounds (the ones on which the genre lives or dies), Kent is a natural. She favors crisp compositions and unfussy editing, transforming the banal house itself into a subtle, shadowy threat."

Scott Foundas, *Variety*: "This meticulously designed and directed debut feature from writer-director Jennifer Kent manages to deliver real, seat-grabbing jolts while also touching on more serious themes of loss, grief and other demons that cannot be so easily vanquished."

Staff, *New York Daily News*: "So many horror films trade depth for a thrill. *The Babadook* has both. It dispenses with cheap scares and draws tension from a slowly enveloping dread. And when you think you know where it's going, that's when it goes in for the kill."

If you liked this, you might also like:

Oculus (2013).

#44 *Henry: The Portrait of a Serial Killer* (1986)

He's not Freddy. He's not Jason. He's real.

Why it made the list:

Much of this film's effectiveness comes as a result of its being made with a low budget ($110,000); *Henry: Portrait of a Serial Killer's* minimalist production values actually lend the film more of a bleak, gritty atmosphere than it probably would have had otherwise. This coupled with Henry's ho-hum workaday approach to the murders he commits make director John McNaughton's character study a truly frightening cinematic experience. There are no simple jump scares to be had here. Instead, McNaughton simply provides us with a warts-and-all examination of a man who kills innocent people for seemingly no reason whatsoever. Despite Henry's unreliable assertion that he had a problematic childhood, the unapologetic film forgoes attempts to psychoanalyze him and explain away his homicidal tendencies, and the film is better for it. That Henry is not held responsible for the grisly acts he commits, coupled with the facts that he could be living right next door to us and that he selects his victims at random, only serve to make the film all the more frightening. McNaughton, who had been a documentary filmmaker prior to this, films the proceedings as if this were a documentary, sometimes making it difficult to remember that what we're seeing isn't real.

Synopsis:

Henry (Michael Rooker) murders complete strangers on a regular basis. Unlike other movie psychos, he seems to have no real reason for doing

the things he does. He doesn't seem to find any satisfaction in the act of murder, and there is no sexual release for him. He simply is what he is: A cold-blooded killer with an insatiable appetite for bloodletting. Henry then pulls his dim-witted roommate Otis (Tom Towles) into his bloody world of mutilation and dismemberment, imparting the wisdom he's gained on the subject after many years of killing. When the emotionless Henry seemingly falls in love with Otis' sister, Becky (Tracy Arnold), it appears that he may be on the verge of an unlikely redemption.

Scariest scene:

The film's scariest and most difficult scene to endure depicts the slaying of a suburban family as seen from the point-of-view of Otis' hand-held camcorder. This incredibly shocking and effective scene looks so real that we as an audience almost forget this is only a movie. The revelation that Henry and Otis are actually watching this footage and are more than a little bit entertained by it only manages to make this frightening scene all the more scary.

Memorable dialogue:

> **OTIS:** I'd like to kill somebody.
>
> **HENRY:** Say that again.
>
> **OTIS:** I'd like to kill somebody.
>
> **HENRY:** Let's me and you go for a ride, Otis.

Did you know?

Michael Rooker was working as a janitor at the time he filmed *Henry: Portrait of a Serial Killer.* The janitor's uniform that he wears in the film was his real uniform. The reason he takes it off before killing his victims is because Rooker didn't want to stain his uniform as he had only one.

Cast:

Michael Rooker (Henry), Tom Towles (Otis), Mary Demus (Dead Woman), Anne Bartoletti (Waitress), Elizabeth Kaden (Dead Wife), Ted Kaden (Dead Husband), Denise Sullivan (Floating Woman), Tracy Arnold (Becky), Monica Anne O'Malley (Mall Victim), Bruce Quist (Husband).

What the critics say:

Peter Travers, *Rolling Stone*: "The movie doesn't shy away from gore: Bodies are kicked, punched, slashed, shot and dismembered. But half of the sixteen murders take place off screen. There's more mayhem in any of the R-rated *Friday the 13th, Nightmare on Elm Street* and *Halloween* movies. Those films offer supernatural villains and cardboard victims; they're easy to shake. Not so *Henry.* The film is no masterpiece, but it is spare, intelligent and thought provoking."

Joe Bob Briggs, *Joe Bob Goes to the Drive-In*: "I was figuring the other day that, in my personal lifetime, I've probably witnessed 157,000 murders by at least 15,000 froth-mouth maniacs. And I have never, ever, in my life, seen a mass-murdering maniac as scary as the one in *Henry: Portrait of a Serial Killer.*"

Roger Ebert, *Chicago Sun-Times*: "Unlike typical 'slasher' movies, 'Henry' does not employ humor, campy in-jokes or a colorful anti-hero. Filmed in the gray slush and wet winter nights of Chicago's back alleys, honky-tonk bars and drab apartments, it tells of a drifter who kills strangers, efficiently and without remorse. The movie contains scenes of heartless and shocking violence, committed by characters who seem to lack the ordinary feelings of common humanity."

If you liked this, you might also like:

Monster (2003).

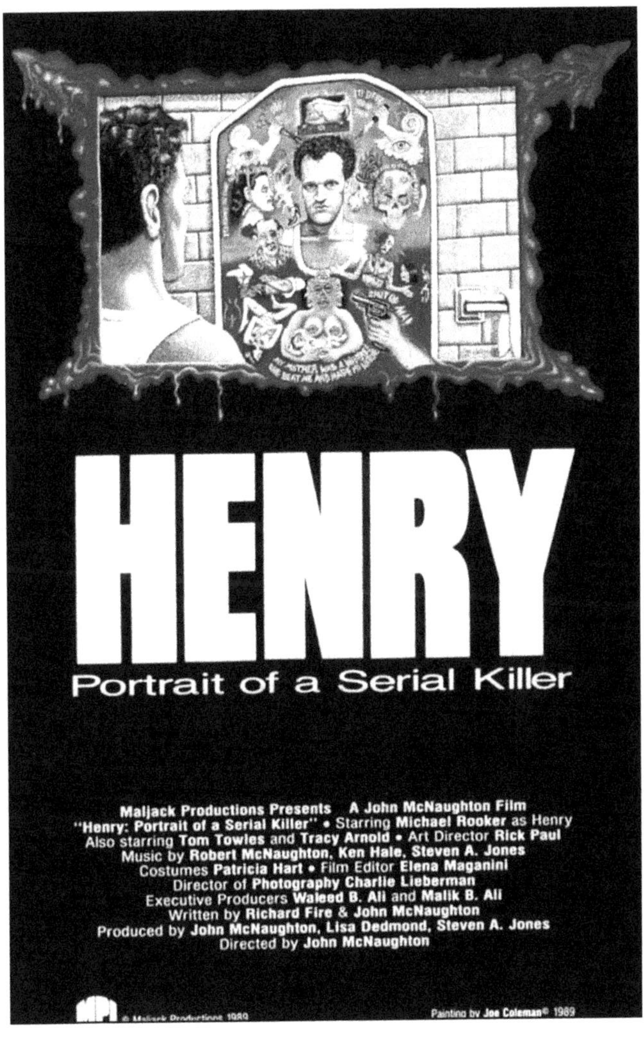

#45 *Phantasm* (1979)

If this one doesn't scare you... you're already dead!

Why it made the list:

Blending elements of science fiction and horror, *Phantasm* overcomes its low-budget indie origins by keeping things surreal, strange and scary. The effective use of dream-like imagery mixed with moments of straight-up shock and gore make the film a true original.

Synopsis:

Jody Pearson (Bill Thornbury) and his younger brother Mike (Michael Baldwin) are struggling to rebuild their lives two years after the deaths of their parents. Jody dreams of going on the road and becoming a musician, but feels he must look after 13-year-old Mike. The mundane details of their day-to-day lives become less important following the mysterious death of Jody's friend Tommy (Bill Cone). Mike spies on Tommy's funeral, and after everyone has left, witnesses the funeral home director and mortician, dubbed the Tall Man, single-handedly lift Tommy's coffin and take it away instead of burying it. Investigating further, Mike discovers small, dwarf-like creatures roaming the grounds of the cemetery and halls of the mausoleum. He convinces Jody that something terrible is happening at the mortuary, and the two band together with Jody's best friend Reggie (Reggie Bannister) to stop the tall man's twisted, unbelievable schemes before they become the next victims.

Scariest scene:

Mike breaks into the mausoleum after hours to see if he can determine what the Tall Man is up to. The hallways, however, are patrolled by flying silver orbs with bad intentions. Mike is pursued by one and can't get away because he is nabbed by the caretaker. He manages to escape the caretaker's grasp just as the orb flies in, and it first spikes the caretaker's head, then drills into his brain, releasing a truly impressive gout of blood.

Memorable dialogue:

> **MIKE:** I know you're not going to believe this, but these things were here, right in the garage, and they were going to get me!
>
> **JODY:** Aw, give me a break, would you?
>
> **MIKE:** They were jumping on the car and making these weird sounds!
>
> **JODY:** You're sure it wasn't that retarded kid, Timmy, up the street?
>
> **MIKE:** No, it was the same things that chased me last night!

Did you know?

The mansion used for the exterior shots of the mausoleum was also seen in the James Bond film *A View to a Kill*, as well as the 1976 horror film *Burnt Offerings*.

Cast:

Michael Baldwin (Mike), Bill Thornbury (Jody), Reggie Bannister (Reggie), Kathy Lester (Lady in Lavender), Terrie Kalbus (Fortuneteller's Granddaughter), Ken Jones (Caretaker), Susan Harper (Girlfriend), Lynn Eastman (Sally), David Arntzen (Toby), Angus Scrimm (Tall Man).

What the critics say:

Kim Newman, *Empire*: "Extremely gory. Horror fans should delight. It has more bizarro gimmicks to the minute than any other horror picture of 1979, including the flying silver balls that bore into your forehead and redistribute your blood all over the place through a sprinkler attachment.

Angus Scrimm, cast as the Tall Man, is a monster worth his own glow-in-the-dark hobby kit. "

Staff, *TV Guide*: "This *tour-de-force* came from a 21-year-old filmmaker Don Coscarelli, who did just about everything on *Phantasm*, a wonderfully creative, bizarre, delightfully terrifying horror film that never fails to surprise. Perhaps because of Coscarelli's youth, *Phantasm* seems the product of a warped teenage imagination, full as it is of creative and original scares rooted in basic fears of abandonment, loneliness, sex, and death. Although viewers leave the theater buzzing about the flying silver sphere, it was only one element in a film filled with unique, personal, witty, and, at the same time, terrifying imagery rarely seen in low-budget horror films."

Almar Haflidason, *BBC*: "As writer and director, Don Coscarelli has a healthy disregard for plot development and is only too happy to leave major questions unanswered. Despite this attitude to film-making he still crafts some excellent sequences of tension and horror, often with a darkly humorous lining. Ideal for Halloween viewing or a dark night, there's plenty of creepy fun to be had here, not least from the fabulously demented Tall Man."

If you liked this, you might also like:

Phantasm II (1988).

#46 The Others (2001)

Sooner or later she'll see them, then everything will be different.

Why it made the list:

The Others is a thought-provoking psychological horror film that explores the possibilities of the living co-existing with the dead. What happens after a person dies has been a heated and passionate on-going debate since the dawn of mankind. *The Others* outlines this discussion very subtly without becoming bogged down with the typical Hollywood haunted house trappings. There's no blood dripping from the walls or demonic howls and screams. Nor are there any distorted faces and figures forming in the darkened windows. The film's success works solely on its atmosphere and the audience's belief in an afterlife.

Synopsis:

Grace Stewart (Nicole Kidman), presumably a widow, shields her ill children from the sunlight. Anne (Alakina Mann) and Nicholas (James Bentley) have an odd condition that is exacerbated by photosynthesis. Curtains are drawn, doors are closed and the children are only allowed to play in the night.

Soon a trio arrives looking for work: Mrs. Bertha Mills (Fionnula Flanagan), Mr. Edmund Tuttle (Eric Sykes) and the mute Lydia (Elaine Cassidy). Grace has only recently been looking for replacements for her previous servants and is slightly put-off by the threesome's seemingly miraculous punctuality. Still, she accepts and hires them.

The young Anne begins telling stories of mysterious goings-ons and the people who are causing them. Nicholas, the younger of the two children, is frightened beyond reason and their mother is incensed at what

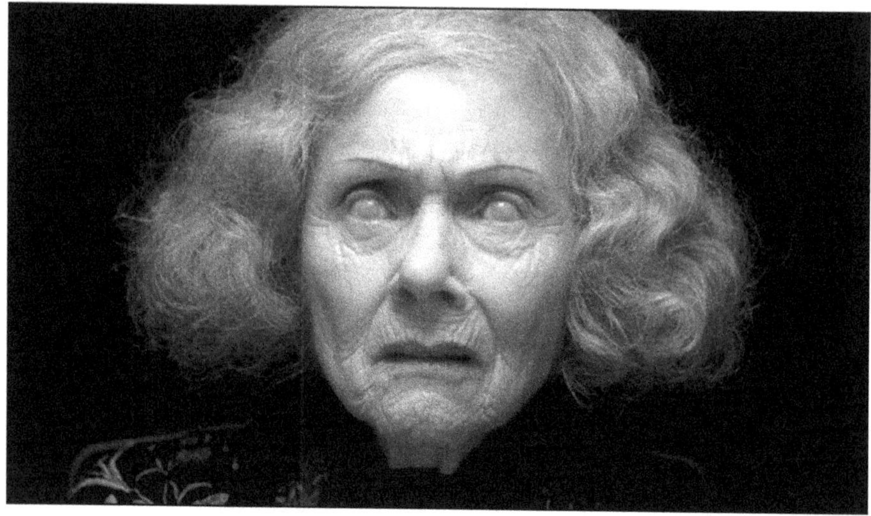

she believes to be tall tales. Anne refuses to relent and eventually her mother begins witnessing the paranormal activity herself.

Scariest scene:

While the film does have its share of obligatory haunted house fixtures (squeaking floors, slamming doors, and sudden screams), the real shocks come at the film's crescendo when Grace is finally hit with the awful truth.

Memorable dialogue:

> **MRS. MILLS:** Sometimes the world of the living gets mixed up with the world of the dead.

Did you know?

Xeroderma pigmentosum is the disease the Stewart children have. It is incredibly rare with only around one thousand people having it worldwide.

Cast:

Nicole Kidman (Grace Stewart), Fionnula Flanagan (Mrs. Bertha Mills), Christopher Eccleston (Charles Stewart), Alakina Mann (Anne Stewart), James Bentley (Nicholas Stewart), Eric Sykes (Mr. Edmund Tuttle), Elaine

Cassidy (Lydia), Renée Asherson (Old Lady), Gordon Reid (Assistant), Keith Allen (Mr. Marlish).

What the critics say:

James Sanford, *Kalamazoo Gazette*: "Writer-director Alejandro Amenabar has assembled a chiller that's thoroughly engrossing without ever grossing us out, and he's gotten an intense, masterfully modulated performance from Kidman that easily ranks among her finest."

James Berardinelli, *ReelViews*: "It's atmospheric, stylish, and spooky. The plot is well thought-out and its secrets and mysteries are unveiled slowly. Unfortunately, it is also cold, distancing, and moves at a glacial pace."

Liam Lacey, *Globe and Mail*: "A welcome change of pace from most contemporary scary stories, where the shocks come with all the subtlety of flashers jumping out of park bushes."

If you liked this, you might also like:

The Sixth Sense (1999).

#47 Cannibal Holocaust (1980)

The men you will see eaten alive are the same men who filmed these incredible sequences.

Why it made the list:

No other movie in cinema history is as notorious for its depiction of on-screen violence and brutality as is Ruggero Deodato's 1980 feature *Cannibal Holocaust*. In the late 1970s and early '80s, a demented and twisted form of the horror genre came into being—the cannibal film. Nothing was too graphic, nothing was too inhumane, and nothing was the least bit sacred. This particular breed of cinema and its creators relished in the idea of breaking down film barriers and taboos.

The proverbial kid gloves were of no use to the producers of this type of entertainment and their viewers were encouraged to hang on tight. These hapless, and sometimes jaded, theater-goers were about to be subjected to visuals unlike any they'd ever seen. *Cannibal Holocaust*, hands down, became the crowning jewel in this questionable and mercifully short-lived cycle of shocking movie making.

As *Cannibal Holocaust* opens, Riz Ortolani's tender soundtrack whispers sweet-nothings into the viewers' ears, while Deodato's camera slowly moves over the lush landscape of the Amazon jungle. It's all very comforting, and if not for the movie's title one might think a benign and inspiring drama was at hand, or a touching love story. However, that's not the case at all. On the contrary; when behind his camera this Italian director, this Ruggero Deodato, is simply and purely a fiend.

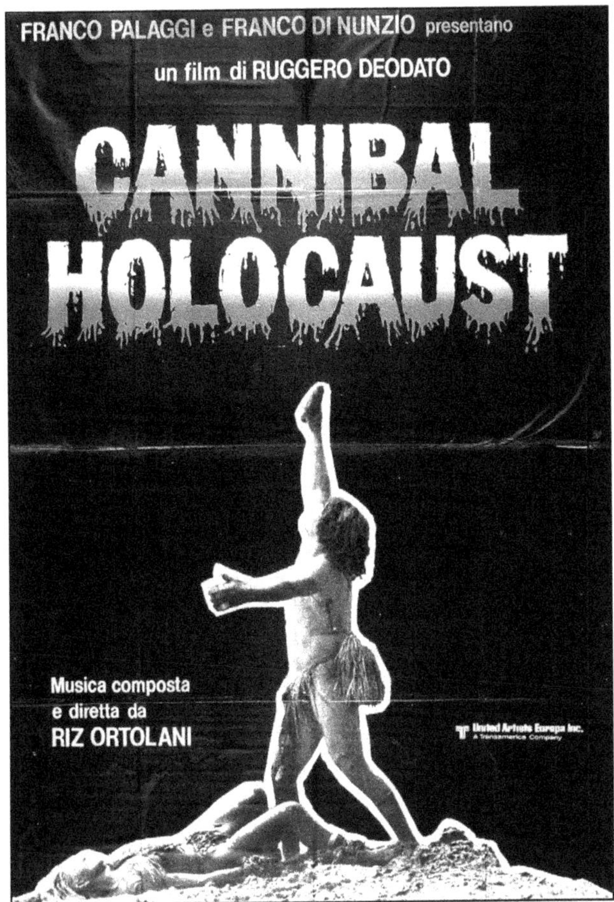

Synopsis:

Professor Harold Monroe (Robert Kerman) is leading a small expedition into the Amazon to locate a lost, and presumably dead, documentary film crew. Monroe is an anthropologist and his interest is piqued because these documentarians were on assignment to record what they believed to be tribes of cannibals. Unbeknownst to Monroe, the filmmakers were more interested in dishonestly staged vulgarism than actual and honest documentation.

Monroe and his cohort Chaco (Salvatore Basile) happen upon an indigenous tribe that has bedecked their dwellings with several shiny film cans. Most are hanging from trees, and the tribesmen seem curiously protective of their finds. It is apparent their mementos mean more to them than just mere decorations. In trade, Monroe offers up a tape recorder and, along with the sounds of the recordings on the tapes, convinces the tribesmen to relinquish the film cans. Monroe is certain that the truth of the documentarians' fate lies within the spools of unexposed celluloid. Monroe packs his newly-acquired belongings and makes his way, post-haste, back to New York City.

Back in New York, Professor Monroe finds himself invited to host a program recounting the tale of the four-member film crew: Alan Yates (Carl Gabriel Yorke), Faye Daniels (Francesca Ciardi), Jack Anders (Perry Pirkanen) and Mark Tomaso (Luca Barbareschi). With some trepidation Monroe accepts, but only if he can preview the found footage before it airs on television. Unusually perplexed at the professor's request, the producers go ahead and grant the green light for Monroe to examine the last known account of Alan Yates and crew.

Upon review of the filmed footage, Professor Monroe discovers that Alan Yates and his team were so starved for sensationalism that they staged many of the on-screen atrocities. Naturally, Yates was comfortable in knowing that he could edit the film upon his return to the mainland, but that accommodation never came to fruition. Alan Yates and his cohorts were about to be exposed for the disrespectful, cruel and savage brutes they were.

Professor Monroe watches on in dismay as Team Yates burns a village and many of its inhabitants. Then he witnesses the ruthless gang-rape of a native girl that ends in her death by impalement. All these things and more were done for the benefit of the camera, for the benefit of a viewing audience, for the benefit of its creators.

In utter disgust, Professor Monroe continues the cinematic onslaught of visceral perversions; perversions brought on by a team of young filmmakers he might have once considered peers or colleagues. It's obvious that Alan Yates will not stop himself from generating a situation that helps develop a unique and shocking camera shot.

Finally, the natives have had enough and launch an attack. They first spear Jack, who is then shot by Alan Yates. Yates wishes to film the natives dismembering and eating Jack. In the filming of this barbarity Faye is captured, raped, and beheaded in front of the camera. Ultimately, Yates and his remaining partner in crime, Mark, are butchered and slaughtered before the very camera they'd used to capture all this unnecessary carnage and misery.

Scariest scene:

Within a few short weeks of its release, *Cannibal Holocaust* found itself garnering a very nasty reputation. With each subsequent market it entered, the rumors about the film's unbridled savagery and vile spirit spread quickly, and rightfully so. There was talk of rape (found to be simulated), animal mutilation (found to be actual), and one god-forsaken sequence where a girl has been impaled like a human skewer (thankfully simulated). Any one or all of these could be considered the scariest scene in *Cannibal Holocaust.*

Memorable dialogue:

> **PROFESSOR HAROLD MONROE:** I wonder who the real cannibals are.

Did you know?

While *Cannibal Holocaust* had a major market release in 1980, it took an additional three years to make its way to Japan. Once the Japanese caught an eye-full of the film, ticket sales erupted. The box office receipts came in second only to *E.T. the Extra-Terrestrial.*

Cast:

Robert Kerman (Harold Monroe), Francesca Ciardi (Faye Daniels), Perry Pirkanen (Jack Anders), Luca Barbareschi (Mark Tomaso), Salvatore Basile (Chaco Losojos), Ricardo Fuentes (Felipe Ocanya), Carl Gabriel Yorke (Alan Yates), Paolo Paoloni (Chief NY Executive), Lionello Pio Di Savoia (Executive), Luigina Rocchi (Native).

What the critics say:

Carol Schwartz, *Video Hound's Cult Flicks & Trash Pics*: "Soul-deadening cannibal exploitation with the malevolent magnetism of a fatal car accident."

Lawrence P. Raffel, *Horror 101*: "There's not one frame of *Cannibal Holocaust* that plays for laughs or comes off as camp. It's serious business through and through … "

Michael Weldon, *The Psychotronic Video Guide*: "This controversial movie [is] a very convincing, clever, subversive, and dishonest feature pretending to condemn everything it shows."

If you liked this, you might also like:

The Green Inferno (2014).

#48 *The House of the Devil* (2009)

Talk on the phone. Finish your homework. Watch TV. Die.

Why it made the list:

Filmmaker Ti West knows a thing or two about ambiance. After carefully studying the moody, atmospheric horror films of the 1970s and 1980s, he mastered the style with this debut offering. *The House of the Devil* is a slow burn for sure, but it's well worth the wait. True students of the genre are sure to love this film as it's got something very few horror films can claim to have—wall-to-wall creepiness, from start to finish. Sure, many viewers are destined to be turned off by the long (but still creepy) build-up sequences in which nothing seems to be happening, but again, the film's payoff is one worth waiting for.

Synopsis:

College student Samantha Hughes (Jocelin Donahue) has just gotten a new apartment and she needs to come up with a couple hundred bucks as soon as possible. Things start to look up when she takes on a babysitting job from a man named Mr. Ulman (Tom Noonan). However, once she arrives at the family's house—conveniently located in the middle of nowhere—she begins to suspect that something else is happening altogether. Ultimately she will learn that she is a key part of a Satanic cult's plan for a ritual on this most special of nights. Will she get out of the house before it's too late?

Scariest scene:

The film's scariest scene is the one in which Sam is bound over a scrawled pentagram and offered up to be Satan's baby mama. In this frightening scene, the ritual is presided over by spooky, robed cult members who force her to drink demon blood.

Memorable dialogue:

> **TITLE CARD:** During the 1980s over 70 percent of American adults believed in the existence of abusive Satanic cults … Another 30 percent rationalized the lack of evidence due to government cover ups … The following is based on true unexplained events …

Did you know?

The film, which takes place in approximately 1983, was intentionally shot using the same techniques and formats as most splatter films from the 1980s.

Cast:

Jocelin Donahue (Samantha), Tom Noonan (Mr. Ulman), Mary Woronov (Mrs. Ulman), Greta Gerwig (Megan), AJ Bowen (Victor Ulman), Dee Wallace (Landlady), Heather Robb (Roommate), Darryl Nau (Random Guy), Brenda Cooney (Nurse), Danielle Noe (Mother).

What the critics say:

Peter Hartlaub, *San Francisco Chronicle*: "This is art house horror, heavily influenced by the scary movies made before Halloween changed the genre. The body count is low, there are no homicidal clowns, none of the main characters get naked and no one has to choose whether to hack off his own arm in order to avoid being drawn and quartered … There's a payoff in *The House of the Devil*, if you have the patience. Some of the scenes seem draggy, but the characters are complex, and their motivations are explained.

Robert Abele, *Los Angeles Times*: "West's assured way with widescreen framing, long takes and silences followed by sharp if unexplainable noise are almost cruelly funny in their heart-stopping pleasures."

Roger Ebert, *Chicago Sun-Times*: "The film may provide an introduction for some audience members to the Hitchcockian definition of suspense: it's the anticipation, not the happening, that's fun."

If you liked this, you might also like:

The Innkeepers (2011).

#49 When a Stranger Calls (1979)

Don't watch it alone.

Why it made the list:

If the basic premise of this film doesn't scare the bejeezus out of you, then you clearly don't have children. This is an example of a film just like an *Exorcist* (1973) or *Pet Sematary* (1989) that will have much more impact on a person who has one or two of the wee small folk wandering around their house. As a general film viewer, it's difficult as hell to sit through the harassing calls and eventual revelations regarding the babysitter. But as a parent, it's downright impossible to sit without squirming once the serial killer starts dialing up old friends after a seven-year stretch in the looney bin.

Synopsis:

Babysitter Jill Johnson (Carol Kane) watches a young couple's children while they enjoy a night on the town. Her tranquility is soon broken when a creepy man begins to make harassing calls to her. With each progressive call, the caller ups the ante and the threats become ever more real and ever more frightening. Jill calls the police department, who ultimately decide to put a trace on the phone. In doing so, they come to a very frightening realization—that the calls are being made from within the house. Let's just say things don't turn out too well for the kids or the parents, and the madman is then locked away for nearly a decade. He will ultimately escape from his looney bin confines and return to wreak havoc once more.

"Unequivocally the most terrifying movie I've ever seen." —AFTER DARK Magazine

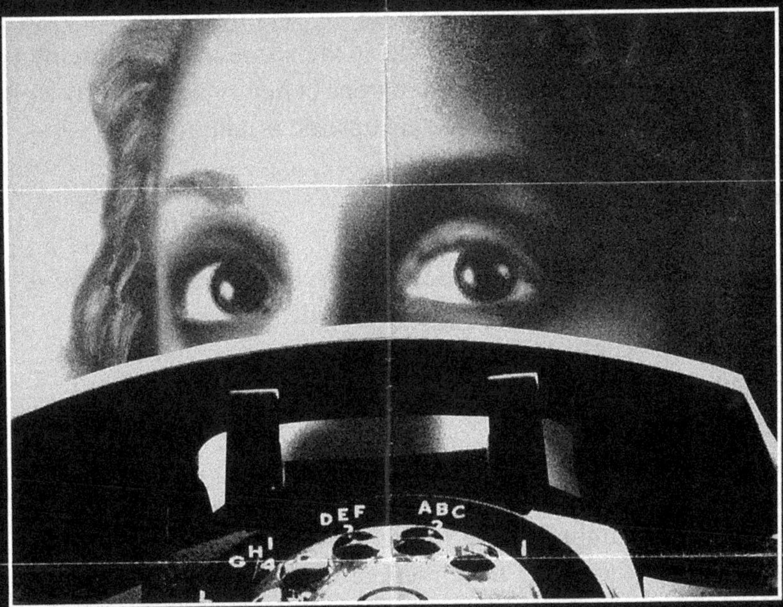

EVERY BABYSITTER'S NIGHTMARE BECOMES REAL...

WHEN A STRANGER CALLS

COLUMBIA PICTURES in association with MELVIN SIMON PRODUCTIONS presents
A BARRY KROST PRODUCTION
CHARLES DURNING CAROL KANE COLLEEN DEWHURST
WHEN A STRANGER CALLS
Also Starring TONY BECKLEY
RACHEL ROBERTS RON O'NEAL Executive Producers MELVIN SIMON AND BARRY KROST
Music by DANA KAPROFF Written by STEVE FEKE and FRED WALTON
Produced by DOUG CHAPIN and STEVE FEKE Directed by FRED WALTON

Columbia Pictures

© 1979 COLUMBIA PICTURES INDUSTRIES, INC.

Scariest scene:

The film's scariest scene is its most iconic—the single scene in which the film is remembered for—and that is the revelation that the presumed-killer/stalker is making the calls within the very house in which the babysitter is located. A close runner-up is the scene in which, many years later, the former babysitter (now a parent in her own right) gets a phone call from a familiar friend at a classy upscale restaurant.

Memorable dialogue:

> **SGT. SACKER:** Jill, this is Sergeant Sacker. Listen to me. We've traced the call … it's coming from inside the house! Now a squad car's coming over there right now, just get out of that house!

Did you know?

The telephone number of the residence where Jill is babysitting (555-2368) is also the number to Jamie Lee Curtis' house in *Forever Young* (1992).

Cast:

Carol Kane (Jill Johnson), Rutanya Alda (Mrs. Mandrakis), Carmen Arenziano (Dr. Mandrakis), Kirsten Larkin (Nancy), William Boyett (Sgt. Sacker), Charles Durning (John Clifford), Ron O'Neal (Lt. Charlie Garber), Heetu (Houseboy), Rachel Roberts (Dr. Monk), Tony Beckley (Curt Duncan),

What the critics say:

Staff, *Variety*: "Thanks to a fine cast, a rich and atmospheric score by Dana Kaproff, and astute direction by co-writer Fred Walton, *Stranger* is unquestionably a scary film. Bridging two distinct storylines, one the standard frightened babysitter alone in a dark house, and the other the subsequent manhunt for an escaped killer, script has chills a-plenty."

Charles Cassady, *Common Sense Media*: "Grim psychothriller with a few teen urban legends."

Staff, *Time Out*, "Not as atmospherically eerie as *Halloween* nor as mechanically effective as *Black Christmas*, but there's one great moment when the husband in bed turns into a stranger."

If you liked this, you might also like:

I Saw What You Did (1988).

#50 *The Descent* (2005)

Afraid of the dark? You will be.

Why it made the list:

I wasn't sure that a film about a group of attractive women going spelunking could be scary. Granted, Neil Marshall (the mastermind behind *Dog Soldiers*) was helming, but I had expectations of a vaguely Jim Wynorski-ish romp underground. In other news, my foot tastes great. What we have here is a terror-filled, underground maze filled with 'crawlers' (subterranean humanoid creatures). Our team of adventurous lady cave explorers picked exactly the wrong time to explore this particular cave system. What Marshall gives us in *The Descent* is exactly that… the viewer hurtles headlong into the dark with these characters, feel the walls close in and pray that somehow, some way they can get back to the surface. The film is visceral; it pulls you along with a mixture of beautiful camera work and a lighting design that is more sleight of hand than expository. Finally, Marshall excels in character development so we actually care about these poor, unfortunate women. That is really the hallmark of *The Descent*. Just when we think we've plumbed the depths of our own fear, we care a bit too much and forced even further down.

Synopsis:

Sarah (Shauna MacDonald), just a year after losing her husband and child in a tragic accident, accompanies her closest friends on an annual cave exploration vacation. The ladies, adrenaline junkies, attempt to get Sarah out of her funk with minimal success. Juno (Natalie Mendoza), this year's leader, chooses a cave system in the remote Appalachians that has largely been ignored and has never been properly mapped… without telling the others. A cave-in insures that the group, with limited supplies, must try

and find the will to survive. Unfortunately for them, they are not alone. The system is inhabited by an indigenous humanoid species that has a particular appetite and can move largely unseen and unheard. What is far more dangerous, though, are the personal revelations that happen through the ordeal including just how much of Sarah's family's death was 'accidental.'

Scariest scene:

Trapped and surrounded, the group gets their first look at the Crawlers... and it is memorable. Sounds reverberate from wall to wall in the cavern, hissing and screeching. The women panic, heading down a tunnel. Their helmet lights do more to confuse them than anything else. They stumble through the dark and the spelunker's frantic attempts at escape show flashes of the eerie, subterranean Crawlers. Then, they pounce! Necks are torn to shreds and the group scrambles. Juno, separated from the rest, prevents the Crawlers from dragging her friend Holly away as a midnight snack, finally engaging in a tooth and nail fight with the creature that she barely escapes. But, like any good horror film, you're never alone in the dark.

Memorable dialogue:

> **BETH:** I am an English teacher, not fucking Tomb Raider!

Did you know?

Soon after the European release in 2005, bombings in July on London buses forced a shift in the marketing. The image of Sarah screaming in a tunnel was the primary image on the buses with an "Outright terror" blurb. These were removed from the London Underground and other mass transit areas.

Cast:

Shauna MacDonald (Sarah), Natalie Mendoza (Juno), Alex Reid (Beth), Saskia Mulder (Rebecca), MyAnna Buring (Sam), Nora-Jane Noone (Holly), Oliver Milburn (Paul), Molly Kayll (Jessica), Craig Conway (Crawler-Scar), Leslie Simpson (Crawler).

What the critics say:

Roger Ebert, *The Chicago Sun-Times*: "This is the fresh, exciting summer movie I've been wanting for months. Or for years, it seems."

Sarah Lilleyman, *Time Magazine*: "Marshall could very well be the Caravaggio of the B-movie."

Alan Jones, *Radio Times*: "Super-scary and vicious, both psychologically and physically, this cleverly produced chill-ride is edgy British horror at its very best."

If you liked this, you might also like:

The Descent: Part 2 (2009).

#51 *The Beyond* (1981)

You will live in fear, the afterlife.

Why it made the list:

Fully capturing the essence of the grindhouse film experience, Lucio Fulci's underground masterpiece revels in every excess his films are known for, from gouged-out eyeballs to grotesque spurting wounds to rotting corpses. The film is filled with genuinely creepy moments, but if it doesn't succeed in frightening you, it will certainly succeed in grossing you out.

Synopsis:

A young New Yorker named Liza Merril (Catriona MacColl) inherits an old hotel in Louisiana, spending all of her money to renovate the place. During these repairs, people begin dying right and left, and Dr. John McCabe (David Warbeck) tries to help her solve the mystery of the location. A blind woman, Emily (Cinzia Monreale), ominously warns Liza to flee the place at once. Later it is discovered that the hotel is one of the seven gates of Hell. Now that it has been opened, the dead shall walk the earth …

Scariest scene:

Filled with scenes that are creepy and scenes that are just flat-out gross, the most frightening scene here has to be the one in which a young girl witnesses her unconscious mother's face slowly melted away with acid. Then, as the girl watches in horror, the oozing acid makes its way towards her. Frightened, she backs away and attempts to open several doors. When she finally finds one that's unlocked, she finds herself face to face with one of Lucio Fulci's gory cadavers.

Memorable dialogue:

> **EMILY [READING]:** Woe be unto him who opens one of the seven gateways to Hell, because through that gateway, evil will invade the world.

Did you know?

The film was originally released under the title *Seven Doors of Death*, directed by one Louis Fuller. Then, years later, after Fulci gained credibility, both he and the film were given new names for the re-release.

Cast:

Catriona MacColl (Liza Merril), David Warbeck (Dr. John McCabe), Cinzia Monreale (Emily), Antoine Saint-John (Schweick), Veronica Lazar (Martha), Larry Ray (Larry), Al Cliver (Dr. Harris), Michele Mirabella (Martin Avery), Gianpaolo Saccarola (Arthur), Maria Pia Marsala (Jill).

What the critics say:

Gerald Peary, *Boston Phoenix*: " … Fulci combines the enterprising low-budget storytelling of Roger Corman with the grisly, gushing-wound acumen of George Romero—*Dawn of the Dead* and way beyond. He also throws in an enthusiastic, obsessive Marquis de Sade cruelty. There are more ways to slit a throat than you can imagine, more ways to gouge out an eyeball—and you'll see them all when enmeshed in the oeuvre of Lucio Fulci. Not for everybody, this medical-student-turned-goremaker, who died of diabetic shock in 1996."

Roger Ebert, *Chicago Sun-Times*: "[M]y favorite scene involves the quick-lime-decomposed corpse, which is now seen in a hospital next to an oscilloscope that flat-lines, indicating death. Yes, the rotting cadaver is indeed dead—but why attach it, at this late date, to an oscilloscope? Could it be because we'll get a shot in which the scope screen suddenly indicates signs of life? I cannot lie to you. I live for moments like that."

Bob Graham, *San Francisco Chronicle*: "The return of director Lucio Fulci's 1981 genre classic *The Beyond* is a sight for sore eyes. [It] is full of Fulci's juicy imagery—of acid face-lifts, chomping tarantulas, rotting corpses and, significantly for a maker of horror films, variations on the theme of eye gouging."

If you liked this, you might also like:

City of the Living Dead (1980).

#52 Near Dark (1987)

Pray for daylight

Why it made the list:

Many years before Kathryn Bigelow won an Oscar for directing *The Hurt Locker*, she helmed this shocker written by Eric Red, whose street cred includes *The Hitcher* and *100 Feet.* Red outdid himself in this Shakespearean tragedy of a road trip. This is a film about vampires, long before the genre was subsumed by teenage girls, and was overlooked a bit because it came out the same year another fun, over-the-top vampire movie debuted in *The Lost Boys.* There was something different about *Near Dark*, though. It was dangerous. It was violent and, most of all, it was terrifying. Granted, at its core, it is a love story just like the other film that year, but this love story literally had teeth. If *The Lost Boys* had a polar opposite, it would be *Near Dark.* This film *felt* real. We didn't have to suspend disbelief as the audience; that was a foregone conclusion. Bigelow foreshadowed a talent for making the unreal about the human condition. She made the undead more human than their prey and showed just how real these nomadic vampires can be. How dangerous. How alluring. Regardless of your take on them, they were terrifying.

Synopsis:

Caleb (Adrian Pasdar) is an Arizona farm boy that falls into a love at first sight scenario with Mae (Jenny Wright) late one night. Little does he know that Mae is part of a nomadic vampire clan led by Jesse (Lance Henrikson). Caleb is bitten and kidnapped into the vampire family. He fights against it, though, even as he is introduced to the seductive power of being a creature of the night. After witnessing the vampires slaughter an entire bar, Caleb manages to escape the clan and makes it home where a transfusion sets him right. The vampires aren't through with Caleb just

yet, though. They come looking for him but this time, with the aid of his real family, Caleb can fight back. He has something to fight for this time, too… Mae's eternal soul.

Scariest scene:

The group of nomadic vampires descends on a small Arizona bar late at night. A few patrons, barflies, are about but nothing out of the ordinary. With their skewed sense of justice, Jesse and his brood slaughter and consume every living thing in the place in a wash of gore and grue.

One particularly thrilling moment sees Severen (Bill Paxton) playing with his food as he leaps on the bar and verbally abuses the bartender (Thomas Wagner). Severen bullies and cajoles, reminding the old man about his imminent demise. In what has to be a movie first, Severen lifts his leg and slices the arteries in the bartender's neck using his spurs. The blood flows.

Memorable dialogue:

> **MAE:** The light that's leaving that star right now will take a billion years to get down here. You want to know why you've never met a girl like me before?
>
> **CALEB:** Yeah. Why?
>
> **MAE:** Because I'll still be here when the light from that star gets down here to Earth in a billion years.

Did you know?

Jason Miller, Father Damien Karras in *The Exorcist*, has a son in each of the 1987 vampire love story films. Joshua John Miller plays Homer in *Near Dark* while his half-brother, Jason Patric, played Michael in *The Lost Boys*.

Cast:

Adrian Pasdar (Caleb Colton), Jenny Wright (Mae), Lance Henriksen (Jesse Hooker), Bill Paxton (Severen), Jenette Goldstein (Diamondback), Tom Thomerson (Loy Colton), Joshua John Miller (Homer), Marcie Leeds (Sarah Colton), Kenny Call (Deputy Sheriff), Ed Corbett (Ticket Seller), Troy Evans (Plainclothes Officer), Bill Cross (Sheriff Eakers),

Roger Aaron Brown (Cajun Truck Driver), Thomas Wagner (Bartender), Robert Winley (Patron in Bar).

What the critics say:

Hal Hinson, *The Washington Post*: "Both outrageous and poetic; it has extravagant, bloody thrills plus something else - something that comes close to genuine emotion."

Jay Boyer, *Orlando Sentinel*: "Long after the picture ends, you're left with potent half-images: strong-but-vague impressions that resemble the remains of dreams."

Peter Travers, *Rolling Stone*: "Bigelow's artful handling of the magic and menace of the night is hauntingly apparent."

If you liked this, you might also like:

The Lost Boys (1987).

#53 *The Uninvited* (1944)

The story of a love that is out of this world!

Why it made the list:

The Uninvited, the directorial debut of Lewis Allen, is an atmospheric, moody thriller that earned cinematographer Charles Lang an Academy Award nomination for Best Black and White Cinematography. Martin Scorsese has named the film as one of the 11 scariest of all time, and Guillermo del Toro listed it as one of the movies that has frightened or disturbed him the most. *The Uninvited* is also regarded as one of the first mainstream Hollywood films to treat its ghostly subject matter in an earnest manner.

Synopsis:

Two Londoners, Roderick "Rick" Fitzgerald (Ray Milland) and his sister, Pamela (Ruth Hussey), are vacationing on the Cornwall coast when they come upon an old abandoned house. Pamela immediately falls in love with the place and wants to buy it with Rick and move in. Rick, a music critic and composer, is initially reticent, but when the house's owner, Commander Beech (Donald Crisp) makes them an exceptional deal, Rick agrees. Beech's granddaughter, Stella Meredith (Gail Russell), is upset. She had lived in Windward House, as it is known, as a child before her mother died from a fall off a nearby cliff, and wishes the home to remain in the family. Her grandfather, however, is adamant that the sale is final. Rick and Pamela move in, but are immediately confronted with evidence that something is not right. The studio on the second floor is damp and chilly while the rest of the house is warm, and harbors a depressive, ugly atmosphere. On Rick's first night in the house, he hears a forlorn sobbing sound. Pamela has heard it, too, and believes it is a ghost. Rick seeks a more practical explanation, but when Stella visits the house for dinner, she senses a spirit that she believes is her mother. Overcome by some unknown force, Stella runs from the house to the same cliff's edge that claimed her mother's life. Rick must acknowledge that the house is, indeed, haunted, and he, Pamela and Stella set out to uncover the mysteries that have led to the presence of the ghosts.

Scariest scene:

After Stella nearly runs off the cliff, Rick and local physician Dr. Scott (Alan Napier) devise a scheme to dissuade her from returning to Windward House. They intend to hold a fake *séance* to convince Stella that the ghost of her mother wants her to stay away. The *séance* turns very real, however, and Stella is possessed by one of the spirits and begins speaking in Spanish as objects fly across the room and a strange chill falls across the proceedings.

Memorable dialogue:

> **RICK**: Loads of people tell me they would've felt it. Even outside that locked door. We didn't. They can't understand why we didn't know what it meant when our dog wouldn't go up those stairs. Animals see the blasted things that appear. Well, my sister Pamela and I knew nothing about such matters. Not then we didn't. We had the disadvantage of being Londoners, just down for a fortnights rest. That 10th day of May, 1937 was the end of our holiday.

Did you know?

The song "Stella By Starlight" was written specifically for this movie and is featured several times. In the movie Roderick Fitzgerald "writes" it for Stella Meredith.

Cast:

Ray Milland (Roderick "Rick" Fitzgerald), Ruth Hussey (Pamela Fitzgerald), Donald Crisp (Commander Beech), Cornelia Otis Skinner (Miss Holloway), Dorothy Stickney (Miss Bird), Barbara Everest (Lizzie Flynn), Alan Napier (Dr. Scott), Gail Russell (Stella Meredith), David Clyde (Ben), Betty Farrington (Carmel's Ghost).

What the critics say:

Bosley Crowther, *New York Times:* "The one thing—and the only thing—about this film is that it sets out to give you the shivers—and will do so, if you're readily disposed. Ray Milland and Ruth Hussey do nicely as the couple who get themselves involved, being sufficiently humorous in spots to seem plausibly real. Gail Russell is wistful and gracious as a curiously moonstruck girl, and Cornelia Otis Skinner is quite chilly as a Mrs. Danvers by remote control. Lewis Allen has handled the direction in such a persistent way that the shocks come at regular intervals."

Geoff Andrew, *Time Out:* "The real strength of the film, though, is its atypical stance part way between psychology and the supernatural, achieving a disturbingly serious effect."

Stephen Whitty, *Newark Star-Ledger:* "The film was a bit of a breakthrough for Golden Age Hollywood—back then, ghosts were seen as comical creatures, always going West or taking Topper for a ride. Scary spectres stuck mostly to Dickens, or occasional dream sequences. *The Uninvited*, however, played it straight—and helped establish some of our favorite haunted-house movie clichés (the suspiciously low rental, the dog that won't enter a room, the "cold spot")."

If you liked this, you might also like:

Dead of Night (1945).

#54 Let's Scare Jessica To Death (1971)

Something is after Jessica. Something very cold ... very wet ... And very dead.

Why it made the list:

Let's Scare Jessica to Death is a truly underrated film and is one of the greatest psychological horror films ever made. It's an understated film that ranks right up there with Robert Wise's *The Haunting*. Writer/director John D. Hancock does a superb job of leaving the audience guessing whether or not Jessica has really experienced the events in the film, or if they were a figment of her imagination. This film is a bit of slow burn. It's also a minor masterpiece, low budget be damned. If you haven't seen it, and chances are that you haven't, you should check it out as soon as you can. Much credit also goes to cinematographer Robert M. Baldwin, who does a terrific job here, as well as to conductor Orville Stoeber, whose creepy-as-hell score provides the film with creepy atmospherics from start to finish.

Synopsis:

Jessica (Zohra Lampert) has just been released for a six-month stint in a mental facility. She's unsure of herself, but hopes to start a new life. She and her hubby, along with a family friend, move to a remote farmhouse. When they move in, they meet Emily (Mariclare Costello), who has been living in the house. They get to know her a little bit and eventually ask her to stay. Jessica then sees a dead body beneath the water in the lake, but no one believes her. Jessica and her family then learn that a girl named Abigail Stone once drowned in the lake back in 1880. Her body was never found, and local folklore says that Abigail is still alive somewhere and living as a vampire. When Jessica begins to notice unexplainable scars on all the townsfolk and then finds a photograph of Abigail that looks suspiciously like Emily, then start to get weird and Jessica doesn't know if she's really seeing these things or just going crazy.

Scariest scene:

This film is frightening from beginning to end. However, the most frightening scene finds Jessica waking up to see that her husband has a scar on his neck. She then turns and sees Emily closing in on her neck, as though she is going to bite it. Then a group of dead-eyed townsfolk show up in her bedroom, and things just get creepier and creepier from there.

Memorable dialogue:

> **JESSICA:** I was just looking at the picture. It looks so much like you.
>
> **EMILY:** My lord, it does. Gee, how weird. What's the matter?
>
> **JESSICA:** Nothing. It's just, uh, it does look very much like you.
>
> **EMILY:** It's an old print. It could look like anybody.
>
> **JESSICA:** No, it's … it's the eyes.

Did you know?

Director John D. Hancock was nominated for an Oscar the same year *Let's Scare Jessica to Death* was released. This was for the short film *Sticky My Fingers … Fleet My Feet.* Two years later, Hancock would direct the film he is best known for, *Bang the Drum Slowly*, starring Robert De Niro.

Cast:

Zohra Lampert (Jessica), Barton Heyman (Duncan), Kevin O'Connor (Woody), Gretchen Corbett (The Girl), Alan Manson (Sam Dorker), Mariclare Costello (Emily).

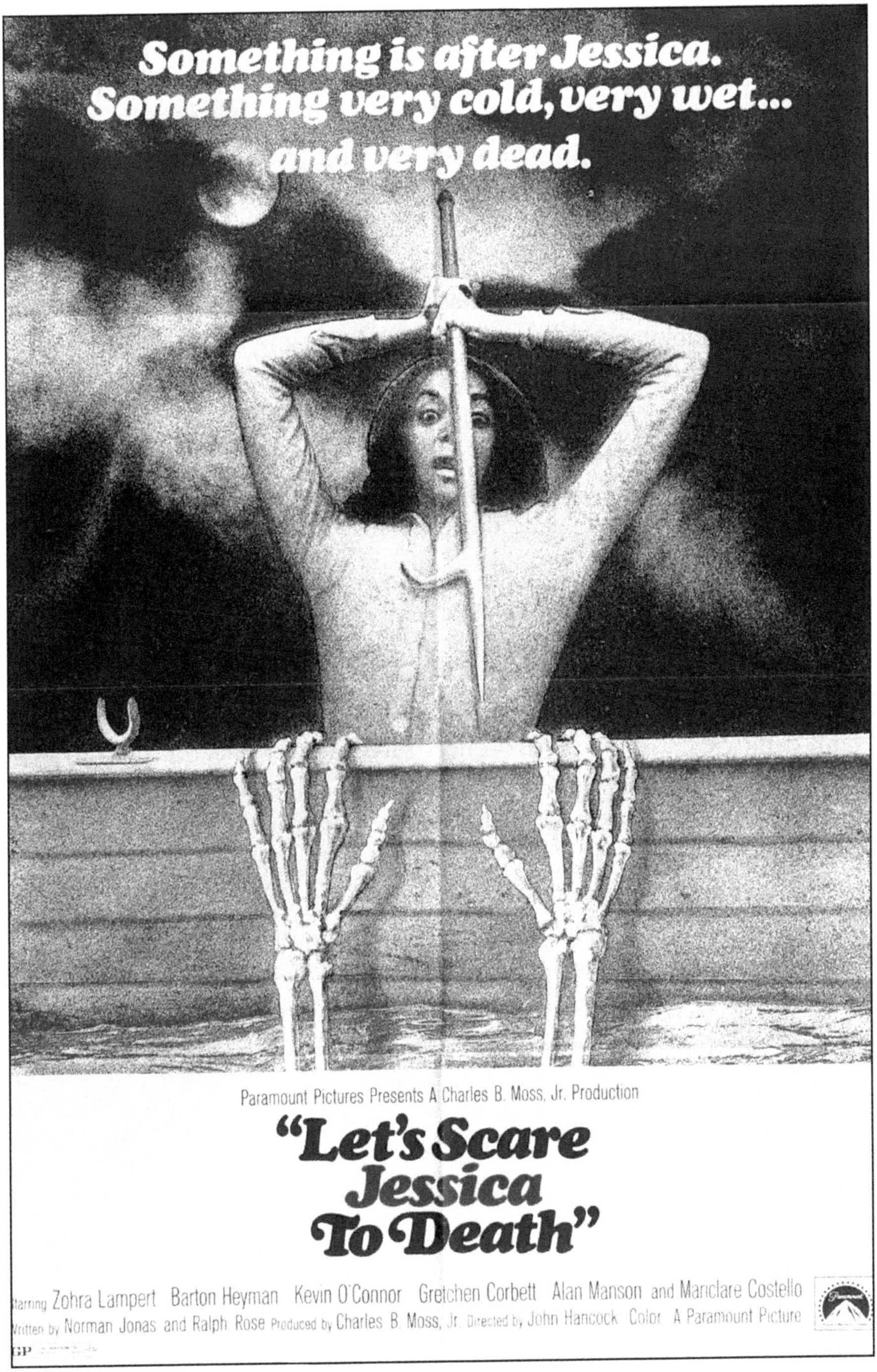

Something is after Jessica.
Something very cold, very wet...
and very dead.

Paramount Pictures Presents A Charles B. Moss, Jr. Production

"Let's Scare Jessica To Death"

Starring Zohra Lampert Barton Heyman Kevin O'Connor Gretchen Corbett Alan Manson and Mariclare Costello
Written by Norman Jonas and Ralph Rose Produced by Charles B. Moss, Jr. Directed by John Hancock Color A Paramount Picture

GP

What the critics say:

Staff, *DVD Verdict*: "*Let's Scare Jessica to Death* is all about creep and dread, and fans looking for gore or thrills are going to be irritated by the plodding picture. I admired how well the film captured the thin line between nightmare and delusion, which made this a solid little ghost story."

Freddie Young, *Full Moon Reviews*: "[T]he script is well written and the ideas that are being presented are engaging. The idea of Jessica being mentally unstable and then watching her hear and see things that may or may not be there makes one a participant in this mystery of 'Is she crazy or are these things really there?' Honestly, I was never really sure what was up with Jessica. A part of me believes the supernatural aspect really did happen, but sometimes we see what we want to see. So who's to say that what Jessica really did experience was actually on the level? Not many films manage to do that these days, and that's probably why so many people like this film."

Ken Phipps, *The Onion A.V. Club*: "It's a classic B-movie move of making much out of little, and while *Let's Scare Jessica to Death* isn't quite a top-rank B-movie classic, it at least offers further proof that all the teen idol stars and CGI effects—or a logical plot, for that matter—mean nothing if they don't make you scared to turn out the lights."

If you liked this, you might also like:

Children Shouldn't Play with Dead Things (1972).

#55 *Peeping Tom* (1960)

Look out! Take care, you are being watched. We repeat, take care for you are now alone with a killer. We warn you, don't let him see the fear in your eyes. For this is what he seeks and this is why he kills.

Why it made the list:

Revered British movie director Michael Powell was known well enough for such classics as *The Red Shoes* and *Black Narcissus*, but his real infamy had yet to come. In 1960, the brave filmmaker unleashed *Peeping Tom* upon an unsuspecting theater-going public who simply weren't ready for his brand of on-screen violence and depravity. *Peeping Tom* was so reviled by the press and the public that Powell found his filmmaking career in serious trouble. He retreated to Australia so he could continue working.

A release date comparison will reveal that *Peeping Tom* came out the same year as Alfred Hitchcock's *Psycho*. Both films have been analyzed alongside one another time and time again. Still, *Psycho* is an American black-and-white shocker and *Peeping Tom*, in dazzling color, belonged to the English, whether they wanted it or not … and they didn't. The most infamous critical quote leveled at the film was, "The only really satisfactory way to dispose of *Peeping Tom* would be to shovel it up and flush it swiftly down the nearest sewer. Even then the stench would remain."

Synopsis:

Handsome Mark Lewis (Carl Boehm) is an introvert of severe proportions. By day, he is a film crew technician for a British film company, and by night he takes cheesecake photos for a girlie magazine. All the while, he subverts his shyness through the viewfinder of a hand-held movie camera. In Mark's world, nothing is tangible or real. Nearly everything he sees is filtered through a camera lens, thus saving him from any harsh realities.

Mark is very well aware of his social ineptness, but continues to seek solace in and around his camera. At one nudie photo shoot, Mark caresses his camera as though he were executing some sort of sexual foreplay. Then, within an instant, he thrusts the camera to his eye and begins snapping photos with wild abandon while he continues his surreal and metaphoric act of love making. Unfortunately, for many a female earmark, this young man's madness hardly stops here.

As Mark's day-to-day life progresses, so does his psychosis; a psychosis known as scopophilia, which is similar to voyeurism. Mark's dementia is traced back to his childhood where his father (Michael Powell), a scientist, used the youngster as a guinea pig. Mark's father was apparently obsessed with capturing the look of human fear on film and he virtually terrorized his own son while forcing a camera upon him. This stuck with the young Mark and in time the student would surpass the teacher.

Mark's tweaked condition is only fully satiated when he kills. Equipped with his camera and a deadly rigged tripod, Mark hits the

streets in search of female victims. He woos them with the allure of the camera, a photo shoot and celluloid immortality.

Once she is primed and ready, Mark extends, or erects, his tripod leg and unsheathes it, revealing a sharpened dagger. The demented cameraman then moves in closer for the kill; but not before presenting a mirror for the victim to watch herself as she dies. The entire episode is caught on film as her killer has purposely left the camera running.

Once home, the sexually frenzied psychopath watches wide-eyed as his victims watch themselves die. However, Mark eventually tires of the stalk-and-slash charade. He has become jaded, and quite frankly disappointed in the outcome of his own cinematic work. He finally stages his *tour de force*—the filming of his own suicide.

Scariest scene:

The murder of Mark Lewis' co-worker Vivian is undoubtedly the film's most nerve-rattling sequence. Vivian is an actress and a dancer. Mark plays upon Vivian's vanity and convinces her to shake a few moves for him and his camera. Here, for the first time, viewers get to witness Mark's entire silver tongue routine that leads Vivian to dance herself literally to her death.

Memorable dialogue:

> **MARK:** Do you know what the most frightening thing in the world is? It's fear.

Did you know?

There is a bit of a cinematic family reunion happening during one of Mark Lewis' home movies. Mark's father is played by "Peeping Tom" director Michael Powell. Mark, as a child, is played by Michael Powell's son Columba, and Powell's real-life wife appears as Mark's mother.

Cast:

Karlheinz Böhm/Carl Boehm (Mark Lewis), Moira Shearer (Vivian), Anna Massey (Helen Stephens), Maxine Audley (Mrs. Stephens), Jack Watson (Chief Insp. Gregg), Shirley Anne Field (Pauline Shields), Pamela Green (Milly), Columba Powell (Mark as a Child), Michael Powell (Mark's Father), Frankie Reidy (Mark's Mother on Deathbed).

What the critics say:

Michael Weldon, *The Psychotronic Encyclopedia Of Film*: "[F]ascinating and unflinching horror classic … Formerly known only to some lucky late-night TV viewers and completist horror fans, this film received belated critical acclaim when Martin Scorsese arranged for a limited release in 1980 … Don't miss it."

Jonathan Ross, *The Incredibly Strange Film Book*: "Michael Powell's *Peeping Tom* and Alfred Hitchcock's *Psycho* (both 1960) remain two of the most effective and interesting horror films ever made, and both attracted vitriolic criticism, especially in Britain."

Michael Wilmington, *Chicago Tribune*: "Michael Powell's great flesh-crawling 1960 shocker … is a profoundly unsettling movie that unnerves audiences not through gore but by building up an atmosphere of fear, desire, and mounting madness."

If you liked this, you might also like:

Psycho (1960).

#56 Session 9 (2001)

Danver's lunatic asylum opened 1855. Condemned 1984. Secrets. Possession. Madness. Murder.

Why it made the list:

Few films on this list will stick with the viewer as long as Brad Anderson's *Session 9*. The film has a subtle and overt sense of realism that's missing from most horror movies. Filmed in a fly-on-the-wall quality that is inescapable, it's as though the viewer is standing in the corner of the room as the storyline creeps, crawls, unhinges and unfolds.

Synopsis:

The Hazmat Elimination Company, owned by Gordon Fleming (Peter Mullan), is hired to remove the asbestos from the abandoned Danvers Asylum. His team, led by Phil (David Caruso), is eclectic but efficient. They take a projected three week job and attempt completion in a mere seven days.

Gordon is a middle-aged new father and he's not coping well at all. His relationship with his wife is strained and his company is slowly going under. He is emotionally unstable and susceptible to the energies of the supernatural. His new workplace has a plethora of negative vibes for him to assimilate.

Team member Mike (Stephen Gevedon) discovers a pile of reel-to-reel audio tapes interviewing patient Mary Hobbes. Mary has multiple personalities, one of which is the bad-natured "Simon." Simon's caustic sensibilities are seemingly released from the magnetic tape and find their way into Gordon's psyche. The newly-possessed Gordon reacts accordingly and his subsequent acts leave a bloodied trail of carnage, corpses, and confusion.

Scariest scene:

The film's narrative basically oozes slowly from the screen. While there are a few shock-and-awe moments, the real jolt hits when the viewer realizes Gordon has not only murdered his employees, but also his wife and child.

Memorable dialogue:

> **DOCTOR:** And where do you live, Simon?
>
> **SIMON:** I live in the weak and the wounded, Doc.

Did you know?

Director Brad Anderson lived in Boston near the Danvers Mental Hospital. His frequent passing-by of the deserted facility inspired him to make *Session 9*.

Cast:

David Caruso (Phil), Stephen Gevedon (Mike), Paul Guilfoyle (Bill Griggs), Josh Lucas (Hank), Peter Mullan (Gordon Fleming), Brendan Sexton III (Jeff), Charley Broderick (Security Guard), Lonnie Farmer (Voice of Doctor), Larry Fassenden (Craig McManus), Jurian Hughes (Voice of Mary Hobbes).

What the critics say:

Peter Travers, *Rolling Stone*: "*Session 9*, a spine-tingler directed with fierce finesse by Brad Anderson, puts an asbestos-removal crew (Peter Mullan, David Caruso, Stephen Gevedon, Josh Lucas, Brendan Sexton III) into an abandoned asylum and lets the scares rip without mercy."

Kevin Thomas, *Los Angeles Times*: "Brad Anderson's *Session 9* is an ingeniously scary movie. With the most effectively minimalist approach since *The Blair Witch Project*, Anderson and his co-writer Stephen Gevedon took as their inspiration one of the most ominous buildings in America, the abandoned Danvers Mental Hospital outside Boston."

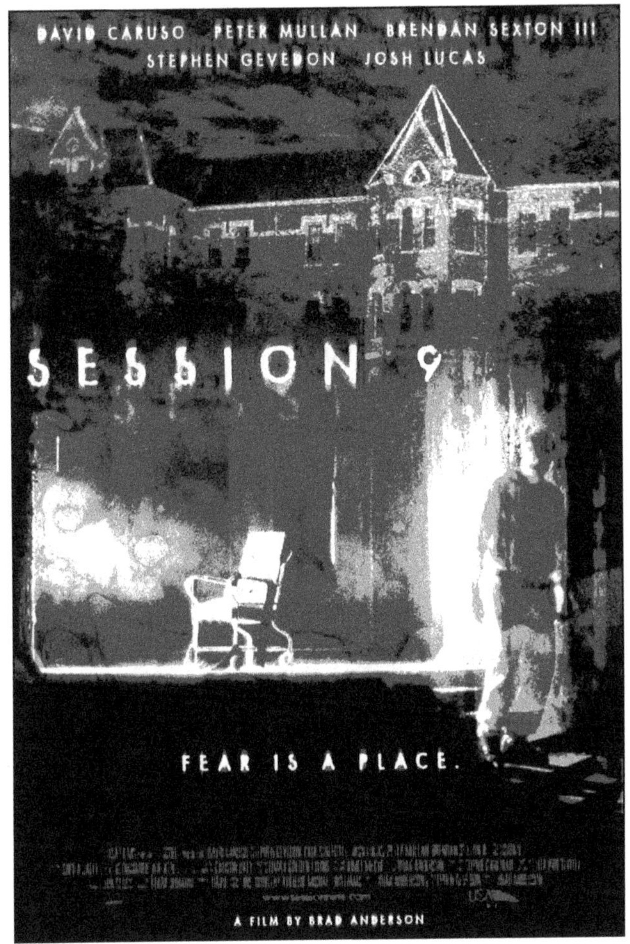

Staff, *Bloody Disgusting*: "*Session 9* isn't just a cheap, hack `n' slash, instantly-forgettable type horror film, but a psychologically probing, deeply unsettling journey off the edge and into the abyss of the human mind. The film is old school in a lot of ways, particularly in that it doesn't just rely on cheap shocks to scare the living daylights out of us. Indeed, the scariest moments in the film are those that involve disembodied voices, eerie visuals, and the mere suggestion that something horrible is about to happen. This is the stuff bad dreams are made of."

If you liked this, you might also like:

The House of the Devil (2009).

#57 Ghost Story (1981)

The time has come to tell the tale.

Why it made the list:

John Irvin's 1981 film *Ghost Story*, adapted from the novel by Peter Straub, is an elegant and straight-faced throwback to horror films of yesteryear. It's chilling and atmospheric, but most of the true fear lies in the eyes and expressions of the four doomed old men who know they have a price to pay for sins they committed long ago. It also features one of the most distinguished ensembles ever captured on film in Fred Astaire, John Houseman, Melvyn Douglas, and Douglas Fairbanks Jr. The performances of these legendary actors, coupled with terrific camerawork by Jack Cardiff and astounding makeup by Dick Smith, make *Ghost Story* a can't-miss proposition for horror film buffs.

Synopsis:

Four old men, known collectively as "The Chowder Society," meet each week to exchange horror tales and sip cognac by firelight. When bad things begin happening and people around them start to die, they start to understand that they are being stalked by a vengeful apparition of a woman they accidentally killed some fifty years before. As the old men start dropping like flies, the remaining members of the club begin to wonder how much time they have left before they meet their own gruesome demise.

Scariest scene:

While any scene featuring Dick Smith's gruesome zombie makeup would suffice as being the film's scariest, it's the more subtle sequences in which the old men await their inevitable death that are the most frightening. It's not what the actors say, but what they don't say—the knowing looks and deafening silences—that make these scenes as effective and haunting as they are.

Memorable dialogue:

> **EVA:** I will take you to places you've never been. I will show you things that you have never seen, and I will see the life run out of you.

Did you know?

The pipe organ used in the film is the exact same organ played by Lon Chaney in *The Phantom of the Opera.*

Cast:

Fred Astaire (Ricky Hawthorne), Melvyn Douglas (Dr. John Jaffrey), Douglas Fairbanks Jr. (Edward Charles Wanderly), John Houseman (Sears James), Craig Wasson (Don Wanderly/David Wanderly), Patricia Neal (Stella Hawthorne), Alice Krige (Eva Galli/Alma Mobley), Jacqueline Brookes (Milly), Miguel Fernandes (Gregory Bate), Lance Holcomb (Fenny Bate).

What the critics say:

Bryan Pope, *DVD Verdict*: "From a technical standpoint, the film is handsomely mounted. At times it's even beautiful, thanks to the evocative New England locales (combined with Albert Whitlock's excellent matte work) and Jack Cardiff's vivid cinematography. If nothing else, *Ghost Story* made me want to call my travel agent and plan a New England holiday. Philippe Sarde's score is interesting and unpredictable. Sometimes lush; sometimes just plain quirky. But it's usually very effective."

Roger Ebert, *Chicago Sun-Times*: "If you like ghost stories, you will appreciate that they cannot be told with all sorts of ridiculous skeletons leaping out of closets, as in Abbott and Costello. They must be told largely in terms of fearful and nostalgic memory, since (by definition) a ghost is a ghost because of something that once happened that shouldn't have happened. *Ghost Story* understands that, and restrains its performers so that the horror of the ghost is hardly more transparent than they are."

Gregory Joseph, *Dreamscape*: "While the plot of *Ghost Story* could be the premise for a fine revisionist-William Castle film, neither the script nor the acting in *Ghost Story* point to camp or nostalgia. The four leads are all veteran actors who can command attention here, yet there are no attempts made in their performances to belie the simple fact that these old men inhabit frail bodies—bodies most likely not strong enough to survive the hazards of 1980's horror."

If you liked this, you might also like:

Lady in White (1988).

#58 *The Changeling* (1980)

Whatever you do ... don't go into the attic.

Why it made the list:

Although roughly a third of the film is spent on the mystery behind the ghost's death (and is therefore not as much fun), the other two-thirds are a terrific little haunted house story. The film is deftly directed by Peter Medak, and extremely well-acted by cinema legends George C. Scott and Melvyn Douglas. John Coquillon does a great job behind the camera, and composer Rick Williams' haunting score helps maintain a genuinely creepy atmosphere. Not only is *The Changeling* a great haunted house story, but it's also the most effective type of haunted house story—the kind that implies more than it shows; scares are given by sounds, shaking chandeliers, and things as mundane as running faucets. There is no CGI here, nor should there be. Director Medak delivers a highly-effective film just by sticking to the basics.

Synopsis:

Composer John Russell (George C. Scott) loses his wife and daughter in an automobile accident. After four months of grieving, he has decided to try and move on. He has accepts a job teaching, and moves into a giant old house. He soon realizes that he isn't alone there, and that's when all the fun begins. After hearing strange sounds and witnessing the unexplainable, he discovers a closed-off room in the attic. The room appears to have been a small child's room many years before. After a séance reveals that a murder transpired in the house, John finds himself doing the ghost's bidding and trying to figure out how the murder took place and who benefited from it.

Scariest scene:

While there's an extremely affecting scene involving a returning rubber ball, the film's most frightening scene comes at the end of the picture. John wakes up from a fall and finds himself lying on the floor in the front room of the house. The chandeliers are shaking and a fire is slowly making its way down the bannister. Then John sees changeling Joe Carmichael, in a sort of trance, walking up the stairs to a fiery death.

Memorable dialogue:

> **DEWITT:** I understand you lost your wife and daughter a little while ago. Maybe it shook you up. Maybe too much … Maybe you need help.
>
> **JOHN:** I'd like you to leave now.
>
> **DEWITT:** We can see that you get it … Do you understand what I'm saying?
>
> **JOHN:** Out! Now!
>
> **DEWITT:** Listen to me, Russell! You've got something of the Senator's … He wants it back. It's a little gold medal, a family heirloom. He lost it. He thinks you've got it.

Did you know?

The Changeling is based on events which allegedly took place in the 1960s at Henry Treat Rogers Mansion in Denver, Colorado, while author Russell Hunter was staying there. The Chessman Park neighborhood does not exist. Its name, however, is a nod to Cheesman Park in Denver, where the actual haunting took place.

Cast:

George C. Scott (John Russell), Trish Van Devere (Claire Norman), Melvyn Douglas (Senator Joe Carmichael), Jean Marsh (Joanna Russell), John Colicos (Capt. DeWitt), Barry Morse (Dr. Pemberton), Madeleine

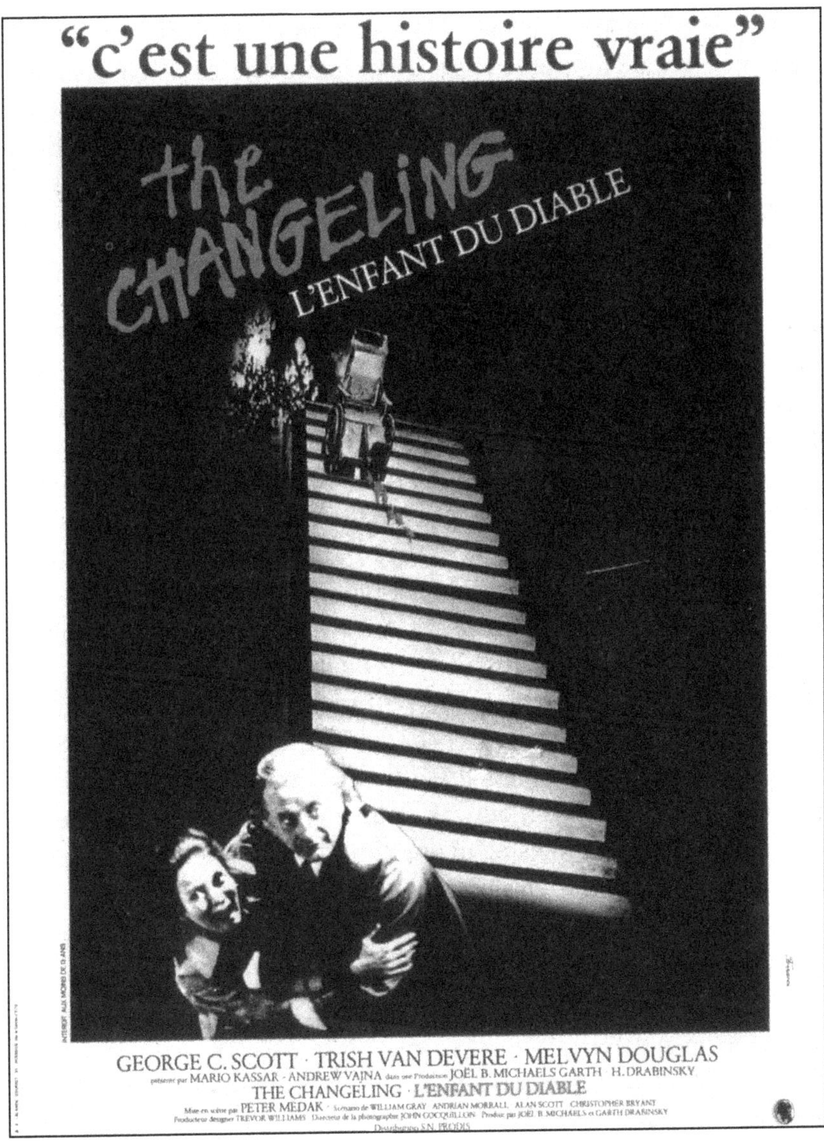

Sherwood (Mrs. Norman), Helen Burns (Leah Harmon), Frances Hyland (Mrs. Elizabeth Grey), Ruth Springford (Minnie Huxley).

What the critics say:

Phil Chandler, *DVD Cult*: "Following the successful release of John Carpenter's *Halloween* in 1978, and Sean Cunningham's *Friday the 13th* in 1980, the slasher craze was well under way. The "have-sex-and-die" theme was prevalent in practically every genre release. Then, a small independent distributor called Associated Film Distribution unleashed this $7 million Canadian film into the marketplace. In place of sex and gore, *The Changeling* offered legitimate acting and supernatural suspense. *The Changeling* went on to become a sleeper hit (and still holds up today), while those terrible slasher films have gone the way of disco."

Captain Midnight, *The Midnight Monster Show*: "The story is engrossing and the acting is top flight; it's just about what you'd expect from a film with George C. Scott and Melvyn Douglas in starring roles. There are some unnerving and creepy scenes, but this is definitely not *Poltergeist* or *The Ring*; there are no girls with long black hair hanging in their faces appearing before a big jump scare, nor are there major special effects."

Daniel Stephens, *DVD Times*: "Medak knows how to use the medium to effectively convey the horrors of what Russell's character goes through. It goes as far as to 'show up' many of Hollywood's latest efforts in the genre, like the similar themed *The Haunting* (1999), in that 'horror,' be that 'fear' instilled in the audience, or something unexplainably awful on screen does not have to exist visually and sonically, but must question a person's own ideological, ethical, and/or religious beliefs to the point where a gray area is manifested in one's mind that defies explanation in its consequence, motivation or otherwise."

If you liked this, you might also like:

The Innocents (1961).

#59 *The Wicker Man* (1973)

From the writer of Frenzy *and* Sleuth.

Why it made the list:

After winning first prize at the 1974 Festival of Fantastic Films in Paris, *The Wicker Man* was later dubbed "the *Citizen Kane* of horror movies" by *Cinefanstique* Magazine. The film was later ranked 485th on *Empire Magazine's* list of *The 500 Greatest Movies of All Time*. But what exactly makes this film so special? *The Wicker Man* is a one-of-a-kind chiller that deftly utilizes psychological horror to achieve its scares. Sure, it's a slow burn, but the film pays off in spades with that deliciously iconic burning wicker man scene. The script is top notch, the acting first rate (especially Edward Woodward and Christopher Lee), and the direction is masterful to say the least. *The Wicker Man* made this list because it truly is one of the finest, most frightening horror films ever produced.

Synopsis:

Sgt. Howie (Edward Woodward) travels to a remote island to investigate the disappearance of a little girl. Howie is a Christian and is horrified to find the Islanders praising pagan gods. He also finds orgies, premarital sex, general immorality, and the elementary school teachings of fornication. Everywhere Howie goes, he is stonewalled, told that the little girl he is searching for never existed. Howie starts to piece together clues when he discovers a series of photographs, each depicting a young girl named as the May Queen.

Scariest scene:

The scariest scene of the film comes at the end when Howie finds himself part of a sacrificial ritual in which he is placed inside a giant wicker man and set ablaze. As the wicker man burns around him, Howie recites from the Bible, seeking supernatural assistance that will never come.

Memorable dialogue:

> **SGT. HOWIE:** And what of the true God? Whose glory, churches and monasteries have been built on these islands for generations past? Now sir, what of him?
>
> **LORD SUMMERISLE:** He's dead. Can't complain, had his chance and in modern parlance, blew it.

Did you know?

In 1989, screenwriter Anthony Shaffer wrote a treatment for a proposed sequel titled *The Loathsome Lambton Worm*, but director Robin Hardy passed on the project. Hardy later directed his own sequel, *The Wicker Tree* (2011), which also features actor Christopher Lee. At the time of this writing, Hardy was working on a third installment in the *Wicker Man* trilogy.

Cast:

Edward Woodward (Sgt. Howie), Christopher Lee (Lord Summerisle), Diane Cliento (Miss Rose), Britt Ekland (Willow McGregor), Ingrid Pitt (Librarian), Lindsay Kemp (Alder MacGregor), Russell Waters (Harbor Master), Aubrey Morris (Gravedigger), Irene Sunter (May Morrison), Donald Eccles (T.H. Lennox).

What the critics say:

Staff, *Variety*: "Anthony Shaffer penned the screenplay which, for sheer imagination and near-terror, has seldom been equaled."

Staff, *TV Guide*: "It remains a fine example of occult horror that remains with the viewer well past its conclusion."

James Berardinelli, *Reel Views*: "A film that defies categorization, *The Wicker Man* can be considered to be a horror film, a psychological thrill-

er, a musical, or a melodrama. In reality, since it includes elements of each of those types, it literally has something for just about everyone. And, because there's a richness and intelligence to the story that leads to an unexpected climax, few viewers leave *The Wicker Man* unshaken. This is one of those motion pictures whose final images stay with audience members, haunting their steps after the end credits have rolled."

If you liked this, you might also like:

Witchfinder General (1968).

#60 Jacob's Ladder (1990)

The most frightening thing about Jacob Singer's nightmare is that he isn't dreaming.

Why it made the list:

This is beautiful film from Adrian Lyne. This film is a living nightmare, specifically Jacob Singer's living nightmare, and Lyne has created a New York, and a Vietnam, that is filled with waking nightmares, hallucinations and true terror. We feel for poor Jacob. He has lost so much and, it appears, the world is not done taking from him. The presentation is visceral, evocative and features a tour de force performance by Tim Robbins. The film itself is a downward spiral into a man's psyche and we can never tell the difference between his real fall and a manufactured one. When we find that Singer's issues may have credence, that nightmare scenario gets very real, very quickly. The demons in this film, the half-seen horrors… all of it builds and builds until, like Jake, we can't take it anymore.

Synopsis:

Jacob Singer (Tim Robbins) is wounded in Vietnam, facing the horror of war. He wakes up in a New York subway in a city that is just as cruel and unforgiving as the jungles of Vietnam. Jacob's life is one of loss. He is divorced, his son has died and he currently lives with his lover Jezzie (Elizabeth Pena). Jacob's world slowly unravels. He hallucinates about his time in Vietnam, about his son and the world around him devolves into a Hell on Earth. Jacob, more and more, feels that there is a conspiracy around him. Something happened to his platoon in Vietnam, something that government did. They changed them, over there, and he is paying the price now. He is in a race against time to find out exactly what happened and if he can stop it before more people get hurt.

Scariest scene:

Hands down, the most terrifying scene in the film starts out innocuously enough. Attending a house party with Jezzie, Jake is talked into dancing. Uncomfortable, he begs off only to see everyone in the room get sexually charged. He turns to find Jezzie dancing seductively. Then, we hear the flapping of wings. Jake is horrified (and so are we) as a demonic, winged thing 'dances' with Jezzie. She virtually has sex with the thing, including its dragon-like tail, and she is injured by the thing… but continues the dance. Jake is shocked as the thing rips a claw through Jezzie's head. He falls back and blacks out.

Memorable dialogue:

> **MICHAEL:** I'd only been in jail 13 hours, I thought 'Nam couldn't be any worse.
>
> **JACOB:** Shows how little you knew.
>
> **MICHAEL:** Yeah, really.

Did you know?

The James Brown song, "My Thang," was playing during the sexually-charged party scene. This is from a 1974 double album called *Hell.*

Cast:

Tim Robbins (Jacob Singer), Elizabeth Pena (Jezzie), Danny Aiello (Louis), Matt Craven (Michael), Pruitt Taylor Vince (Paul), Jason Alexander (Geary), Patricia Kalember (Sarah), Eriq La Salle (Frank), Ving Rhames (George), Brian Tarantina (Doug).

What the critics say:

John Hartl, *Seattle Times*: "For hours and days after you've seen it, you'll still be putting it together in your head. While all of it is gripping, it doesn't come together until the final scene, which is jolting, transcendent, unexpected yet inevitable."

Gary Thompson, *Philadelphia Daily News*: "*Jacob's Ladder* is unique. Rarely is such an unconventional screenplay given this full-blown, $25 million studio treatment. It is a curiosity – a mutant of a movie in an industry that specializes in clones."

Stephen Rea, *Philadelphia Enquirer*: "A friend, after seeing *Jacob's Ladder*, griped, "I wasn't afraid of dying – until I saw this movie." Put that blurb in an ad and see who shows up at the multiplexes."

If you liked this, you might also like:

Angel Heart (1987).

#61 *Horror of Dracula* (1958)

The chill of the tomb won't leave your blood for hours ... after you come face to face with Dracula!

Why it made the list:

Following their hit 1957 film *The Curse of Frankenstein*, England's legendary Hammer Studios turned their attention to Bram Stoker's famous vampire Count Dracula. (They had won a lawsuit by Universal Studio saying they had the right to make their own monster films as long as they didn't resemble those made by Universal.) In this new Dracula film, loosely adapted from Stoker's novel, all the elements that had made *The Curse of Frankenstein* a hit were present; vivid color, action, lots of blood, and overt eroticism. At the time of the film's release, its violence and bloodshed—tame by today's standards—elicited outrage from film critics who called it crude and distasteful. Some have called the film the greatest horror movie ever made. (We consider it the 61st scariest movie ever made.) No matter where you rank the film on your own personal list of horror films, it certainly deserves inclusion to any such list.

Synopsis:

Jonathan Harker (John Van Eyessen) goes to work for Count Dracula (Christopher Lee) in Germany, pretending to catalog his impressive library. However, Harker is secretly on a mission to kill Dracula, who is a vampire. Harker ultimately fails in his attempt to kill the blood-sucker and soon finds himself one of the walking dead. When Dracula targets Harker's fiancée, Lucy Holmwood (Carol Marsh), Harker's colleague and fellow vampire hunter Dr. Van Helsing (Peter Cushing) tries to save her. Van Helsing attempts to convince Lucy's brother, Arthur (Michael Gough), that his family is in danger, but Arthur refuses to listen. Soon

Dracula sets his sights on Arthur's wife, Mina (Melissa Stribling), and Van Helsing and Arthur are forced to track down the vampire in an effort to stop him before she too becomes one of the Count's walking dead followers.

Scariest scene:

When Harker stakes Count Dracula's undead mistress, he then turns to the master vampire's coffin to find that it's now empty. Harker's mouth falls open in sheer horror, and we the audience feel that along with him. He looks up to the door to the cellar where Dracula is now entering, blocking any possible exit. This briefest of moments when Harker knows his fate has been sealed is the single most frightening scene of the film. (Nevermind why Harker staked the woman first rather than Dracula, or why Dracula left the cellar and then returned—presumably to make a dramatic entrance—only a moment later. Logic be damned, it's a chilling scene.)

Memorable dialogue:

> **ARTHUR:** Gerda, would you fetch another bottle?
>
> **GERDA:** I don't like to. You know what happened last time I disobeyed Mrs. Holmwood's orders.
>
> **ARTHUR:** What do you mean?
>
> **GERDA:** Madam told me the other day that on no account was I to go into the cellar …

Did you know?

Melissa Stribling, who plays Mina Holmwood, found difficulty emoting in a way that satisfied director Terence Fisher in the scene in which she has just been bitten by Dracula. After several takes, Fisher finally told Stribling to pretend she'd just had the best sex of her life and that it had lasted all night long. With this motivation, Stribling performed the scene with a satisfied expression on her face, pleasing the director with only one take.

The TERRIFYING Lover–
who died – yet lived!
Universal-International presents A Hammer Film Production
PETER CUSHING
DRACULA
(Cert. X) Adults only
MICHAEL GOUGH
MELISSA STRIBLING
CHRISTOPHER LEE Dracula
In Eastman Colour processed by Technicolor
Screenplay by JIMMY SANGSTER Associate Producer ANTHONY NELSON-KEYS
Produced by ANTHONY HINDS Directed by TERENCE FISHER
Executive Producer MICHAEL CARRERAS
Distributed by Rank Film Distributors Ltd.
DON'T DARE SEE IT ALONE!

HORROR OF DRACULA
ALL NEW!
in Brilliant TECHNICOLOR!
starring
PETER CUSHING
also starring
MICHAEL GOUGH
and MELISSA STRIBLING
with
CHRISTOPHER LEE
as DRACULA
Screenplay by JIMMY SANGSTER
From the novel by BRAM STOKER
Directed by TERENCE FISHER
Associate producer: ANTHONY NELSON-KEYS
Produced by ANTHONY HINDS

Cast:

Peter Cushing (Dr. Van Helsing), Christopher Lee (Count Dracula), Michael Gough (Arthur), Melissa Stribling (Mina), Carol Marsh (Lucy), Olga Dickey (Gerda), John Van Eyssen (Jonathan Harker), Valerie Gaunt (Vampire Woman), Janina Faye (Tania), Barbara Archer (Inga).

What the critics say:

Staff, *Variety*: "Both director Terence Fisher as well as the cast have taken a serious approach to the macabre theme that adds up to lots of tension and suspense. Peter Cushing is impressive as the painstaking scientist-doctor who solves the mystery. Christopher Lee is thoroughly gruesome as Dracula, and Michael Gough is suitably skeptical as a bereaved relative who ultimately is persuaded to assist Cushing."

Steve Biodrowski, *Cinefantastique*: "At a clipped eighty-two minutes, this is one of the most effective and tightly structured horror films ever made; in fact, some have gone so far as to call it the greatest horror film of all time."

Staff, *TV Guide*: "The film moves quickly and forcefully from one scene to the next, keeping the audience on their seat edges. Lush sets, rousing musical score, spirited acting and a direct attitude toward undead sensuality heighten the vampiric illusion. The result is a terrific combination of the intellectual and visceral that continues to work today."

If you liked this, you might also like:

The Brides of Dracula (1960).

#62 The Creature From the Black Lagoon (1954)

Not since the beginning of time has the world beheld terror such as this!

Why it made the list:

Generally regarded as the final canonical Universal Monster, *The Creature from the Black Lagoon* is an entry that has had an indelible effect on an entire generation of filmgoers. As most critics agree, the story itself is rather hackneyed. A generic plot that could have led to a generic 'monster' film was indeed a possibility. What we have here, though, is a genre-bending aquatic monster film that relied heavily on the environment to create an audience panic. The Creature, you see, actually swam and it was fast! The underwater cinematography, advanced for its time, captures the menace beneath the surface and—combined with a brilliant and terrifying costume design—director Jack Arnold almost had all the pieces for a very convincing monster. Casting Ricou Browning, an accomplished water entertainer, to play the underwater Creature and Ben Chapman as the Creature on land cemented the 'this could really happen' idea of the film.

Synopsis:

Playing out like a water-based King Kong, a group of researchers looking for fossils along the Amazon discover what they believe to be a missing link: the Gill Man, a humanoid creature that lived underwater. Dr. Reed (Richard Carlson), and his team, succeed in capturing the beast, much to the chagrin of their native guides and Reed's fiancée, Kay (Julie Adams). Of course, the Creature breaks free and succeeds in kidnapping the beautiful Kay. It is a race against time as the Creature wishes to keep the young woman as his bride, which would certainly result in her death.

Scariest scene:

Using the skills of Ricou Browning, the Creature's scariest scene comes 20 years before Spielberg terrified us with *Jaws*. Young Kay (Julie Adams) goes for a leisurely swim in the lagoon. She is unaware of any danger, but something lurks below her. The Creature appears and, as we see from underwater, matches her swimming speed stride for stride as he stares up at the young woman. Her blissful ignorance is never shattered and the Creature doesn't make a move, but it feels as if he is simply playing with his food.

Memorable dialogue:

> **ELIZABETH**: Open the door, Henry! Henry!
>
> **MARK WILLIAMS**: Come on, come on!
>
> **DAVID REED**: You talking to me Mark or something out there?
>
> **MARK WILLIAMS**: Both David, they won't believe it back home, none of them, I wouldn't have believed it myself sitting out here waiting for some monster to appear: that's why we've got to take him.
>
> **DAVID REED**: Why won't they believe Mark?
>
> **MARK WILLIAMS**: Because we deal with known quantities, with knowledge we've accumulated up to now.
>
> **DAVID REED**: We've just begun to learn about the water and its secrets, just as we've only touched on outer space. We don't entirely rule out the possibility that there might be some form of life on another planet, and why not some entirely different form of life in a world we already know is inhabited by millions of living creatures?

CREATURE
FROM THE
BLACK LAGOON
Starring
RICHARD CARLSON · JULIA ADAMS
RICHARD DENNING · ANTONIO MORENO · NESTOR PAIVA · WHIT BISSELL
DIRECTED BY JACK ARNOLD · SCREENPLAY BY HARRY ESSEX AND ARTHUR ROSS · PRODUCED BY WILLIAM ALLAND · A UNIVERSAL-INTERNATIONAL PICTURE

Did you know?

Bud Westmore was credited for nearly 50 years as the sole creator of the Gill-Man costume. The original designer, though, was ex-Disney artist Millicent Patrick.

Cast:

Richard Carlson (David Reed), Julie Adams (Kay Lawrence), Richard Denning (Mark Williams), Ben Chapman (The Creature on Ground), Ricou Browning (The Creature in the Water), Antonio Moreno (Carl Maia), Nestor Paiva (Lucas), Whit Bissell (Dr. Edwin Thompson), Bernie Gozier (Zee), Henry Escalante (Chico).

What the critics say:

Dave Kehr, *The Chicago Reader:* "Jack Arnold has a flair for this sort of thing, and if there really is anything frightening about a man dressed up in a rubber suit with zippers where the gills ought to be, Arnold comes close to finding it."

Staff, *TV Guide*: "Imbued with great atmosphere by director Jack Arnold, the film is genuinely frightening, but also elicits a certain amount of pathos for the creature."

Steve MacFarlane, *Slant Magazine*: "What distinguished Jack Arnold's pictures from mutant spinoffs/ knockoffs is even more imperative to sci-fi today than it was in 1954: wonderment."

If you liked this, you might also like:

The Wolf Man (1941)

#63 An American Werewolf in London (1981)

This is the story of two yong American students traveling through England on a night of the full moon. Fate let one live and now everything is changing, changing, changing …

Why it made the list:

Director John Landis was best known for his comedies *National Lampoon's Animal House* and *The Blues Brothers*. But with his 1981 feature *An American Werewolf in London*, he fused his smart and sharp wit with straight up horror. It was an odd combination that Landis executed with an iron-fisted, take-no-prisoners approach. The comedy disarms the viewer so that when the horror comes into play it's all the more alarming. In addition to Landis' masterful direction, Rick Baker's impressive special FX set a new standard for horror cinema.

Synopsis:

Two American college students, David Kessler (David Naughton) and Jack Goodman (Griffin Dunne), are hiking to Paris, France, by way of London, England. Along the way they are attacked by a werewolf. Jack is killed in the onslaught, but David's life is spared when local townsfolk shoot and kill the wolf. The wolf is immediately revealed to be a man; a man stricken with the fabled lycanthropy, a condition brought on by the bite of a werewolf that causes a person to transform into a wolf-like creature during a full moon. David was bitten and scratched by the wolf.

David is taken to a hospital where his wounds are treated. He is interrogated by the police who do not believe his werewolf tales. Later, David is visited by his dead and decomposing friend Jack. At first David believes

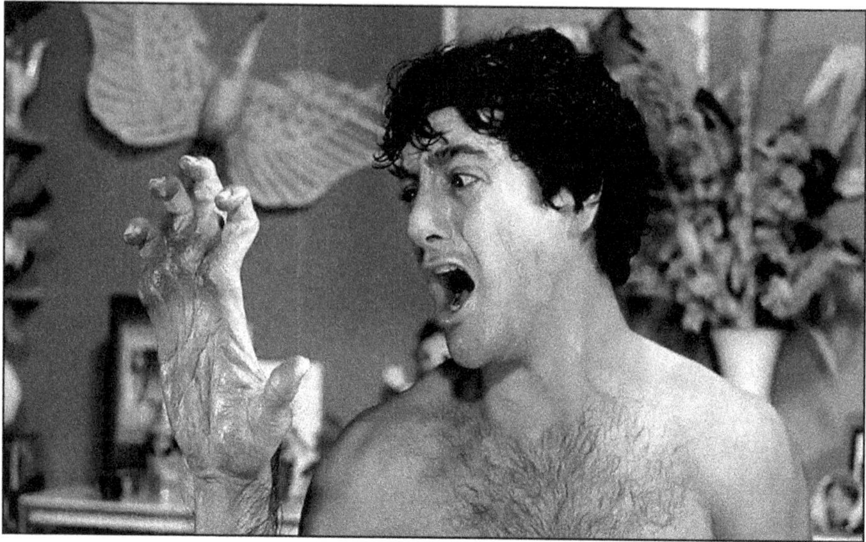

himself to be hallucinating but slowly comes around to the notion that he is in fact infected by the dreaded lycanthropy disease.

Just days after his attack a full moon is on the rise and David begins a harrowing transformation. Once in full wolf-man mode, David launches into a killing spree by which London hasn't seen since the days and nights of Jack the Ripper.

Scariest scene:

David's first mutation into a werewolf is undoubtedly the film's centerpiece and its scariest moment. It is a long and grotesque sequence that, even by today's standards, would shake up an audience.

Memorable dialogue:

> **DAVID:** Look at me. Here I sit in a porno theater in Piccadilly Circus talking to a corpse.

Did you know?

Because of director John Landis' success with *National Lampoon's Animal House* and *The Blues Brothers*, studio executives pressured the filmmaker to cast Dan Aykroyd and John Belushi in the two lead roles.

Cast:

David Naughton (David Kessler), Griffin Dunne (Jack Goodman), Lila Kaye (Barmaid), Paddy Ryan (First Werewolf), Jenny Agutter (Nurse Alex Price), Anne-Marie Davies (Nurse Susan Gallagher), John Woodvine (Dr. J. S. Hirsch), Frank Oz (Mr. Collins / Miss Piggy), Don McKillop (Inspector Villiers), Paul Kember (Sergeant McManus).

What the critics say:

Kim Newman, *Empire*: "Carnivorous lunar activities rarely come any more entertaining than this."

Staff Writer, *Variety*: "A clever mixture of comedy and horror which succeeds in being both funny and scary, *An American Werewolf in London* possesses an overriding eagerness to please that prevents it from becoming off-putting."

Tom Huddleston, *Time Out*: "Not just gory but actually frightening, not just funny but clever, *American Werewolf...* has its flaws, but these are outweighed by the film's many, mighty strengths."

If you liked this, you might also like:

Wolf (1994).

#64 The Night of the Hunter (1955)

Towering above all others, a motion picture that will not be easily matched... or forgotten!

Why it made the list:

This film is terrifying in the sense that it is a grotesquerie. A grotesquerie that mirrors our everyday life so completely that we get lost in the atmosphere of it. It can feel surreal, at times, but Charles Laughton's only credited directorial effort resonates with us, even over 50 years later. Pair that with Robert Mitchum's portrayal of one of the silver screen's most evil villains, and the result is nothing short of paralyzing. The sense of menace, especially for Mitchum's targets (a pair of children), is palpable, making this the prototypical psychological horror film.

Synopsis:

A criminally insane religious fanatic, Harry Powell (Robert Mitchum), shares a cell with Ben Harper (Peter Graves). Harper tells Powell about a ten-thousand-dollar heist that he hid with Harper's wife and kids before he is executed. Posing as a reverend, Powell hunts down Willa Harper (Shelley Winters) and seduces her to get close to the money. He terrorizes Willa's children and has no compunctions whatsoever about killing anyone that gets close. The entire plan is well within Harry's wheelhouse: he is a serial seducer and murderer of rich widows. The entire town falls for Harry, except the Harper kids. They lead Powell on a chase across the countryside where the children are found by Rachel Cooper (Lillian Gish), who runs an orphanage and helps to stop Powell... but can anyone really?

Scariest scene:

Harry Powell has told the children that their mother is away and, like anything terrifying in this film, we go right to the river. Beautiful in its own way, Willa Harper's corpse, bound to a submerged car, flows with the tide. Her hair, like the underwater vegetation, reaches out, dancing on the tide. She is cold and alone, much like her children. A fisherman manages to hook the car and sees Willa's dead body. The look that comes over his face is filled with terror, and so is ours.

Memorable dialogue:

> **HARRY POWELL:** Ah, little lad, you're starin' at my fingers. Would you like me to tell you the little story of Right Hand-Left Hand - the story of good and evil? *[He raises his left hand]* H-A-T-E! It was with this left hand that old brother Cain struck the blow that laid his brother low. *[He raises his right hand]* L-O-V-E. You see these fingers, dear hearts? These fingers has veins that run straight to the soul of man. The right hand, friends! The hand of love! Now watch and I'll show you the story of life. These fingers, dear hearts, is always a-warrin' and a-tuggin', one agin the other. Now, watch 'em. Ol' brother Left Hand. Left hand, he's a-fightin'. And it looks like LOVE's a goner. But wait a minute, wait a minute! Hot dog! LOVE's a winnin'? Yes, siree. It's LOVE that won, and ol' Left Hand HATE is down for the count!

Did you know?

The character of Harry Powell was patterned after Netherlands-born, but American hanged, serial killer, Harry Powers (Herman Drenth) that would murder women after luring them with "Lonely Hearts" ads in local newspapers.

Cast:

Robert Mitchum (Harry Powell), Shelley Winters (Willa Harper), Peter Graves (Ben Harper), Rachel Cooper (Lillian Gish), Billy Chapin (John Harper), Sally Jane Bruce (Pearl Harper), James Gleason (Birdie Steptoe),

Evelyn Varden (Icey Spoon), Don Beddoe (Walt Spoon), Gloria Castillo (Ruby).

What the critics say:

Eleanor McKeown, *Electric Sheep*: "Laughton made a unique and sublimely stunning film. It enchants, haunts and frightens in equal measures."

Wendy Ide, *Times UK*: "It's overwrought and lurid; the story is grotesque and so are the characters. It's unlike anything else before and since. And that is why this strident psychological horror stands up now as one of the great pieces of American genre cinema."

Michael Wilmington, *The Chicago Tribune*: "One of the great movie horror tales, with one of the greatest of all movie villains."

If you liked this, you might also like:

Cape Fear (1962).

#65 The Sixth Sense (1999)

I see dead people.

Why it made the list:

While much attention has been given to its surprise "twist" ending, *The Sixth Sense* is an effectively creepy film in its own right. The color palate helps establish a sense of gloom and dread with its emphasis on various hues of gray and brown. The occasional splashes of color serve as "clues" to the real nature of the otherworldly goings on. Haley Joel Osment delivers a supremely convincing performance as the little boy haunted by visions of dead people, and was nominated for an Academy Award for Best Supporting Actor.

Synopsis:

Dr. Malcolm Crowe (Bruce Willis) is a decorated child psychologist. One night, while celebrating an award given to him by the city of Philadelphia with his wife, Anna (Olivia Williams), Crowe is confronted in his own home by a former patient, who, in obvious mental torment, shoots the doctor and then kills himself. Six months later, still troubled by his inability to help this patient, Crowe takes on a new case. Young Cole Sear (Haley Joel Osment) is having trouble in school and is obviously deeply troubled. His devoted and loving mother, Lynn (Toni Collette) is at the end of her rope. Dr. Crowe tries to get Cole to communicate his problems, but the boy is reticent, fearing he'll be labeled a "freak." Finally, after a particularly traumatic event at a birthday party, Cole admits to Dr. Crowe that he sees "dead people." Dr. Crowe, meanwhile, is having problems of his own. Anna won't talk to him, and his marriage seems to be falling apart. He resolves to bring relief to the boy and to bridge the problems in his marriage, but what he doesn't realize is that the ghosts Cole sees are real, and they won't go away easily.

Scariest scene:

Cole encounters a particularly troublesome spirit in his own home, a young girl whose power to disrupt his safe space and seemingly manifest a physical presence terrifies and moves the boy to try to begin to exert some kind of control over the terrors that have taken over his life.

Memorable dialogue:

> **COLE:** I see dead people.
>
> **DR. CROWE:** In your dreams?
>
> **COLE:** [Shakes his head.]
>
> **DR. CROWE:** While you're awake?
>
> **COLE:** [Nods.]
>
> **DR. CROWE:** Dead people like, in graves? In coffins?
>
> **COLE:** Walking around like regular people. They don't see each other. They only see what they want to see. They don't know they're dead.
>
> **DR. CROWE:** How often do you see them?
>
> **COLE:** All the time. They're everywhere.

Did you know?

The Latin phrase Cole speaks in the church when he first meets Malcolm: "*De profundis clamo ad te domine*" translates to "Out of the depths, I cry to you, O Lord." These are the first few words of Psalm 130 in the *Book of Psalms.*

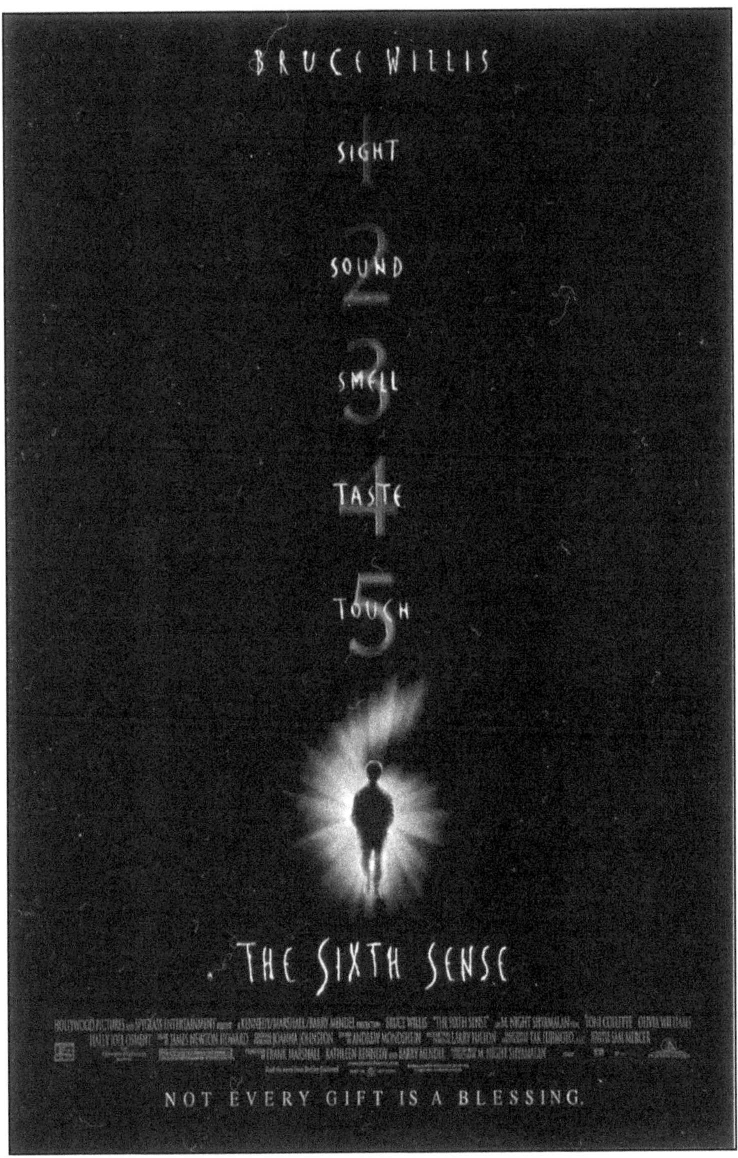

Cast:

Bruce Willis (Dr. Malcolm Crowe), Haley Joel Osment (Cole Sear), Toni Collette (Lynn Sear), Olivia Williams (Anna Crowe), Trevor Morgan (Tommy Tommasino), Donnie Wahlberg (Vincent Grey), Peter Tambakis (Darren), Jeffrey Zubernis (Bobby), Bruce Norris (Stanley Cunningham), Glenn Fitzgerald (Sean).

What the critics say:

Carrie Rickie, *Philadelphia Inquirer*: "While the film about a troubled boy tormented by visions and by schoolmates stars Bruce Willis as a child psychologist, *The Sixth Sense* rests squarely on Osment's hunched little shoulders. He carries the movie, a lyrical and eerie meditation upon loss and hurt and healing, like Atlas swatting away ghosts with his free hand. So transparent is Osment as an actor, and so rare, that the pain on his face stabs you in the heart."

David Denby, *The New Yorker*: "The movie is an admirable attempt at injecting some honest feeling into a curdled commercial genre, and it pays off in the end with a genuine shock that leaves one amazed."

John Anderson, *Los Angeles Times*: "Mixing weird rhythms and gothic-Catholic iconography—static shots of church friezes, petrified statuary and the Latin muttered by Cole when he seeks sanctuary among the pews, *Sixth Sense* is off-kilter from the start, rich in a kind of matter-of-fact horror. Because what Malcolm doesn't know, what he can't possibly suspect until Cole eventually bares his soul, are the depths and echoes of the boy's possible 'disorder.'"

If you liked this, you might also like:

Stir of Echoes (1999).

#66 Dead Alive (1982)

On this picturesque block. In this manicured home. Something evil, something terrifying, something horrifying is haunting Lionel.

Why it made the list:

Dead Alive is universally considered the bloodiest motion picture of all time. Now, blood and gore alone plainly will not make for a scary movie. The reason this picture is so unnerving is that director Peter Jackson knows no bounds or limits. He breaks down the barriers and rules of horror filmmaking at every turn. Jackson's nauseatingly morbid film has the audience in his hands. Time after time he rubs their faces in his unrelenting cinematic carnage, intense bad taste and over-the-top humor. A first-time viewer either resigns himself to the graphic blood-spattered mess or simply gets up to leave.

Synopsis:

Mama's boy Lionel Cosgrove (Timothy Balme) is still hanging on to those proverbial apron strings. Vera Cosgrove (Elizabeth Moody), his Mum, is the paint-by-numbers domineering mother who revels in exploiting her son's love and affections for her. It's a twisted relationship not at all unlike the one Norman Bates has with his mother in Alfred Hitchcock's *Psycho*.

The two visit the local zoo and Mum is bitten by the exotic Sumatran rat monkey. Lionel takes Mum home in an attempt to nurse her back to health. What the young lad doesn't know yet is that he cannot help her. The rat monkey bite has infected her with a deadly virus that caused her to die and then be reborn as a zombie.

Attempting to keep his mother's condition a secret, Lionel stages scene after scene of normalcy for his neighbors, family members, and newcomers. However, it's to little success. Mum's dietary needs have changed since her death. First she eats a dog and then moves on to houseguests. With every caller and every Mum's bite, the virus spreads until Lionel's house is swarming with the undead.

Scariest Scene:

The sheer magnitude of onscreen violence has been amplified to a feverish pitch by the film's climax. Director Peter Jackson severely encroaches upon his viewers' comfort zones. When Lionel's house is finally overrun with flesh-eating brain-dead zombies, he enters equipped with a modified lawnmower as a weapon. Audience's sensors become overloaded during the resultant slaughter.

Memorable dialogue:

> **PAQUITA:** Your mother ate my dog!
>
> **LIONEL:** Not all of it.

Did you know?

Nearly 80 gallons of theatrical blood were used in the final sequence alone.

Cast:

Timothy Balme (Lionel Cosgrove), Diana Penalver (Paquita Maria Sanchez), Elizabeth Moody (Vera Cosgrove), Ian Watkin (Uncle Les), Brenda Kendall (Nurse McTavish), Stuart Devenie (Father McGruder), Jed Brophy (Void), Stephen Papps (Zombie McGruder), Murray Keane (Scroat), Glenis Levestam (Nora Matheson).

What the critics say:

David Stratton, *Variety*: "[*Dead Alive*] is one of the bloodiest horror comedies ever made, and that will be enough to ensure its success in both cinemas and, especially, on video. It's also the best to date from Kiwi gore specialist Peter Jackson, who goes for broke with an orgy of bad taste and splatter humor. Some will recoil from the gore, but this wasn't made for them."

Staff, *Time Out*: "The finale, in which Lionel reduces a horde of flesh-eaters to a mulch of blood, flesh and offal with the aid of a flymo, is probably the goriest scene ever."

Owen Gleiberman, *Entertainment Weekly*: "*Dead Alive* is one outrageously gruesome set piece after another, a movie in which the human characters are boring but the limbs, eyeballs, and—especially—intestinal tracts have an exuberant life of their own. There are no rules in Jackson's slapstick carnival of gore."

If you liked this, you might also like:

Bad Taste (1987).

#67 Deep Red (1975)

The maker of Suspiria *now takes you on a journey through the macabre, the bizarre … the unnatural.*

Why it made the list:

Few films have managed to exploit the darkness the way master filmmaker Dario Argento's giallo *Deep Red* does. The picture revels in its tension-building "what's-hiding-in-the-shadows?" method of filmmaking. This, coupled with an abundance of creepy atmospherics, will have viewers sitting on the edge of their seats, overcome with anxiety. Despite an abundance of gore, nothing we see on film is quite as frightening as what we imagine to be hiding in every darkened corner. The storyline is a bizarre, disjoined one that leaves the viewer constantly guessing. Throw in a few unsettling images and a couple of creepy baby doll heads, and you've got a genuinely effective and uncompromising thriller/horror picture from one of the genre's all-time greats working at the peak of his powers.

Synopsis:

Deep Red wastes no time getting down to it; the film opens with two shadowy figures fighting until one of them is brutally murdered with a hatchet. The film then takes us to a lecture by psychic medium Helga Ulmann (Macha Meril), who has a vision of a brutal murder that is about to take place. When Helga is chopped to bits as a result of this vision, pianist Marcus Daly (David Hemmings) embarks upon an investigation. In the process of this probe, Marcus encounters several more bloody murders at the hands of the hatchet-wielding madman. And now it appears that the killer is after him …

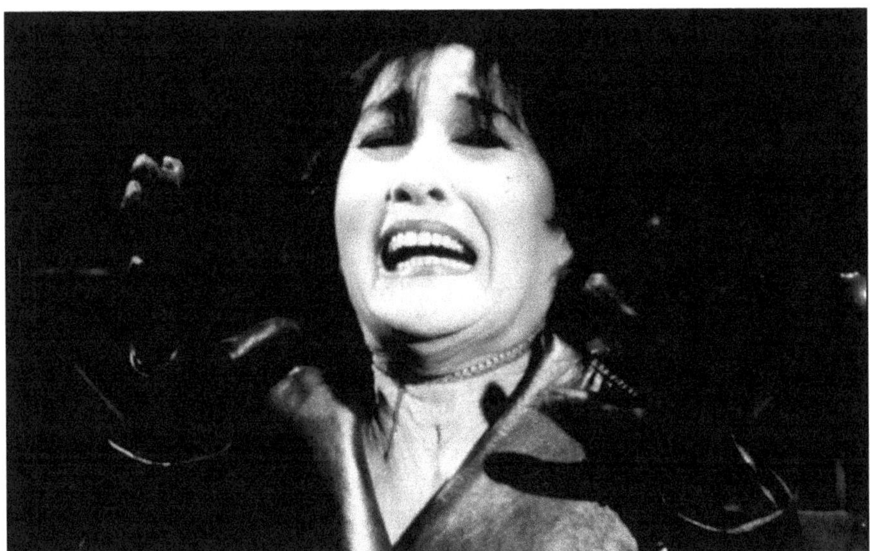

Scariest scene:

The film is filled with eerie sequences in which characters stare into the darkness and analyze every creaking floorboard, waiting for the killer to emerge and hack them to pieces. Each of these scenes is equally effective, so it's difficult to point out one scene as being the most frightening. And any time that damned children's song plays in the film (that accompanies the murders), things get super-creepy really fast.

Memorable dialogue:

> **MARC:** Gianna! Gianna! There's someone in the house—absolutely trying to kill me, you know?

Did you know?

Close-up shots of the killer's hands, donning black leather gloves, actually feature the hands of director Dario Argento.

Cast:

David Hemmings (Marcus Daly), Daria Nicolodi (Gianna Brezzi), Gabriele Lavia (Carlo), Macha Meril (Helga Ulmann), Eros Pagni (Supt.

Calcabrini), Giuliana Calandra (Amanda Righetti), Piero Mazzinghi (Bardi), Glauco Mauri (Professor Giordani), Clara Calamai (Marta), Aldo Bonamano (Carlo's Father).

What the critics say:

Sweetback, *Daily Grindhouse*: "It feels almost cliché to say that it's one of the very best the genre ever produced. That it's visually stunning, expertly composed and even—for one of the few times in Argento's career—has a strong screenplay. The set pieces are bigger and the murders bloodier than ever before—and the subtle supernatural overtones cleared a path for *Suspiria*. It's perhaps Argento's masterpiece and the film that would go on to define his career. But it's also a supremely satisfying film, so overflowing with style that an unprepared viewer can almost be overwhelmed by the cavalcade of visual and aural stimuli on display."

Shane M. Dallmann, *Images Journal*: "The ultimate art of display is the filmmaker's. Argento's world dominates, and the characters only live in it. Only the viewers of the film see the unusual camera angles or the extreme close-ups of certain peculiar objects … [T]his is one of Argento's finest films."

Staff, *Empire Magazine*: "Undoubtedly the finest of Argento's thrilling horrors, this one takes the radical step, for the director at least, to concentrate on a plot that equals the shocking visuals of his other works. David Hemmings is well cast and is given a great script which genuinely frightens."

If you liked this, you might also like:

Tenebrae (1982).

#68 The Legend of Hell House (1973)

For the sake of your sanity, pray it isn't true!

Why it made the list:

A quiet British film with very little special effects (falling chandeliers and tossed-around chairs aside), *The Legend of Hell House* relies on subtleties like whispering voices, creaking floorboards, and ambiance to scare its audience. It is also quite effective, save for a really horrendous ending that pits Roddy McDowell against the ghost, and … well, you'll just have to see it to believe how craptastic it is. Ending notwithstanding, the film offers a good 80 minutes of sheer creepiness. It also doesn't hurt that it was written by legendary novelist Richard Matheson, of *I Am Legend* fame.

Synopsis:

A wealthy man sends a handpicked team of specialists (a physicist, a young psychic, and the only survivor of the previous visit) to investigate a house that is supposedly haunted and "evil." Their mission is to determine whether or not there is life after death. Each is paid 100,000 pounds for their participation. The only catch? Almost everyone who has ever visited the house has either gone insane or been killed in some mysterious fashion.

Scariest scene:

It's difficult to pinpoint one truly scary scene as there really isn't one. *The Legend of Hell House* is more about sustaining a sense of dread throughout its running time, and it manages to do that handily (again, save for its goofball conclusion). Long moments of silence are punctuated by the loud, shrill screams of actress Gayle Hunnicut, and those prove to be as frightening as anything in the film.

Memorable dialogue:

> **ANN:** What did he do to make this house so evil, Mr. Fischer?
>
> **FISCHER:** Drug addiction, alcoholism, sadism, bestiality, mutilation, murder, vampirism, necrophilia, cannibalism, not to mention a gamut of sexual goodies. Shall I go on?
>
> **ANN:** How did it end?
>
> **FISCHER:** If it had ended, we would not be here.

Did you know?

When novelist/screenwriter Richard Matheson learned that *Hell House* would be made into a feature, he expressed his desire that real-life couple Richard Burton and Elizabeth Taylor star in the film.

Cast:

Pamela Franklin (Florence Tanner), Roddy McDowell (Benjamin Franklin Fischer), Clive Revill (Dr. Barrett), Gayle Hunnicutt (Ann Barrett), Roland Culver (Mr. Deutsch), Peter Bowles (Hanley).

What the critics say:

Staff, *DVD Verdict*: "The appeal of *Legend of Hell House* lies in its stylish direction, opulent sets, and Matheson's tense (though confusing) story. Director John Hough has had a less-than-stellar career, though it's hard to fault him for that after witnessing *Hell House*. Hough makes interesting and effective use of 'deep focus,' keeping subjects in the foreground and background focused in the viewer's attention. Often, the subjects are the four principal characters, though the house is equally prominent in our attention. This use of deep focus brings us closer to the characters, though its unnatural connection between them throws off our sense of geography and disorients us."

Andrew Hershberger, *Cinescape*: "*The Legend of Hell House* is a remarkably effective little thriller that provides the bulk of its chills in the first two-thirds—the final third is bogged down with the inclusion of a ghost-eradicating machine and a semi-goofy final confrontation with the individual behind the malice. A prime example of suggestion over showing, the movie concentrates on the actions of the spirits—opening/closing doors, moving objects, possession—rather than the age-old standby of translucent figures in whiteface. As a result, the audience is treated to a series of hair-raising events that may be the work of the deceased, or might simply be manifestations of the mediums' subconscious."

Kurt Dahlke, *DVD Talk*: "The brilliance of *Hell House* lies in a 'veddy British' attitude; matter-of-fact, proper and unwavering. Spectral antics aren't dolled up in splashy effects or arch trappings, just laid out with straightforward earnestness; no one in the house displays more attitude than they would on any other day at work. This coolness brings the fear right into the real world, giving Hell House more than the usual share of scares. Chillingly delightful is the way characters will become aware of something sinister, staring into an empty space while no more than hushed whispers and choked atmosphere telegraph the trauma."

If you liked this, you might also like:

House on Haunted Hill (1959).

#69 The Amityville Horror (1979)

For God's sake, get out!

Why it made the list:

What do you get when you mix a supposedly "true story" and a horror film? A crowd-pleasing, box office smash! In 1974, Butch Defeo massacred his parents and four siblings at 112 Ocean Avenue, Amityville, New York. A year and a month later, George and Kathy Lutz bought the house and moved in. They lasted 28 days. The validity of the Amityville haunting makes for creepy fun and remains a perfect blend of fact, fiction, and Hollywood entertainment to this day.

Synopsis:

Newlyweds George and Kathy Lutz, along with their three children, move into a large, colonial style home in Long Island that was previously the location of a gruesome family massacre. Soon afterwards Father Delaney, a close family friend, comes to bless their new home and in doing so releases the anger of a demonic entity. The entity drives the priest away and then turns its full wrath upon the unsuspecting new occupants. While Father Delaney wrestles with his fear and cowardice, George Lutz is plagued by fatigue, sickness, cold, and explosive bouts of rage. The rest of the Lutz family members are visited by horrific specters, voices, and other demonic activity. It seems apparent that the only hope the Lutz's have of surviving their ordeal lies with Father Delaney. Will he find his courage in time to help or will the evil inside the house possess George, spurring him on to reenact the tragic events of the Defeo slaughter?

Scariest scene:

The most frightening scenes are of the exterior of the house itself with its eerily lit, evil Jack-o-lantern window "eyes"! It's unsettling as hell how the light in those windows go from a warm yellow to a hellish red as the haunting progresses. The cinematographer took full advantage of the natural creepiness of the house and made it even more horrifying with tints of various distressing colors. The house literally looks demonic.

Memorable dialogue:

> **KATHY LUTZ:** I just wish that … all those people hadn't died here. I mean … ugh! A guy kills his whole family. Doesn't that bother you?
>
> **GEORGE:** Sure, but … houses don't have memories.
>
> **THE HOUSE:** GET OUT!

Did you know?

At the time of its release the film was one of the highest grossing independent films of all time and American International Pictures' biggest hit.

Cast:

James Brolin (George Lutz), Margot Kidder (Kathy Lutz), Rod Steiger (Father Delaney), Don Stroud (Father Bolen), Murray Hamilton (Father Ryan), John Larch (Father Nuncio), Natasha Ryan (Amy), K.C. Martel (Greg), Meeno Peluce (Matt), Michael Sacks (Jeff).

What the critics say:

Staff, *Variety*: "Flies swarm where they shouldn't; pipes and walls ooze ick; doors fly open; and priests and psychic sensitives cringe and flee in panic. It's definitely a house that audiences will enjoy visiting, especially if unfamiliar with the ending."

Ryan Turak, *Shock Till You Drop:* "Social subtext aside, if there's one thing that *The Amityville Horror* will always be remembered for, it's the house itself – arguably the most instantly identifiable edifice in horror history with its Dutch gambrel roof design and quarter-circle windows that give it the appearance of having two evil eyes. To this day, no other haunted house can compare. As James Brolin's George Lutz says, "houses don't have memories," but as *The Amityville Horror* proves, houses themselves can be unforgettable."

Staff, *UrbanCinefile:* "This isn't the kind of film that makes you jump at every turn. It's creepy in a cumulative kind of way, as a normal family is tipped over into their dark side, when ghosts of the past make themselves known. Sure, all the filmmaking tools are put to good use—the tinkling wind chimes, the creaky stairs that go down to the dark cellar, and of course the mandatory nighttime thunderstorm that allows the shadows to jump even more ominously."

If you liked this, you might also like:

Burnt Offerings (1976).

#70 *Black Sunday* (1960)

Stare into these eyes ... discover deep within them the unspeakable terrifying secret of Black Sunday.

Why it made the list:

Shot way back in 1960, Mario Bava's *Black Sunday* is one of the creepiest films you'll ever see. Fully utilizing the black-and-white film on which it was shot, it uses every dark shadow to its benefit. One of the greatest Italian horror films ever produced, *Black Sunday* is perhaps the most underrated (and criminally underseen) film in this bunch. It would be ranked much higher on this list, but the years have not been particularly kind to it. Although it's still extremely creepy and atmospheric, its story and acting have not aged well.

Synopsis:

In the seventeenth century, Princess Asa Vajda (Barbara Steele) and her lover, Javutich (Arturo Dominici), are killed for worshiping the devil and practicing witchcraft. First they have spiked masks nailed to their faces, and then they are burned at the stake. But before Princess Vajda dies, she unleashes a powerful spell on the unsuspecting townsfolk—one that will affect the town for generations to come. All hell breaks loose two hundred years later when Dr. Andre Gorobec (John Richardson) unwittingly frees the witch from her slumber, bringing her back to wreak havoc on the earth once more.

Scariest scene:

The film is filled with many downright creepy, shudder-inducing scenes, but it's difficult to pinpoint a "scariest scene" here. Perhaps it is the scene

in which Dr. Andre Gorobec comes face to face with the newly-risen Princess Asa Vajda and is enticed to come forward, kiss her, and drain his blood so that she may have everlasting life.

STARE INTO THESE EYES
discover deep within them the unspeakable terrifying secret of "BLACK SUNDAY"
BLACK SUNDAY
...the most frightening motion picture you have ever seen!
PLEASE NOTE
The producers of BLACK SUNDAY recommend that it be seen only by those over 12 years of age!
starring BARBARA STEELE
JOHN RICHARDSON · IVO GARRANI
ANDREA CHECCHI
A GALATEA-JOLLY FILM PRODUCTION · Directed by MARIO BAVA · AN AMERICAN-INTERNATIONAL PICTURE

Memorable dialogue:

> **PRINCESS ASA VAJDA**: You will never escape my vengeance, or of Satan's! My revenge will seek you out, and with the blood of your sons, and of their sons, and their sons, I will continue to live forever! They will restore me to the life you now rob from me!

Did you know?

This was American International Pictures' highest-grossing film at the time it was released, exceeding grosses for *Goliath and the Barbarians* and Roger Corman's *House of Usher*.

Cast:

Barbara Steele (Katia Vajda/Princess Asa Vajda), John Richardson (Dr. Andre Gorobec), Andrea Checchi (Dr. Thomas Kruvajan), Ivo Garrani (Prince Vajda), Arturo Dominici (Igor Javutich/Javuto), Enrico Olivieri (Prince Constantine Vajda), Antonio Pierfederici (Priest), Tino Bianchi (Ivan), Clara Bindi (Inn Keeper), Mario Passante (Nikita the Coachman).

What the critics say:

Eugene Archer, *New York Times*: "It will leave its audiences yearning for that quiet, sunny little motel in *Psycho*."

Keith Phipps, *The Onion A.V. Club*: "Working, as usual, on a low budget, Bava turned 1960's *Black Sunday* into an experience akin to wandering into someone else's nightmare. The shadow-drenched, black-and-white film is ostensibly a gothic tale of vampires and witches, but the lurid, overheated, sexually-charged, and (for its time) graphically violent images soon overwhelm the plot, suggesting what might have happened if Val Lewton and Alfred Hitchcock had ever teamed up."

Derek Adams, *Time Out*: "The visual style still impresses, but the story beneath it has become too formularised for the film to retain all its original power."

If you liked this, you might also like:

The Masque of the Red Death (1954).

#71 *Pet Sematary* (1989)

Sometimes dead is better.

Why it made the list:

Based on the Stephen King novel of the same name, and boasting a screenplay by King himself, *Pet Sematary* spends much of its first half focused on the characters' relationship with and fear of death. In the second half, things really ramp up as madness and supernatural terror come to the fore, though death definitely remains a constant, looming presence.

Synopsis:

The Creed family of Chicago relocates to the small town of Ludlow, Maine. The father, Louis (Dale Midkiff) is a doctor who has taken a position at the University of Maine. A path behind their house leads to a small clearing with a sign that says "Pet Sematary." Their neighbor, Jud Crandall (Fred Gwynne), explains that children from the area have brought their pets to be buried there for decades. The road that runs in front of the Creed's house is frequented by fast-moving trucks, and many pets, Jud tells them, have died on that road. Later, while Louis' wife, Rachel (Denise Crosby) and children, Ellie (Blaze Berdahl) and Gage (Miko Hughes) are visiting her parents in Chicago for Thanksgiving, Ellie's cat, Church, is found dead in Jud's front yard. Jud, feeling that Ellie is too young to understand death, shows Louis a place beyond the pet cemetery, an old Indian burial ground. He instructs Louis to bury the cat there. Church returns home the next day, alive but very different. When a tragic accident on the road later takes the life of his beloved son, Louis' grief is too much, and he decides to take Gage to the Indian burial ground. Neither he nor his family and friends can possibly be prepared for what happens next.

Scariest scene:

Despite knowing what the burial ground turned his son into and the death and destruction that followed his return, Louis buries his murdered wife there anyway, then goes home to await her return. When she arrives, he is quick to embrace her, and she is just as quick to grab a butcher knife from the kitchen table.

Memorable dialogue:

> **JUD:** The soil of a man's heart is stonier, Louis. A man grows what he can, and he tends it. 'Cause what you buy, is what you own. And what you own … always comes home to you.

Did you know?

Two twin actresses played the role of Ellie Creed. Blaze Berdahl, however, received the main credit for the role while her sister Beau Berdahl is credited as "Ellie Creed II."

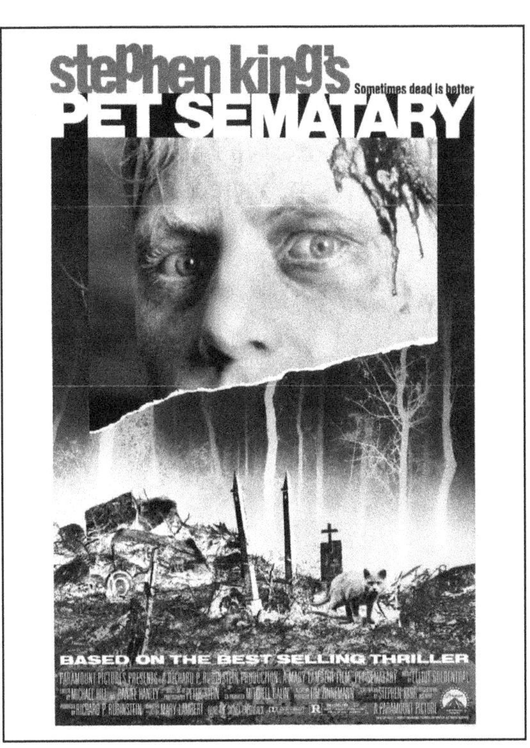

Cast:

Dale Midkiff (Louis Creed), Fred Gwynne (Jud Crandall), Denise Crosby (Rachel Creed), Brad Greenquist (Victor Pascow), Michael Lombard (Irwin Goldman), Miko Hughes (Gage Creed), Blaze Berdahl (Ellie Creed), Susan Blommaert (Missy Dandridge), Mara Clark (Marcy Charlton), Kavi Raz (Steve Masterson).

What the critics say:

A.J. MacReady *Horror View*: "This is a well-done flick, certainly, but a feel-good story it ain't. It's dark and depressing and horrible things happen to good people, over and over again. It's like the harshest parts of life in that respect. Regardless, it's effective and creepy and awesomely gory when it needs to be and just flat out twisted nasty. Lambert's direction is solid, assured and has no qualms whatsoever about punching you in the gut."

Steve Hutchison, *Tales of Terror*: "*Pet Sematary* is a dark, sad story that excels at exploiting one of the deepest and most visceral fear humans have: losing someone near, a pet or someone from their family. The film bathes in an aura of sadness and it is terribly scary. It's without a doubt one of the creepiest supernatural horror films in history."

Staff, *Cinefessions*: "The best part of the film is definitely Gwynne's performance, but a close second is the incredible special effects work. There is one character who is creepy enough to give nightmares thanks to the effects (Zelda). In an era that saw 'body horror' and extreme graphic content become all the rave, *Pet Sematary* absolutely holds its own."

If you liked this, you might also like:

Cemetery Man (1994).

#72 *The Devil's Backbone* (2001)

The living will always be more dangerous than the dead.

Why it made the list:

Mexican director Guillermo del Toro (*Cronos*) is one of the finest filmmakers working today, so when he decided to craft a ghost story about a dead boy in an orphanage, he naturally made a film that excels on nearly every level. *The Devil's Backbone* isn't just horror—it aspires to be so much more (and succeeds in damn near every way imaginable)—but nonetheless it remains one of the creepiest films around. Again, it's a beautiful film that's poetic on many levels, but that beauty doesn't make it any less effective as a chiller.

Synopsis:

It's 1939, and the Spanish Civil War is finally at its end. Carlos (Fernando Tielve), a ten-year-old boy who's recently become an orphan due to the war (but doesn't yet know), is taken to live in an orphanage in the middle of nowhere. While there, his entire life will change as he struggles to fit in with the other boys. Soon things become complicated when Carlos starts seeing a ghostly figure in the darkness. He eventually learns that the ghost is that of a young boy named Santi (Junio Valverde), who may have been killed by one of the caretakers. As Carlos sets out to find out what really happened to Santi, he will soon learn that the living are far more dangerous than the dead.

Scariest scene:

The scenes in which Carlos follows the dead boy Santi are the scariest in the film. They are extremely atmospheric, capturing a feeling of overwhelming dread. Credit Guillermo del Toro for actually showing the ghost throughout the film—a difficult feat for any filmmaker to pull off. And each and every time we see the dead boy sneaking through the darkness, it remains chillingly effective.

Memorable dialogue:

> **CASARES:** What is a ghost? A tragedy condemned to repeat itself time and again? An instant of pain, perhaps. Something dead which still seems to be alive. An emotion suspended in time. Like a blurred photograph. Like an insect trapped in amber.

Did you know?

Guillermo del Toro, a big fan of world cinema, chose to present Santi's ghost in the film in a style similar to the white-faced ghosts found in Japanese horror films such as *Ringu*.

Cast:

Marisa Paredes (Carmen), Eduardo Noriega (Jacinto), Federico Luppi (Dr. Casares), Fernando Tielve (Carlos), Inigo Garces (Jaime), Irene Visedo (Conchita), Jose Manuel Lorenzo (Marcelo), Francisco Maestre (El Puerco), Junio Valverde (Santi), Berta Ojea (Alma).

What the critics say:

Roger Ebert, *Chicago Sun-Times*: "Any director of a ghost film is faced with the difficult question of portraying the ghost. A wrong step, and he gets bad laughs. The ghost in *The Devil's Backbone* is glimpsed briefly, is heard sighing, is finally seen a little better as a dead boy. What happens at the end is not the usual action scene with which lesser ghost films dissipate their tension, but a chain of events that have a logic and a poetic justice. *The Devil's Backbone* has been compared to *The Others*, and has the same ambition and intelligence, but is more compelling and even convincing."

Andrew J. Rausch, *Screem*: "*The Devil's Backbone* really shouldn't be much more than a simple E.C. Comics-style story of supernatural revenge, but in Del Toro's hands, it becomes something much more—it's both elegant and poetic. This film is the cinematic equivalent of the divine poem that makes you weep or the song that makes you yearn for your lost love. It's as powerful as anything ever captured on celluloid, which is somewhat of a rarity in terms of supernatural-themed films."

Jonathan Holland, *Variety*: "One of the pic's strengths is the way it suggests that these glimpses may be the product of Carlos' disturbed mind as he seeks companionship. The script creates genuine tension between real and supernatural explanations, and when the kids' nighttime whisperings about ghosts are proven to be true ones, it feels like a vindication of the imaginative way that kids see the world."

If you liked this, you might also like:

The Orphanage (2007).

#73 *Return of the Living Dead* (1985)

The dead are refusing to remain buried. They've come back to life and they're hungry, and they're not vegetarians.

Why it made the list:

Director Dan O'Bannon's *Return of the Living Dead* is less of an unofficial sequel to George A. Romero's *Night of the Living Dead* as it is a parody of zombie movie mythology. O'Bannon wrote what he'd learned from reading horror comics as a youngster. He injected his film with a super-charged serum of high octane wit, blood, guts, gore and humor. In short, O'Bannon's first feature film is a runaway train of unpredictable and visceral assaults on the viewer's senses.

Synopsis:

The Uneeda Medical Supply Company, in Louisville, Kentucky, has just hired its latest employee, Freddy (Thom Mathews). Freddy's orientation has started on the fourth of July and Uneeda's manager, Frank (James Karen), is going to show the newbie the ropes. Dragging his feet on the boring preliminaries, Frank decides to give Freddy an earful (and eyeful) about what, and who, is in the basement. Frank lets Freddy in on a little-known secret—the 1968 zombie film *Night of the Living Dead* was based on an actual incident. Frank also recounts that the U.S. government had been toying with a reanimating agent called Trioxin 245. Continuing on, Frank explains that a 55 gallon barrel drum, containing one of the undead corpses, was accidentally sent to the Uneeda Medical Supply.

Frank leads Freddy to the basement. Before either one of them are truly aware of what has happened, the zombie (Allan Trautman) is accidentally released from his barrel home of 15 years. Apparently, being pickled in the experimental Trioxin 245, for over a decade, has not set well with this new-

ly-animated corpse. He's hungry too, and he makes no bones about what he wants: brains! This unfortunate incident will ultimately set forth a chain of events that will have the undead rising from their graves all around.

Scariest scene:

It's a miracle of filmmaking that any sequence whatsoever within this zombie send-up would be even remotely frightening, yet the film does have its moments. Snatching first prize would be the newly-released barrel zombie, lunging manically towards the cast members/camera. Second prize goes to every moment spent with the Half Lady Corpse. Both scenes are spook house business for sure, but to resign this film solely to the black comedy corner would be doing these horror movie creators a great disservice.

Memorable dialogue:

BURT: If that is a re-animated body, we're gonna have to kill it.

FREDDY: How do you kill something that's already dead?

BURT: How do I know, Fred? Let me think!

FRANK: It's not a bad question, Burt.

Did you know?

Some zombie extras were asked to eat cow brains. Director Dan O'Bannon vowed that he would not make anyone do something he would not do, so he ate cow brains, as well.

Cast:

Clu Gulager (Burt), James Karen (Frank), Don Calfa (Ernie), Thom Mathews (Freddy), Beverly Randolph (Tina), John Philbin (Chuck), Jewel Shepard (Casey), Miguel A. Núñez Jr. (Spider), Brian Peck (Scuz), Linnea Quigley (Trash).

What the critics say:

Michael Weldon, *The Psychotronic Video Guide:* "A movie that manages to be scary, surprising, and funny."

Pete Vonder Haar, *Film Threat*: "A fresh and immensely entertaining take on the zombie genre."

Felix Vasquez Jr., *Cinema Crazed:* "For pure eighties, punk rock, walking dead, brain eating mayhem, this is the film to watch."

If you liked this, you might also like:

Fido (2006).

#74 *The Hitcher* (1986)

The terror starts the moment he stops.

Why it made the list:

The Hitcher slathers the screen with nearly every conceivable and alarming notion about picking up a stranger along the road. The movie's title is the film's set up. There's little explanation of the story's background, keeping the exposition at a minimum, and that is to the filmmaker's credit.

The picture portrays the protagonist Jim Halsey as a truly amenable character, almost forcing the audience to become accepting of him. This allows *The Hitcher* to successfully work in a way that other slasher flicks cannot. Unlike the *Friday the 13th* movies and their ilk, the protagonist is truly the film's hero. Moreover, Rutger Hauer's turn as the psychopathic John Ryder is unnerving, caustic, and damned convincing.

Synopsis:

Halsey (C. Thomas Howell) is delivering a car from Chicago to San Diego by way of Texas as a means of cheap transportation to California. The road is long and desolate until he happens upon a hitchhiker. Playing the Good Samaritan, Halsey picks up the stranger and almost immediately regrets his genial intentions. The hitchhiker, John Ryder (Rutger Hauer), has an extremely nasty disposition and begins taunting Halsey. Abruptly, a switchblade is brandished and held to Halsey's throat. True to his sadistic nature, Ryder wastes no time in telling graphic detailed accounts of people he has contentedly murdered.

Ryder insists that Halsey stop Ryder from murdering again. If he doesn't comply then he will summarily dismember Halsey's body and leave him dead by the roadside. Halsey reacts by kicking his assailant out the passenger door and into the road. Relieved, though falsely so, Halsey

continues his road trip only to encounter his attacker time and time again with dead bodies piling up along the way.

Ryder manages to frame Halsey for the murders and a cat and mouse scenario between Ryder, Halsey, and the police is underway.

Scariest scene:

Once Jim Halsey picks up John Ryder the scares are virtually non-stop for its 99 minute duration. Ryder is relentless in his pursuit of Halsey and stops at nothing to let him know his intentions. However, the time the two spend together at the beginning of the film, whilst trapped in a moving vehicle, are certainly the most disturbing. Honorable Mention: While chowing down on some steak fries, Halsey nearly bites into a strategically placed disembodied finger snatched from one of Ryder's earlier victims.

Memorable dialogue:

> **JOHN RYDER:** Do you know what happens to an eyeball when it gets punctured? You got any idea how much blood jets out of a guy's neck when his throat's been slit?

Did you know?

Screenwriter Eric Red got his inspiration for the narrative from The Doors' song "Riders on the Storm" and its line, "There's a killer on the road."

Cast:

Rutger Hauer (John Ryder), C. Thomas Howell (Jim Halsey), Jennifer Jason Leigh (Nash), Jeffery DeMunn (Captain Esteridge), John M. Jackson (Sergeant Starr), Billy Greenbush (Trooper Donner), Jack Thibeau (Trooper Preston), Armin Shimerman (Interrogation Sergeant), Gene Davis (Trooper Dodge), Jon Van Ness (Trooper Hapscomb).

What the critics say:

Staff, *The New York Post*: "A hair-raising, gut wrenching, heart-stopping journey into hell that combines every terrifying tale about evil hitchhikers in one dark and diabolically unnerving adventure … It will leave you so frightened you won't want to stop for the next red light."

Jeffery M. Anderson, *San Francisco Examiner*: "A gruesome cult classic."

Staff, *TV Guide*: "Feature debuts don't come much better than director Robert Harmon and screenwriter Eric Red's sleek, dream-like thriller about a naïve college boy who crosses paths with devil in the flesh after taking a wrong turn on some lost highway."

If you liked this, you might also like:

Duel (1971).

#75 *Zombi 2* (1979)

We are going to eat you!

Why it made the list:

Legendary Italian director Lucio Fulci's *Zombi 2* (released as *Zombie* in the United States) remains as powerful as it was when it was released in 1979. Novelist Stephen King once said that if he couldn't scare you, then he would try to gross you out. Well, that's *Zombi 2* in a nutshell. It's not the scariest film ever made—even though it may well be the best zombie movie of all time—but it does not lack in gross-out moments. Sure, several scenes are downright frightening, but a whole slew of them are just sickeningly gross. The film also loses points for a plodding first half; it doesn't really get going until the final 20 minutes, but man, what an amazing 20 minutes those are!

At the time of the film's initial release, censors didn't know what to make of it as it was more gruesome than anything which had preceded it. The film was banned or trimmed in many countries, most notably Great Britain. Today the make-up and special effects still hold up; *Zombi 2's* zombies make the walkers from The *Walking Dead* look as tame as kittens in comparison.

Synopsis:

When a seemingly-empty ship floats into New York, a couple of patrolmen investigate, discovering a flesh-hungry zombie onboard. When the daughter of the ship's captain sets out with a newspaper reporter to find out what happened to her father and his crew, their journey takes them to Matul Island, where they team up with Brian, an ethnologist, and his lover Susan. On the island they soon discover that a devastating disease is transforming the locals into rabid, flesh-eating zombies.

Scariest scene:

Everyone remembers two iconic scenes from *Zombi 2*. The first is the ridiculously over-the-top zombie vs. shark fight, which remains one of the most amazing things ever captured on celluloid. The second memorable scene is the one in which a woman's eyeball is gouged out in slow motion. While those scenes are the film's most iconic, neither of them compares in terms of fear to the feeling of dread and impending doom at the end of the film when we are shown hundreds of zombies shambling along the Brooklyn Bridge.

Memorable dialogue:

> **ANN:** What exactly did my father die of, Dr. Menard? And the boat's crew … what happened to them?
>
> **PETER:** What's this about the dead coming back to life again and having to be killed a second time?

Did you know?

Although the film is titled *Zombi 2*, it isn't actually a sequel to any other film. Producers opted to slap that title on it after George Romero's *Dawn of the Dead* was released to great acclaim in Italy as *Zombi*. There is no relation between the two films.

Cast:

Tisa Farrow (Anne Bowles), Ian McCulloch (Peter West), Richard Johnson (Dr. David Menard), Al Cliver (Brian Hull), Auretta Gay (Susan Barrett), Stefania D'Amario (Nurse), Olga Karlatos (Paola Menard), Nick Alexander (Brian Hull, Voice), Ugo Bologna (Anne's Father), Ramon Bravo (Underwater Zombie).

What the critics say:

Staff, *The Video Graveyard*: "[E]verything I heard about this movie was true and it exceeded my expectations as far as being a gross-out. It also introduced me to the world of Eurohorror and it did not take long for me

WE ARE GOING TO EAT YOU!

ZOMBIE
...THE DEAD ARE AMONG US!
Jerry Gross presents "ZOMBIE" starring Tisa Farrow • Ian McCulloch • Richard Johnson • Al Cliver
Story and Screenplay by Elisa Briganti • Produced by Ugo Tucci and Fabrizio De Angelis for Variety Film
Color by Metro Color • Directed by Lucio Fulci • Distributed by The Jerry Gross Organization
There is no explicit sex in this picture.
However, there are scenes of violence which may be considered shocking.
No one under 17 will be admitted.

to seek out as many zombies, cannibals, and tales of stylized murder as I could find. Reflecting on it years later, I like the movie even more today as I am able to see past all the gore and appreciate that this is director Lucio Fulci arguably at his finest."

George Pacheco, *Examiner*: "At this point, what else needs to be said about Lucio Fulci's *Zombie* that rabid Italian cinephiles haven't already cut, ingested and dissected? Originally released in 1979, and marketed as a sequel to George Romero's massively popular and influential *Dawn of the Dead*, Fulci's *Zombie*, a.k.a. *Zombi 2*, caused a fervent firestorm in England as one of the original 'video nasties' and managed to impress horror fans around the globe with its unique, stylistic vision, gut-munching, eye-gouging, throat-tearing zombie chaos."

Kurt Dahlke, *DVD Talk*: "*Zombie* is a towering achievement in spaghetti splatter—one of the all-time great living dead movies. The plot, which attempts to marry Romero's flesh-eaters to their voodoo roots, isn't much, but it sets in motion set piece after set piece of iconic mayhem, all of which manage to be creepy, audacious, and stomach-churning at the same time."

If you liked this, you might also like:

City of the Living Dead (1980).

#76 REC (2007)

Just one witness. A video camera.

Why it made the list:

Directors Jaume Balagueró and Paco Plaza deliver a ton of scares in a tight 78-minute running time in this Spanish language film The setting, a cramped, claustrophobic apartment building, is used to great effect, and is almost a character in its own right. The first-person, faux-documentary camera work keeps viewers disoriented and filled with dread at what might be hiding just around the next corner.

Synopsis:

Television host Angela (Manuela Velasco) and her cameraman Pablo (Pablo Rosso) are spending the evening with the night shift at a local firehouse for the program *While You Were Asleep*. A call comes in to the station that an old woman is trapped in her apartment. Angela and Pablo accompany firemen Manu (Ferran Terazza) and Alex (David Vert) to the building, where they find a police cruiser already on the scene. Upon entering the building, the foursome and a pair of policemen endure a gruesome encounter in the old woman's apartment that leaves one of the police officers terribly wounded. When they try to remove the officer from the scene, they find the doors barred and a voice from outside informs them the building is locked down and under quarantine. Some kind of infection is spreading inside, turning its victims into raving, flesh-hungry abominations. Angela and Pablo are determined to capture the ordeal on film, and document a night of panic and terror.

Scariest scene:

After the building's power goes out, the only light is from Pablo's camera.

He and Angela take refuge in a penthouse apartment, but the camera light gets broken, plunging them into darkness. Pablo turns on the night vision system and records as the pair is attacked by the source of the infection, a young woman transformed into a terrifying, ravenous creature.

Memorable dialogue:

> **ANGELA:** So besides your father, who do you live with?
>
> **JENNIFER:** With my mommy, my daddy, and my dog Max.
>
> **ANGELA:** Your dog isn't here, either, right? I can't see him.
>
> **JENNIFER:** No, he's not.
>
> **ANGELA:** Do you love your dog?
>
> **JENNIFER:** Yes.
>
> **ANGELA:** Why isn't he here?
>
> **JENNIFER:** He's at the vet.
>
> **ANGELA:** What's wrong with him?

JENNIFER: He got sick.

Did you know?

The closing passages really were shot in complete darkness, using an infra-red camera. The actors had no idea what was taking place as they couldn't see a thing.

Cast:

Manuela Velasco (Angela Vidal), Ferran Terazza (Manu), Jorge-Yamam Serrano (Policia Joven), Pablo Rosso (Pablo), David Vert (Alex), Vicente Gil (Policia Adulto), Martha Carbonell (Sra. Izquierdo), Carlos Vicente (Guillem Marimon), Maria Teresa Ortega (Abuela), Manuel Bronchud (Abuelo).

What the critics say:

Mark Salisbury, *Total Film*: "*[REC]* serves up horror that's frenzied and hardcore. Spanish directors Jaume Balagueró and Paco Plaza show everything through the filter of Pablo's camera, plunging the audience directly into the chaos. Then the power goes out in the building, blacking the frame and leaving the camera spotlight as the only illumination. Then that fades, night-vision mode clicks in and things get really creepy."

Nigel Floyd, *Time Out*: "Suffice it to say that nothing in the previous work of joint directors Jaume Balagueró and Paco Plaza prepared us for the nerve-shredding intensity of the ensuing scenes. A brilliantly staged early scare signals that the safety rails are off and, despite an unexpected, last-minute swerve into the supernatural realm, the edge-of-the-seat tension is sustained to the very last second."

Vincent Canby, *New York Times*: "*[REC]* is a shock-a-minute mini-masterpiece of sound design, tricky jolts, and wonderfully distressing tension. Once we get knee-deep in the non-stop creeps 'n' carnage, there's little denying that *[REC]* is a whole lot of ferociously scary fun."

If you liked this, you might also like:

Hollow (2011).

#77 *The Howling* (1981)

Imagine your worst fear a reality.

Why it made the list:

Not only did *The Howling* pay fond tribute to the 1940's-era werewolf, but it effectively reimagined the hairy man-wolf creature with anxiety issues into a 1980s vicious, bloodthirsty predator, replete with gory, real-time transformations and a script that crackled with wit, humor, and chills aplenty!

Synopsis:

News anchor Karen White has been contacted by serial killer Eddy Quist who wishes to give her an exclusive interview - provided she follow his implicit instructions. Eddie leads Karen, who is alone and defenseless (but trailed a few minutes behind by policemen), to a seedy adults only establishment where the two meet face to face. What Eddie has summoned Karen to witness is so overpoweringly horrific that the anchorwomen passes out just as the cops bust in and shoot Eddie to death. Once revived, Karen can't recall what she witnessed moments before Eddie died. Nevertheless, Karen is deeply traumatized by the events and is prompted by noted psychologist George Waggner to bring her husband and come to the Colony, a sort of strange new age group therapy place he has concocted a short distance from the city. While Karen and Bill try to adjust to the eccentric group at the Colony, Karen's best friends and co-workers Terry and Chris continue to investigate Eddie Quist—whose body suddenly vanishes from the city morgue. Eventually, all signs point to the strange Colony where Karen White will discover much more than she ever bargained for!

Scariest scene:

Terry has followed Eddie Quist's trail to the Colony. She decides to break into Dr. Waggner's office and take a look at his files. Dr. Waggner had treated Eddie once and she figures a look at the good Doctor's confidential notes may be able to shed light on Eddie's actions before he was killed. After some poking around Terry finds exactly what she's looking for. Terry makes an anxious call to her boyfriend but she doesn't get to say much. Unfortunately, somebody else has been keeping a close eye on Terry's activities ... somebody who doesn't want her talking. With her boyfriend on the line too many miles away to help, Terry comes face to face with the terrifying secret of the Colony and pays the price for it.

Memorable dialogue:

> [looking in what was Eddie Quist's morgue locker]
>
> **CHRIS:** He's not here!
>
> **MORGUE ATTENDANT:** He was here this morning!
>
> **TERRY FISHER:** Look at the door!
>
> **CHRIS:** You think somebody took him?
>
> **MORGUE ATTENDANT:** Well, he didn't just get up and walk away!

Did you know?

In the scene where Terry calls Chris from Dr. Waggner's office, we see a picture of Lon Chaney, Jr. on the wall. Chaney played the Wolf Man in five movies (*The Wolf Man*, 1941, *Frankenstein Meets the Wolf Man*, *House of Frankenstein*, 1944, *House of Dracula*, 1945, and *Bud Abbott And Lou Costello Meet Frankenstein*, 1948). He is the only actor that played a Universal monster in the original film and all of its sequels.

Cast:

Dee Wallace (Karen White), Patrick Macnee (Dr. George Waggner), Dennis Dugan (Chris), Christopher Stone (Bill), Belinda Balaski (Terry), Kevin McCarthy (Fred Francis), John Carradine (Erle Kenton), Slim Pickens (Sam Newfield), Elisabeth Brooks (Marsha Quist).

What the critics say:

Staff, *Variety:* "There are good one-liners throughout, some delivered straight-faced by Kevin McCarthy as an empty-headed TV news producer and Dick Miller as the colorful expert on werewolves. And in a picture like this, John Carradine and Slim Pickens only have to open their mouths to get a laugh from long-time appreciative fans.
But this is supposed to be a horror film, after all [from the novel by Gary Brandner]. And it definitely is in a good old-fashioned way, complete with a girl venturing out alone with a flashlight to investigate a weird noise. In large part the picture works because of the make-up effects created by Rob Bottin."

Staff, *TV Guide:* "A wonderful combination of horror, laughs, and state-of-the-art special effects from director and Roger Corman alumnus Joe Dante, screenwriter John Sayles, and makeup artist Rob Bottin."

Jeremy Zoss, *Film Threat:* "*The Howling* is still one of the better werewolf films out there. While the werewolves look a bit 'muppetesque' today, at the time they were top notch. The design of the creatures is unique, mixing elements of wolf and man more equally than most other werewolf films. But what works the best about *The Howling* is the mood. With a somber, hopeless feel straight out of *Taxi Driver* and a great ending, the film's atmosphere far overshadows the thin plot and dated effects. Everyone involved with the making of the film treats it very seriously, from director Joe Dante and writer John Sayles to the cast and effects artists. This serious, straight-faced attitude is what made the movie work; a lot of hard work was put into creating a moody, frightening film. Although the film may have lost some of its bite over the years, it will always remain one of the most respected werewolf films ever."

If you liked this, you might also like:

The Company of Wolves (1984)

#78 *Dead Calm* (1989)

In the middle of nowhere there is nowhere to hide.

Why it made the list:

Being trapped in a boat on the open sea with a homicidal maniac aboard is enough to cause even the most hardened of humankind a bit of uneasiness. Terry Hayes' screenplay for *Dead Calm* is a marvel of simplicity in that it revolves around only three key players and *that* simplicity keeps the tensions high. Phillip Noyce's direction is grand while maintaining the necessary feelings of hopelessness and claustrophobia. The ocean is vast and overwhelming, but the real horror is contained within the small confines of a boat. This limits the protagonists' abilities for escape and survival.

Synopsis:

John and Rae Ingram (Sam Neill and Nicole Kidman) are aboard their yacht Saracen in the middle of the Pacific Ocean. Surprisingly, castaway Hughie Warriner (Billy Zane) comes adrift in a dinghy. The Ingrams have suffered the loss of their toddler to an automobile accident. They feel that some alone time at sea will help ease their pain and heal their emotional wounds. Gate-crasher Warriner couldn't care less about their gloomy situation and in due time turns their misery into pure terror.

Warriner recounts a tale of food poisoning that claimed the lives of his shipmate and four passengers aboard his original ship, the now sinking Orpheus. John Ingram becomes suspicious of Warriner's telling. While Warriner sleeps, Ingram sets out in the dinghy to investigate the doomed vessel. This arrangement leaves Warriner and Rae alone. Warriner awakens to find himself locked inside his cabin and realizes that John has gone to the Orpheus to check out his story. Enraged at this turn of events, Warriner goes on a violent rampage tearing down doors and walls to get to Rae. Rae is brutalized and terrorized. John discovers evidence that Warriner murdered his shipmate and passengers.

While delving further into the mystery of the sinking Orpheus, John accidentally traps himself in the hull of the boat as it slowly fills with water. The time John spends trying to save his life is more time for Warriner and Rae to continue getting to know one another. They play a cruel game of cat and mouse.

Scariest scene:

After the film's one false ending, Hughie Warriner seemingly returns from the dead. Rae, with her eyes closed, is washing her hair. Warriner approaches from behind and places his bloodied hands on her head. Rae, thinking it's her husband, carries on a whimsical conversation with her vengeful attacker. It's a heart-pounding sequence that is punched home when Rae finally realizes what the viewer already knows.

Memorable dialogue:

> **WARRINER:** You think I'm making this up!
>
> **RAE:** No, I don't.
>
> **WARRINER:** You sound so much like them, Rae, it's scary!

Did you know?

Dead Calm was based on the 1963 novel of the same name by Charles Williams. Director extraordinaire, Orson Welles, began a film version of *Dead Calm* in the late 1960's called *The Deep*. However, due to the death of star Laurence Harvey the project was never completed.

Cast:

Nicole Kidman (Rae Ingram), Sam Neill (John Ingram), Billy Zane (Hughie Warriner), Rod Mullinar (Russell Bellows), Joshua Tilden (Danny), George Shevtsov (Doctor), Michael Long (Specialist Doctor), Lisa Collins ('Orpheus' Cruise Girl), Paula Hudson-Brinkley ('Orpheus' Cruise Girl).

What the critics say:

Sheila Benson, *Los Angeles Times*: "Take an ocean voyage of full-masted fright with *Dead Calm*, a spare, smart, seductive piece of moviemaking with enough tension to keep us all hyperventilating for hours."

Roger Ebert, *Chicago Sun-Times*: "*Dead Calm* generates genuine tension, because the story is so simple and the performances are so straightforward. This is not a gimmick film (unless you count the husband's method of escaping from the sinking ship), and Kidman and Zane do generate real, palpable hatred in their scenes together."

Caryn James, *New York Times*: "Phillip Noyce's *Dead Calm* is an unsettling hybrid of escapist suspense and the kind of pure trash that depends on dead babies and murdered dogs for effect. In it, John and Rae Ingram are a husband and wife alone on their yacht in still waters. They are joined by a classic intruder, the mysterious stranger, who in this case doesn't arrive nearly soon enough."

If you liked this, you might also like:

Inhumanoid (1996).

#79 Scanners (1981)

Their thoughts can kill!

Why it made the list:

David Cronenberg delivers a paranoiac thriller with heaps of visual style and big moments of gory special effects. *Scanners* explores themes of isolation, unimaginable powers, and, ultimately, the meaning of being human.

Synopsis:

Cameron Vale (Stephen Lack) is a homeless man with telepathic powers. He spends his days in a shopping mall, scrounging for food and shelter, until a security and weapons company called ConSec finds him and brings him to meet Dr. Paul Ruth (Patrick McGoohan). Dr. Ruth explains that Vale is a scanner, one of about 200 people on the planet with powerful psychic abilities. At first, Vale cannot control his powers, but with Dr. Ruth's help, he learns how to use them successfully in a variety of ways. ConSec and Dr. Ruth want Vale to track down a group of scanners led by a man named Darryl Revok (Michael Ironsides). Revok wants to destroy ConSec because it stands in the way of his plans to use scanners to achieve power on a massive scale. With the help of a sympathetic fellow scanner named Kim Obrist (Jennifer O'Neill), Vale searches both for Revok and for answers to the mysteries surrounding the existence of the scanners. The pair discover that Revok is not merely recruiting existing scanners, but is using a drug called Ephemerol to create new ones. Together, they must find and stop Revok before it is too late.

Scariest scene:

Although *Scanners* is well known for an early scene in which a man's head literally explodes into a mass of blood and gore, the final showdown between Vale and Revok delivers true suspense and bloody, disturbing special effects galore.

Memorable dialogue:

> **VALE:** What did you need Keller for?
>
> **REVOK:** ConSec had hardware. It had contacts. Keller could see the future.
>
> **VALE:** The future? You murdered the future.
>
> **REVOK:** That's negative, Cam. Defeatist. Disappoints me to hear you talk that way. You're starting to sound like them. There's a whole generation of scanners soldiers just a few months away from being born. We'll find them. Train them to be like us. Not like Obrist and their band of cripples. We'll bring the world of normals to their knees. We'll build an empire so brilliant, so glorious. We'll be the envy of the whole planet.

Did you know?

The exploding head sequence was accomplished by filling a latex head with dog food and rabbit livers, and shooting it from behind with a 12-gauge shotgun.

Cast:

Jennifer O'Neill (Kim Obrist), Stephen Lack (Cameron Vale), Patrick McGoohan (Dr. Paul Ruth), Lawrence Dane (Braedon Keller), Michael Ironside (Darryl Revok), Robert Silverman (Benjamin Pierce), Lee Broker (Security One), Mavor Moore (Trevellyan), Adam Ludwig (Arno Crostic), Lee Murray (Programmer 1).

What the critics say:

Dave Kehr, *Chicago Reader*: "One of the most technically proficient of David Cronenberg's early gnawing, Canadian-made horror. The premise—warring factions of telekinetic killers are sent out by two mysterious corporations—is vague but suggestive, and it's developed with a creepy psychological resonance."

Derek Adams, *Time Out*: "Part conspiracy thriller, part political tract, it is Cronenberg's most coherent movie to date, drawing a dark world in which corporate executives engineer human conception to produce ever more powerful mental samurai. And he punctuates it with spectacular set piece confrontations which really do dramatise the abstract, ingenious premise."

Vincent Canby, *New York Times*: "The performances are quite satisfactory, including that of the beautiful Jennifer O'Neill, who, though she is the film's nominal star, plays what is really a secondary role. Major credit for the film's visual spectacle is shared by Dick Smith, who earlier did the make-up for *The Exorcist* and *Little Big Man*, and Gary Zeller, who most recently worked on the special effects for *Altered States*."

If you liked this, you might also like:

Brainscan (1994).

#80 *Hellraiser* (1987)

Hellraiser, beyond any terror you have imagined. A nightmare, unlike anything you have witnessed.

Why it made the list:

In 1987, *Hellraiser* was seriously pushing the boundaries of what was acceptable on the big screen. It's shocking that the MPAA allowed director Clive Barker to get away with so much in the blood and gore department. Sadly, too many horror film directors chicken out and cut away, or make sudden edits when the carnage occurs. Barker's camera stays in there, and when things start to get nasty and dig in, the viewer sees what he sees. Barker's directorial debut may be far too visceral to appeal to every fan of horror films, but its inclusion within a list of this type is quite certain.

Synopsis:

Frank (Sean Chapman) is bored, really bored. So bored, in fact, that he dumps a load of cash on what appears to be a gold-encrusted Rubik's Cube prototype. Frank retreats to a sweltering, disgusting room and sits shirtless working the puzzle and sweating. Beads of perspiration pour from Frank as he concentrates, caressing and fondling the golden cube.

Finally success is attained, and the puzzle box begins to shift and spin. The room darkens. The walls appear to widen, and soon chains with meat hooks begin flying in from all four corners of the room. The hooks slash and lash into Frank's flesh, ripping and tearing him completely asunder. Frank has been transported, in bloodied pieces, to an alternate reality where pleasure and pain are indivisible.

Frank's brother Larry (Andrew Robinson) is moving into the old family house; the very house where Frank cured his boredom. Larry ap-

pears to be under some duress. His second wife Julia (Clare Higgins) is clearly a high-maintenance kind of gal. She seems to be upset by just about everything possible. There's more trouble in paradise as Larry's teenage daughter, Kirsty (Ashley Laurence), apparently abhors her stepmother.

"I HAVE SEEN
THE FUTURE OF
HORROR FICTION,
AND HIS NAME IS
CLIVE BARKER..."
STEPHEN KING
HELLRAISER
THERE ARE NO LIMITS
NEW WORLD PICTURES IN ASSOCIATION WITH
CINEMARQUE ENTERTAINMENT B.V. PRESENTS
AN IMPRESSIONISTS PRODUCTION "HELLRAISER"
STARRING ANDREW ROBINSON • CLAIRE HIGGINS • ASHLEY LAURENCE
SCREENPLAY BY CLIVE BARKER BASED ON HIS NOVEL "THE HELLBOUND HEART"
EXECUTIVE PRODUCERS CHRISTOPHER WEBSTER AND MARK ARMSTRONG
PRODUCER CHRISTOPHER FIGG DIRECTED BY CLIVE BARKER
NEW WORLD PICTURES
BILLING NOT CONTRACTUAL

While moving a mattress up a staircase, Larry slices his hand open on a protruding nail. He goes searching for Julia so she can help bandage the gaping wound. He finds her in the attic where Frank had earlier rid himself of all apathy and tedium. Larry's wounded hand is gushing blood onto the old floor boards. The wood planking seems to absorb, or rather drink up Larry's blood.

Later that evening, peculiar sounds are heard coming from the attic. It is deduced that rats are the culprits, but rats are not the problem. Somehow, Frank has been reborn. His essence was left in limbo beneath the attic floor and Larry's blood partially revived him. Frank now resembles a skinned corpse—a skinned corpse that can drag itself across a floor and talk.

Julia finds Frank first and they reminisce of old times when Frank and she were having an affair. Frank insists that Julia bring him more victims for more blood. She obliges and a veritable blood bath begins. Julia bludgeons her male guests into submission and Frank extracts the sanguine fluid through his finger tips. With each feeding frenzy, Frank becomes more and more whole until eventually he is again completely human.

The owners of the chains and meat hooks are not at all happy Frank has escaped their world. These four demonic and disfigured invaders, led by Pinhead (Doug Bradley), are called Cenobites. Frank summoned the Cenobites with the box he had manipulated. In their domain, they are the rulers of the pleasures of the flesh and are on the hunt for Frank.

Pinhead and his leather-clad S&M wrecking crew will stop at nothing to capture Frank. Everyone and everything in their wake is good for the taking. Hooks and chains fly about and bodies are torn and strewn apart until Frank is safely returned home to the Cenobites, piece by piece.

Scariest scene:

Frank's reanimation in the attic hits pay dirt. It's a baffling scene where skinless human limbs crash through hardwood floors; bones form and slimy intestines, with other bits of vitals and innards, crawl toward their bodily homes. Honorable mention goes to Frank's second dismemberment.

Memorable dialogue:

PINHEAD: We'll tear your soul apart.

Did you know?

Electronic/Industrial band Coil originally scored *Hellraiser*. The studio promptly had the film re-scored to avoid paying out royalties. Clive Barker has been stated as saying Coil was, "the only group I've heard on disc whose records I've taken off because they made my bowels churn." The pieces the group recorded can be heard on their albums *Unnatural History II: Smiling in the Face of Perversity* and *The Unreleased Themes for Hellraiser.*

Cast:

Andrew Robinson (Larry), Clare Higgins (Julia), Ashley Laurence (Kirsty Cotton), Sean Chapman (Frank), Oliver Smith (Frank the Monster), Doug Bradley (Pinhead), Nicholas Vince (Chatterer), Simon Bamford (Butterball), Grace Kirby (Female Cenobite).

What the critics say:

Michael Weldon, *The Psychotronic Video Guide*: "It's a classic, the first bloody S&M fantasy/horror hit."

Carol Schwartz, *Videohound's Cult Flicks and Trash Pics*: "The story plays out like a somewhat maniacal soap opera (family tensions, cheating) laced with Barker's disturbingly unforgettable images."

Leonard Maltin, *Leonard Maltin's Movie Guide*: "Grisly but stylish directorial debut by famed horror novelist Clive Barker; ugly fun all the way."

If you liked this, you might also like:

The Midnight Meat Train (2008).

#81 *Vacancy* (2007)

How can you escape ... if they can see everything?

Why it made the list:

Vacancy is a throwback to the gritty, grimy horror movies of yesteryear. Its script, direction, camerawork, score, and acting are terrific, but none of those are the reason why this film made the list. Why, you ask? Because *Vacancy* is good old fashioned scare-a-minute fun. It's got its fair share of jump scares, creepy ambiance, and some VHS home movies (played by the characters in the film) that are as unforgettably creepy as anything this side of *Ringu* (1998).

Synopsis:

Young married couple David (Luke Wilson) and Amy (Kate Beckinsale) Fox find themselves stranded in the middle of nowhere in the middle of the night when their car breaks down on the side of the road. Classic movie trope that works every time. But in this instance, there's not an old creepy castle nearby, but an old creepy motel straight out of the Vietnam era. Frank Whaley's hotel caretaker is hands down the creepiest hotel caretaker fright cinema has seen since Norman Bates conversed with his mama and slashed the hell out of Janet Leigh.

The couple begins to quarrel, but find themselves distracted by some VHS tapes left in their room. When they put the tapes into the dusty old VCR, they discover that they're snuff films depicting couples fighting off masked attackers—and they were all filmed within this very room!

Scariest scene:

David and Amy's initial discovery of the snuff films (and their gradual realization of what exactly they depict) is by far the scariest moment in the film. The tapes themselves are creepy, grainy and amateurish, giving them a feel of frightening authenticity, and the moment of realization is as scary as anything horror has seen in a good long time.

Memorable dialogue:

> **MASON:** Everything alright, Mr. Fox?
>
> **DAVID:** Uh, no, because the asshole in the room right beside us keeps banging on the walls and won't stop. You got any ideas?
>
> **MASON:** The room beside you?
>
> **DAVID:** Yeah, room three. Uh, I go over there to talk with the guy to try to get him to stop, but he just kind of keeps doing it. So, uh, I gotta say I don't know what his problem is.
>
> **MASON:** It's very strange, seeing as you folks are the only guests I've got in here tonight.

Did you know?

The snuff films were the first scenes of the film shot.

Cast:

Luke Wilson (David Fox), Kate Beckinsale (Amy Fox), Frank Whaley (Mason), Ethan Embry (Mechanic), Scott Anderson (Killer), Mark Casella (Truck Driver), David Doty (Highway Patrolman), Norm Compton (Snuff Victim), Caryn Mower (Snuff Victim), Meegan Godfrey (Snuff Victim).

What the critics say:

Steve Newton, *Georgia Straight*: "Once the fight-for-their-lives plot kicks in, unfortunately named director Nimrod Antal keeps the action intense and well-paced."

Tim Grierson, *Village Voice*: "Perfectly suited to the shabby delights of the hometown drive-in theaters of yesteryear, director Nimrod Antal's creepy cockroach of a thriller feels less horrifying than it does curiously nostalgic ... At a time when so many genre films go splat because of large budgets or big egos, the small-scale pleasures of *Vacancy* are a welcome surprise."

Stax, *IGN Movies*: "*Vacancy* may not be the most wholly original thriller but it has some heart to it and is directed with gritty, old school style by Nimrod Antal. Coupled with the good work done by the leads, *Vacancy* is worth checking into."

If you liked this, you might also like:

Identity (2002).

#82 Sinister (2012)

Once you have seen him, nothing can save you.

Why it made the list:

Scott Derrickson's film *Sinister* is one of the best kept secrets in the genre. Underrated to be sure, this powerful picture packs one hell of a wallop and contains more than just one or two frightening scenes. Today's horror audiences are cynics by nature, and they instantly distrust anything new. Perhaps that explains how *Sinister* has been completely overlooked. Some horror fans might wonder how exactly this film made the list, and to those people I would recommend a second (or, more likely, a first) look at this incredibly well-made little shocker.

Synopsis:

True crime novelist Ellison Oswalt (Ethan Hawke) tries to reignite his fledgling career by investigating a house where a grisly set of murders took place. The first thing Ellison does? Why, he moves his family into their house, of course! He ultimately finds a cache of super 8 snuff films and finds that there were a series of murders which took place across the country—all apparently committed by the same person. But upon closer inspection, Oswalt soon discovers that the perpetrator may not be a person at all, but something much darker and more evil.

Scariest scene:

Similar to the videos in *Ringu* (1998), the snuff films here are scary as all hell. They are expertly crafted to maximize terror. Even scarier is the scene at the end of the film in which Ellison's little girl stands over him with an axe, promising to make Daddy famous again by living out the murders of her family as she depicted them in a drawing. If this doesn't make your blood curdle, nothing ever will.

Memorable dialogue:

> **ELLISON OSWALT:** So, you don't believe in any of that otherworldly stuff, right?
>
> **DEPUTY:** Are you kidding? I believe in all that stuff. I wouldn't sleep one night in this place. Are you nuts? Four people were hung by their necks in the tree in your backyard and that little girl is probably God knows wherever!

Did you know?

Screenwriter C. Robert Cargill says he came up with the name Ellison Oswalt by combining the names of novelist Harlan Ellison and comedian Patton Oswalt.

Cast:

Ethan Hawke (Ellison Oswalt), Juliet Rylance (Tracy), Fred Thompson (Sheriff), James Ransone (Deputy), Michael Hall D'Addario (Trevir), Clare Foley (Ashley), Rob Riley (E.M.T.), Tavis Smiley (Anchor), Janet Zappala (Reporter), Victoria Leigh (Stephanie).

What the critics say:

Dr. Karen Oughton, *Ain't It Cool News*: "So is it scary? The more appropriate question is whether it is effective. This reviewer had to be scraped off the Empire Cinema's ceiling, being particularly prone to jump scares and having bruised Britgeek's arm from grabbing it in fright … The fear (rather than shock) comes from some superb direction and pacing from Scott Derrickson. Scenes capture the action in a balletic form perfectly akin to another world seen in slivery snatches so strangely beautiful and oddly believable that it is impossible to tear your eyes away."

Ty Bru, *Daily Examiner*: "The sounds and the eerie score was the highlight of *Sinister* for me, which up until this point in filmmaking was a style that had been used very little … The demon, Bagul, was incredibly terrifying, as well as the vintage footage that was played through the 110 minute film. No matter how many times the opening scene was shown, the effectiveness never wore off."

Mick LaSalle, *San Francisco Examiner*: "Director Scott Derrickson is in touch with that unsettling part of the night, when the terrors come and the logic of waking life seems like a lie we tell ourselves to keep from screaming. He has a special feel for that most-alone time, that three in the morning zone, when demons, metaphoric or real, come out to dance up and down your head and there's nothing you can do but white knuckle it until daylight."

If you liked this, you might also like:

Sinister 2 (2015).

#83 *Hostel* (2005)

10,000 people are killed in America each year. Over 2,000 with firearms. Americans ... they have no imagination ...

Why it made the list:

Since its initial release, Eli Roth's sophomore effort, *Hostel*, has caught a lot of flak. It's frequently referred to as torture porn, and the more serious film critics (read: Snobs who take themselves way too seriously to give a good review to a horror film) have decried it as a sloppy half-hearted effort. Bullshit, we say. Go back and take a second look at the film and you'll remember how truly frightening it was back in 2005 (and remains today). Despite its having all the gory trappings of something lesser, like *Saw*, Roth's *Hostel* is actually an intelligent movie crafted by a knowing and talented filmmaker. Roth continually ups the ante, masterfully ratcheting up the terror and suspense.

Respected French film critic Jean-François Rauger of *Le Monde* called it the single finest American film of 2005 (and one of the 10 best worldwide), and Bravo named it number one on their (second) list of the 100 most frightening movie moments. Revisit *Hostel* with an open mind and you'll quickly be reminded what all the fuss was about.

Synopsis:

Three backpackers, two American and one Icelandic, make their way across scenic Europe when they are told of a hostel in Slovakia that is "to die for." At this hostel, the European women are said to want nothing more than to have lots of wild sex with male tourists—especially Americans. The three friends naturally go to the hostel, and they discover that all of the tales are true. They soon have numerous sexual adventures and

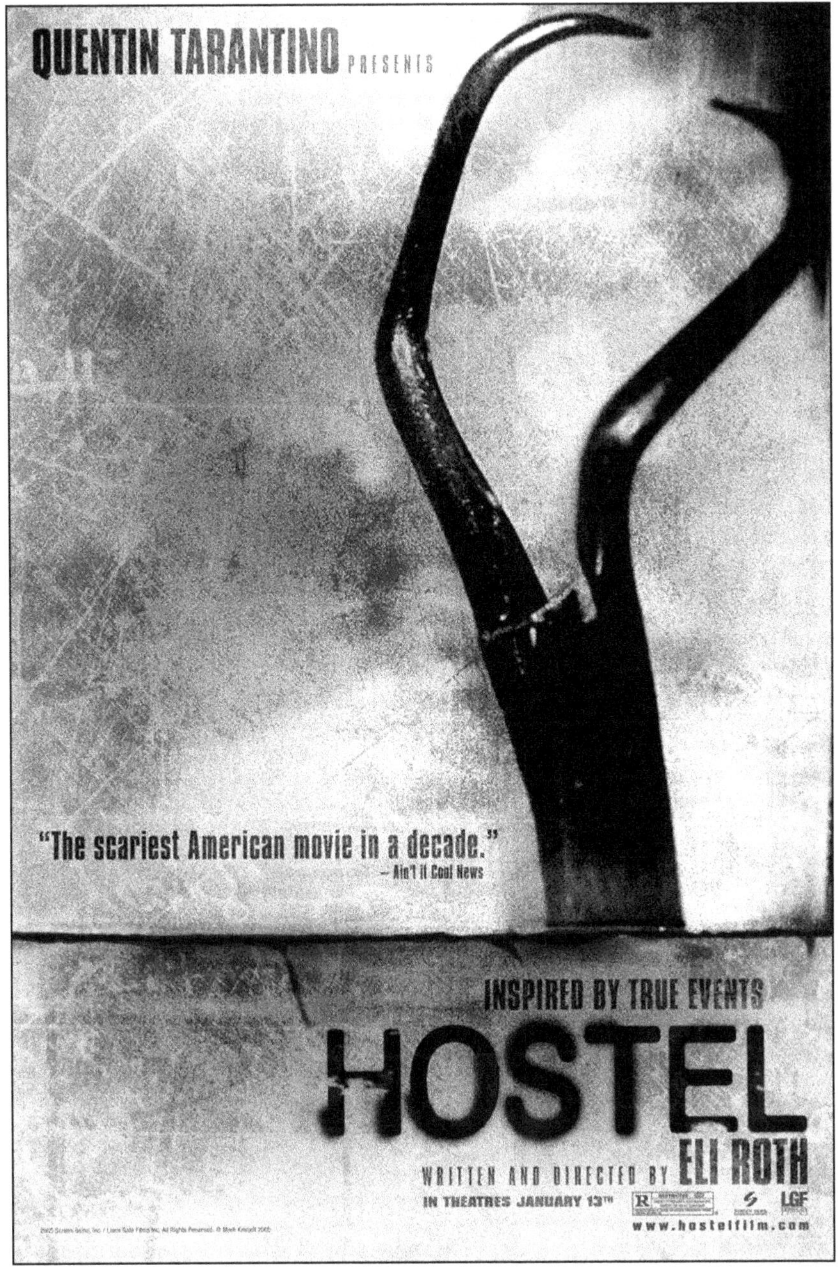

have the times of their lives. However, this fantasy vacation takes a dark turn when they discover that the hostel hides a dirty little secret; the travelers who stay there all seem to disappear …

Scariest scene:

Eli Roth's sick little film is just brimming with stomach-churning scenes and downright disturbing episodes. However, the film's single most frightening scene is the one in which Paxton (Jay Hernandez) wakes up to find himself strapped to a chair in what appears to be a dingy cellar. He is then confronted with a sadistic German who first swipes at him with a pair of scissors, but then turns on the real horror when he turns on a chainsaw with which he intends to dismember the young American. Things look grim from the get-go, but soon become even more bleak when the man cuts off three of Paxton's fingers.

Memorable dialogue:

> **JOSH:** Please! I have money! I'll fucking pay you! Ten times, two times—whatever you want!
>
> **DUTCH BUSINESSMAN:** Pay *me*?
>
> **JOSH:** Yeah!
>
> **DUTCH BUSINESSMAN:** No one is paying me. In fact, I'm the one paying *them*!

Did you know?

A guard outside the torture chamber is watching a porno movie. The camera lingers on the small TV playing the sex film for a moment. Why? Because the movie the guard is watching is *Sex Fever*, a real-life X-rated parody of director Eli Roth's film *Cabin Fever*.

Cast:

Jay Hernandez (Paxton), Derek Richardson (Josh), Eythor Gudjonsson (Oli), Barbara Nedeljakova (Natalya), Jan Vlasak (Dutch Businessman), Jana Kaderbkova (Svetlana), Jennifer Lim (Kana), Keiko Seiko (Yuki), Lubomir Bukovy (Alex), Jana Havlickova (Vala).

What the critics say:

Adam Hakari, *Reel Talk*: "As unusually intelligent as *Hostel* is, it also maintains its more primal side, highlighting an array of increasingly disturbing fates for the film's characters (the most nasty of which is reserved for the film's final minutes) that'll have the most hardened of moviegoers squirming and wanting to put their hands over their eyes."

Bill Gibron, *DVD Verdict*: "While it may seem hard to believe now, *Hostel* will be the *Halloween* of the 2020s. Removed from its immediate surroundings, studied and written about, it will take on an air of importance that will guarantee its place in the legion of classics. It will sit alongside Romero's Dead trilogy (or whatever number he finally stops at), Craven's most memorable fright films, and *Saw* as the reason that true visceral horror returned to the mainstream marketplace."

Kurt Loder, *MTV*: "Does it need to be said that this is not a movie for everybody? Those unentertained by the sight of a gouged eyeball dangling from the end of a wet tendon on a screaming victim's cheek can happily pass it up. But *Hostel* is more artfully horrific than the usual gore flick, and more truly scary. It's a small classic of its awful kind."

If you liked this, you might also like:

Cabin Fever (2002).

#84 *Paranormal Activity* (2009)

What happens when you sleep?

Why it made the list:

Certainly one of the better "found footage" movies, *Paranormal Activity* sets the bar rather high for such fare. Similar to films like *The Haunting*, *Paranormal Activity* works best because it shows relatively little. Much of the horror is implied, and the tension continues to mount as the film's running time ticks away. Although the film does have its share of jump-scares, it does a satisfying job of ratcheting up the tension and making us actually care about the film's protagonists.

Synopsis:

Micah (Micah Sloat) and Katie (Katie Featherston) have just purchased a new house. When strange things start to happen, Micah decides to purchase a camcorder to document these happenings. His hope is to uncover what is causing all of this. However, once the couple starts to document their surroundings, it becomes more and more apparent that they are not alone in the house—something evil resides there with them.

Scariest scene:

At the end of the film, after the couple has stayed an extra night for reasons we cannot possibly fathom, Katie gets out of bed and stands over Micah in a sleep trance. Then she leaves the room, and we hear screaming. Micah jumps out of bed and runs to her aid. Meanwhile, the camera remains static in the couple's bedroom. Moments later, Micah's dead body is thrown across the room into the camera. Then Katie arrives and we learn that Katie has been possessed by the demonic force within the house.

Memorable dialogue:

> **MICAH:** Basically they're these malevolent evil spirits that only exist to cause pain and commit evil for their own amusement. It's pretty creepy. I mean, they stalk people for years, like decades, and sometimes they're really intelligent in the way they do things to freak you out.

Did you know?

Noted director Steven Spielberg had to stop watching the movie midway through because he was creeped out. He finished it during daylight hours the following day, and he loved it.

Cast:

Katie Featherston (Katie), Micah Sloat (Micah), Mark Fredrichs (Psychic), Amber Armstrong (Amber), Ashley Palmer (Diane), Crystal Cartright (Exorcism Nanny), Spencer Marks (Doctor), Randy McDowell (Lt. Randy Hudson), James Piper (Richard).

What the critics say:

Roger Ebert, *Chicago Sun-Times*: "It illustrates one of my favorite points, that silence and waiting can be more entertaining than frantic fast-cutting and berserk effects. For extended periods here, nothing at all is happening, and believe me, you won't be bored."

J.R. Jones, *Chicago Reader*: "The climax is deliciously scary, and Peli gets considerable mileage from the simple matter of lights inexplicably going on in another room."

Peter Keough, *Boston Phoenix*: "Oren Peli in his feature debut has a few jolts in store, and the natural performances of the cast and the aura of reality provided by the video format keep the tension high."

If you liked this, you might also like:

Paranormal Activity 2 (2010).

#85 *Seven* (1995)

Seven deadly sins. Seven ways to die.

Why it made the list:

A grim, gripping thriller about the hunt for a relentless, implacable serial killer, *Seven* injects terror and suspense directly into viewers' veins. From the wildly stylized opening credits, *Seven* keeps tightening the noose, as the grisly tableaux left behind by the killer drive an increasingly desperate pair of detectives to find him before even more awful damage is done.

Synopsis:

A homicide detective just one week from retirement, William Somerset (Morgan Freeman), is assigned to help train his replacement, David Mills (Brad Pitt), a cocky, aggressive young man new to the department. Somerset and Mills respond to their first crime scene, where a morbidly obese man is found dead in his apartment, face down in a plate of spaghetti. The detectives discover that the man's hands and feet were bound before his death. Somerset and Mills clash, and Somerset is given control of the investigation. He soon discovered the word "Gluttony" scrawled on the wall behind the refrigerator in the dead man's apartment. The next day, Mills catches a case in which a lawyer has been murdered in his office, and the word "Greed" is spelled out on the floor in the dead man's blood. The pair realize they are tracking a serial killer who is "preaching" to the world about the seven deadly sins. Somerset reluctantly agrees to stay on until the killer is apprehended after two more victims are discovered. The detectives manage to track the suspect down to his apartment, but he eludes capture and kills again. With just two sins left, Somerset and Mills race against the clock to solve the case.

Let he who is without sin try to survive.
GLUTTONY
GLUTTONY • GREED • SLOTH • ENVY • WRATH • PRIDE • LUST

Scariest scene:

Seven is tense and suspenseful throughout, leading to a truly horrifying climax, but for pure scare value, it's tough to beat an emaciated, bone-white victim covered in blood suddenly coming to life, gasping frantically and throwing a room full of seasoned cops into fits of terror.

Memorable dialogue:

> **DETECTIVE SOMERSET:** This guy's methodical, exacting, and worst of all, patient.
>
> **DETECTIVE MILLS:** He's a nut-bag! Just because the fucker's got a library card doesn't make him Yoda!

Did you know?

All of John Doe's books were real books, written for the film. They took two months to complete and cost $15,000.

Cast:

Brad Pitt (David Mills), Morgan Freeman (Detective Somerset), Gwyneth Paltrow (Tracy Mills), Kevin Spacey (John Doe), R. Lee Ermey (Police Captain), Andy Walker (Dead man), Daniel Zacapa (Detective Taylor), John Cassini (Officer Davis), Bob Mack (Gluttony victim), Peter Crombie (Dr. O'Neill).

What the critics say:

Jonathan Rosenbaum, *Chicago Reader*: "The filmmakers stick to their vision with such dedication and persistence that something indelible comes across—something ethically and artistically superior to *The Silence of the Lambs* that refuses to exploit suffering for fun or entertainment."

Rita Kempley, *Washington Post*: "*Seven*, a grisly social allegory drawn in blood and spawned in despair, casts a lingering, malodorous spell. A buddy-cop thriller recast as Dante's sojourn in Hell, this graphic, allusion-littered film stands the conventions of the genre on end—along with the viewer's hair."

Owen Gleiberman, *Entertainment Weekly*: "*Seven* is a heebie-jeebies thriller, the kind people will go to for a good, cathartic creep-out. The credits sequence, with its jumpy frames and near-subliminal flashes of psycho paraphernalia, is a small masterpiece of dementia—the film itself seems to be breaking down in terror. Balancing out the sleek horror are Freeman and Pitt, who, within a stock old cop-young cop routine, spark each other. Freeman plays nearly every scene in a doleful hush; he makes you lean in to hear his words, to ferret out the hints of anger and regret that haunt this weary knight. It's Pitt's job to blow his cool, which he does with energized grunge charisma, and to act as comic relief."

If you liked this, you might also like:

Zodiac (2007).

#86 *Pumpkinhead* (1988)

Deep in the Appalachian Mountains they say that an act of evil shall never go unpunished. There they tell of a creature who shall come from nowhere. Born from the blood of the innocent to hunt the guilty, and they call it Pumpkinhead.

Why it made the list:

In 1988, *Pumpkinhead* came lurching in as a breath of fresh air for horror film fans who were growing tired of the slasher cycle. Sure, the body count is as great as any Fred Krueger movie, but director Stan Winston chose to cloak his cinematic creation in a nightmare of backwoods folklore. Winston's directorial debut is threatening and at times unpleasant, but sharp and stylish all the way.

Synopsis:

When small town store keeper Ed Harley (Lance Henriksen) is convened upon by a group of rowdy teenagers, his work day goes from tiring to terrifying. The teens are on holiday from the city and intend on exploring a bit of rural America and its simpler amenities. Problem is, they have little or no respect for the local townsfolk, their property or their environs.

Ed Harley tends to his store and watches in dismay as some of the new arrivals mount dirt bikes and begin riding. The flippant and disrespectful teens tear about his property screaming, squalling, and popping wheelies. Ed's only son Billy (Matthew Hurley) is fascinated by all the action, and is enthralled to the point of accidentally finding himself in harm's way. One of the wilder motorcycle riders loses control of his bike and inadvertently hits and injures the young Billy. Ed Harley is mortified and races to his son's care. Frantic and seemingly without remorse, the teens scurry and abandon the scene. Meanwhile Billy Harley dies in his father's arms.

The following day, while still in shock, Ed Harley buries Billy and vows to avenge his early death. The grieving father's revenge will not be of the normal kind. He won't hunt and kill the despicable teens by conventional methods. In Ed Harley's part of the world, there's a "special" kind of death saved just for these types of heathens. Ed Harley knows of an old crone (Florence Schauffler) living deep in the woods who can call up an unfathomable beast driven by bloodlust and pure evil. Through a series of strange rituals that includes a deal with the devil, the ten-foot-tall abomination is brought forth. This satanic entity is called Pumpkinhead (Tom Woodruff Jr.).

All the townsfolk know of Pumpkinhead, and they also know their neighbor and friend has had the damned thing summoned. Pumpkinhead goes about his task of vindication with a boundless amount of intensity and determination. These city folk don't stand a chance in hell or on earth.

Scariest scene:

Every death that Pumpkinhead executes is visceral and very hands-on, so all of the murder sequences are hard to beat. However, when Ed Harley

comes to the realization the hate in his soul feeds Pumpkinhead, the film truly becomes a shocker of near epic proportions.

Memorable dialogue:

> **ED HARLEY:** God damn you!
>
> **HAGGIS:** He already has, son. He already has.

Did you know?

The origin of the film's story was said to be a poem written by Ed Justin. However, little information can be found on the poet, or any of his other works for that matter. This fosters the notion that the producers made up the lyrical piece as part of a fictitious Pumpkinhead folklore.

Cast:

Lance Henriksen (Ed Harley), Jeff East (Chris), John D'Aquino (Joel), Kimberly Ross (Kim), Joel Hoffman (Steve), Cynthia Bain (Tracy), Kerry Remsen (Maggie), Florence Schauffler (Haggis), Brian Bremer (Bunt), George "Buck" Flower (Mr. Wallace).

What the critics say:

Michael Weldon, *The Psychotronic Video Guide*: "This movie is dark, smoky, and dreary … the creature is pretty great … "

Felix Vasquez Jr., *Film Threat*: "In spite of being almost 20 years old, this monster movie is still harrowing, creepy, and better than modern horror fare."

Staff, *TV Guide*: "An old-fashioned, atmospheric, moralistic tale that presents horror steeped in rural folklore and legend."

If you liked this, you might also like:

Jeepers Creepers (2001).

#87 Day of the Dead (1985)

The dead have waited. The day has come.

Why it made the list:

While *Day of the Dead* is easily the weakest of George Romero's original zombie trilogy, it still has much to offer in the way of scares and story. In this third installment, Romero focuses on a ragtag military unit and a mad scientist looking for a cure, all residing inside an abandoned missile silo. Sure, the character motivations are ridiculous; sure, the acting is as wooden as a dime store Indian; sure, the soldiers look less like military men and more like hippies and weirdos in various states of military dress; sure, the plot is plodding and moves along at a glacial speed. But this book isn't the *101 Most Entertaining Horror Films Ever Made*; this book is about scares, and *Day of the Dead*, for all its faults, has got them in spades.

Synopsis:

The entire world has been taken over by zombies, and only a handful of scientists and soldiers survive, living in an abandoned missile silo. The scientists search desperately for a cure to the zombie plague, performing outlandish and gruesome experiments on the creatures. When the soldiers learn that the scientists are using their own men for experimentation and zombie food, they are outraged. Suddenly there's an underground war between the scientists and the soldiers. As all of this plays out, the zombies infiltrate the bunker and all hell begins to break loose.

Scariest scene:

The final 15 minutes or so of the film contain one frightening scene after another as the scientists and soldiers are plunged into darkness along with the ravenous zombies in the catacombs beneath the bunker.

Memorable dialogue:

> **JOHN:** You want to put some kind of explanation on all this? Here's one as good as any other. We're bein' punished by the Creator. He visited a curse on us. Maybe he didn't want to see us blow ourselves up, put a big hole in the sky. Maybe He just wanted to show us He's still the Boss Man. Maybe He figure, we gettin' too big for our britches, tryin' to figure His shit out.

Did you know?

Dr. Logan estimates that the ratio of zombies to human survivors is 400,000 to one. Considering the population of the United States in 1985 was roughly 240 million, this means there are only about 600 survivors in the entire country.

Cast:

Lori Cardille (Sarah), Terry Alexander (John), Joseph Pilato (Rhodes), Jarlath Conroy (McDermott), Anthony Dileo Jr. (Miguel), Richard Liberty (Logan), Sherman Howard (Bub), Gary Howard Klar (Steel), Ralph Marrero (Rickles), John Amplas (Fisher).

What the critics say:

Mike McGranaghan, *Aisle Seat*: "An indisputable classic."

Rob Humanick, *Projection Booth*: "The director's favorite of his zombie trilogy is an unrecognized masterpiece."

Felix Vasquez Jr., *Cinema Crazed*: "One of the most uneasy and unnerving horror movies ever created."

If you liked this, you might also like:

The Dead Next Door (1989).

#88 28 Days Later (2002)

His fear began when he woke up alone. His terror began when he realized he wasn't.

Why it made the list:

Danny Boyle's *28 Days Later* reinvents a tired zombie genre in a way that is both daring and entertaining. Boyle and company's decision to shoot the film on handheld DV cameras was a brilliant one, as this adds to the depressing, fatalistic atmosphere of a world that is nearly empty save for flesh-eating undead creatures bent on the elimination of the human race. A lot of the film's ideas are new, and some are merely new twists on ideas we've seen before, but with *28 Days Later* Boyle has managed to craft a touchstone genre picture that demands equal respect and consideration by future zombie filmmakers as anything George Romero has made.

Synopsis:

Idealistic animal rights activists break into a laboratory, intent on releasing captive chimps that are being used for experimentation. However, what they don't realize is that the chimps are infected with a deadly virus that causes rage. Despite the pleas of the scientists, the activists open the cage doors and release the infected animals, which immediately begin infecting everyone around them.

Twenty-eight days after this event, Jim (Cillian Murphy) awakens from a coma, finding himself alone in an abandoned hospital. He climbs up from his hospital bed and goes searching for other survivors, but finds the streets of London deserted. He then stumbles into a large Catholic church, where he finds a horde of undead humans wishing to eat him. He, along with three other survivors, will make their way through the vast wasteland that is now London, hoping to survive one more night … one more day … one more hour …

When they ultimately discover a military compound, it appears that now they will be safe. However, this is only the beginning for these rag-tag, worn-down survivors. Soon they will face a whole new evil …

Scariest scene:

The film is filled to the brim with chilling scenes, but the most frightening hands-down is the scene in which the survivors attempt to change a flat tire in the tunnel in the seconds before they will be rushed by a hungry horde of the undead.

Memorable dialogue:

> **JIM:** Do you know what I was thinking?
>
> **SELENA:** You were thinking that you'll never hear another piece of original music ever again. You'll never read a book that hasn't already been written or see a film that hasn't already been shot.
>
> **JIM:** Um, that's what you were thinking.
>
> **SELENA:** No, I was thinking I was wrong.
>
> **JIM:** About what?
>
> **SELENA:** All the death. All the shit. It doesn't really mean anything to Frank and Hannah because … Well, she's got a dad and he's got his daughter. So, I was wrong when I was that staying alive is as good as it gets.

Did you know?

The decision to shoot the film on handheld Canon XL1 cameras was not just an aesthetic one. While Boyle believed shooting on the cameras would add to the gritty nature of the film, producer Andrew Macdonald

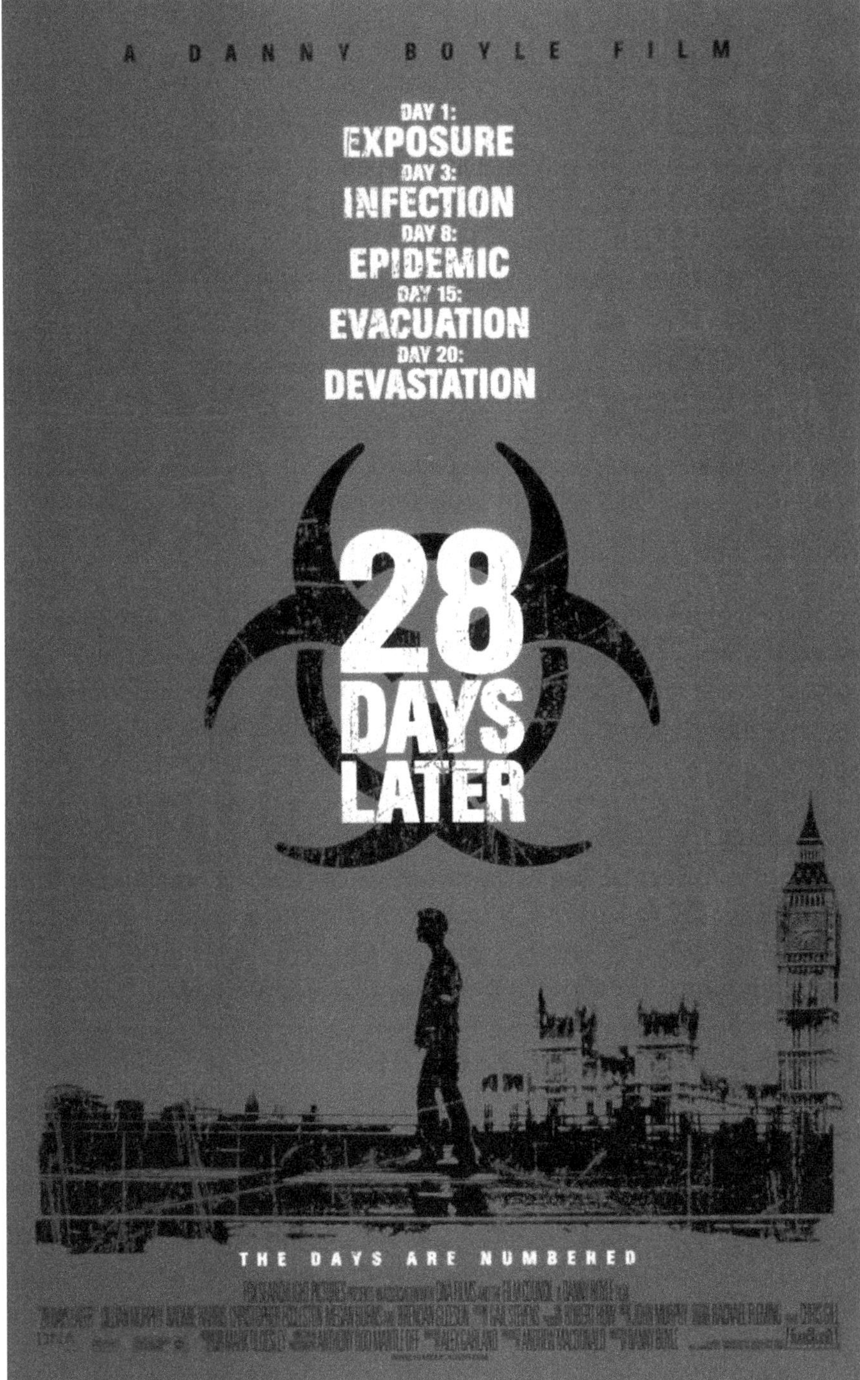
A DANNY BOYLE FILM
DAY 1:
EXPOSURE
DAY 3:
INFECTION
DAY 8:
EPIDEMIC
DAY 15:
EVACUATION
DAY 20:
DEVASTATION
28
DAYS
LATER
THE DAYS ARE NUMBERED

claims that many of the shots captured in the film would have been impossible to shoot with 35mm cameras.

Cast:

Alex Palmer (Activist), Bindu De Stoppani (Activist), Jukka Hiltunen (Activist), David Schneider (Scientist), Cillian Murphy (Jim), Toby Sedgwick (Infected Priest), Naomie Harris (Selena), Noah Huntley (Mark), Christopher Dunne (Jim's Father), Emma Hitching (Jim's Mother).

What the critics say:

Joe Morgenstern, *Wall Street Journal*: "Heedlessly derivative though it may be, *28 Days Later* does what it sets out to do and then some—scare us out of our wits, then get us to apply those wits to an uncommonly intelligent and provocative zombie flick."

Jonathan Rosenbaum, *Chicago Reader*: "Danny Boyle's purposeful direction and Mark Tildesley's imaginative and resourceful production design keep this fresh and edgy; the images of a wasted London and the details of a paramilitary organization in the countryside are both creepy and persuasive."

Mick LaSalle, *San Francisco Chronicle*: "*28 Days Later* is almost a great apocalyptic thriller. It has eerie images, a compelling situation and an unusual capacity to surprise. It incites an irresistible state of unease, the sense of disaster only seconds away, as well as a deep hunger to know what comes next. There's no real relief until its last moments."

If you liked this, you might also like:

World War Z (2013).

#89 *The Last House on the Left* (1972)

Mari, 17, is dying. Even for her the worst is yet to come.

Why it made the list:

Wildly transgressive and sometimes brutally violent, *The Last House on the Left* drew shock and outrage upon its release from some quarters. Horror-meister Wes Craven's first directorial effort, the film reveled in keeping viewers off-kilter. The script, written by Craven, contains moments of quiet reflection followed by sudden, vicious gore, and also features a bizarre, comic-relief subplot featuring two bumbling cops, about which the less said the better. Crude but effectively nasty, *The Last House on the Left* has become an icon of the 70s horror/exploitation movement.

Synopsis:

For her 17th birthday, Mari Collingwood (Sandra Cassell) meets up with her friend, Phyllis Stone (Lucy Grantham) to attend a concert in a nearby city. Mari's parents are concerned, but allow her to go. Mari and Phyllis decide to try to find some marijuana, and while doing so are kidnapped by a pair of escaped convicts and their two accomplices. Mari and Phyllis are then forced by their captors into a twisted, terrifying odyssey of torture, rape, and worse. The tension escalates even further when the criminals stumble upon Mari's parents' house in search of shelter after they've killed both girls.

Scariest scene:

Phyllis briefly manages to escape from the group holding her and Mari captive, but is chased down after a long, harrowing pursuit through the woods. The criminals proceed to kill her slowly, methodically, and gruesomely.

Memorable dialogue:

> **ESTELLE COLLINGWOOD:** Are you folks on vacation?
>
> **KRUG STILLO:** No, we're sort of, um, on a business trip.
>
> **DR. JOHN COLLINGWOOD:** Well what sort of business are you in?
>
> **FRED "WEASEL" PODOWSKI:** Plumbing.
>
> **KRUG STILLO:** Insurance.
>
> **ESTELLE COLLINGWOOD:** Well, which is it?
>
> **SADIE:** You see, we're actually in both. We sell insurance to plumbing companies. You know, in case they steal some toilets or something.

Did you know?

Last House on the Left is loosely based on Ingmar Bergman's 1960 Swedish film *The Virgin Spring.*

Cast:

Sandra Cassell (Mari Collingsworth), Lucy Grantham (Phyllis Stone), David A. Hess (Krug Stillo), Fred Lincoln (Fred "Weasel" Podowski), Jeramie Rain (Sadie), Marc Sheffler (Junior Stillo), Gaylord St. James (Dr. John Collingwood), Cynthia Carr (Estelle Collingwood), Ada Washington (Ada), Marshall Anker (Sheriff).

What the critics say:

Staff, *TV Guide*: "Expertly made on a tiny budget, this drive-in exploitation flick decisively transcends its genre. The extremely graphic violence is never played for thrills; indeed, Craven has said he wanted to resensitize Americans to the reality of violence in the wake of the Vietnam War. Craven—who would go on to polish his themes in the slicker *The Hills Have Eyes*—never for a moment allows the viewer to sympathize with the killers, but he does provide a window of understanding into how seemingly senseless acts of violence occur."

Staff, *Empire Magazine*: "Three decades of notoriety, urban mythology and varying degrees of banishment have done nothing to diminish the shocking impact of Craven's rape-revenge movie. Sartorially dated certainly, but still powerful, disturbing and raw."

David Wood, *BBC*: "The film retains its capacity to shock due largely to the cold, flat, and dispassionate style in which Craven depicts the events. The film, to its credit, details both the initial acts of violation and the revenge that ensues as similarly de-humanising and reprehensible. Far from subtle, it still perhaps ranks as Craven's best work and speaks volumes for the disparity in censorship regarding non-studio fare and the carte-blanche enjoyed by Hollywood productions as they merrily kill, maim, and generally blow people away with unfettered abandonment."

If you liked this, you might also like:

Chaos (2005).

#90 *Salem's Lot* (1979)

Salem's Lot, a town too good to be true. Something is happening. Something terrible.

Why it made the list:

For children of the 1970s, *Salem's Lot* may well have been their first experience with horror cinema. The movie was based on the writings of the parent-approved Stephen King and it aired as a mini-series on prime time television. There was simply no reason for parents to concern themselves with this made-for-TV spook show, or so they thought.

The storyline is simple and believable, and the characters are good and decent folk. Still, at this seemingly harmless movie's heart, lies something dark and sinister. That dark and sinister part is in the form of a vampire named Barlow.

Yet, this vampire looks nothing like the suave and debonair blood suckers of yore. Barlow is bluish in pallor, bald with rat-like fangs and pointed ears. He truly resembles a half-human-half-bat creature. This monster of the night also violently attacks his victims with a verve not seen in vampire films before. Barlow is hellish in both the looks and attitude.

Synopsis:

Novelist Ben Mears (David Soul) returns to his hometown of Salem, Maine to write about the borough's haunted centerpiece, the old Marsten House. For inspiration, Mears intends to set up shop in the subject house and remain there for the duration of his stay. His plans are thwarted by the mysterious Richard K. Straker (James Mason) who has only very recently acquired the property.

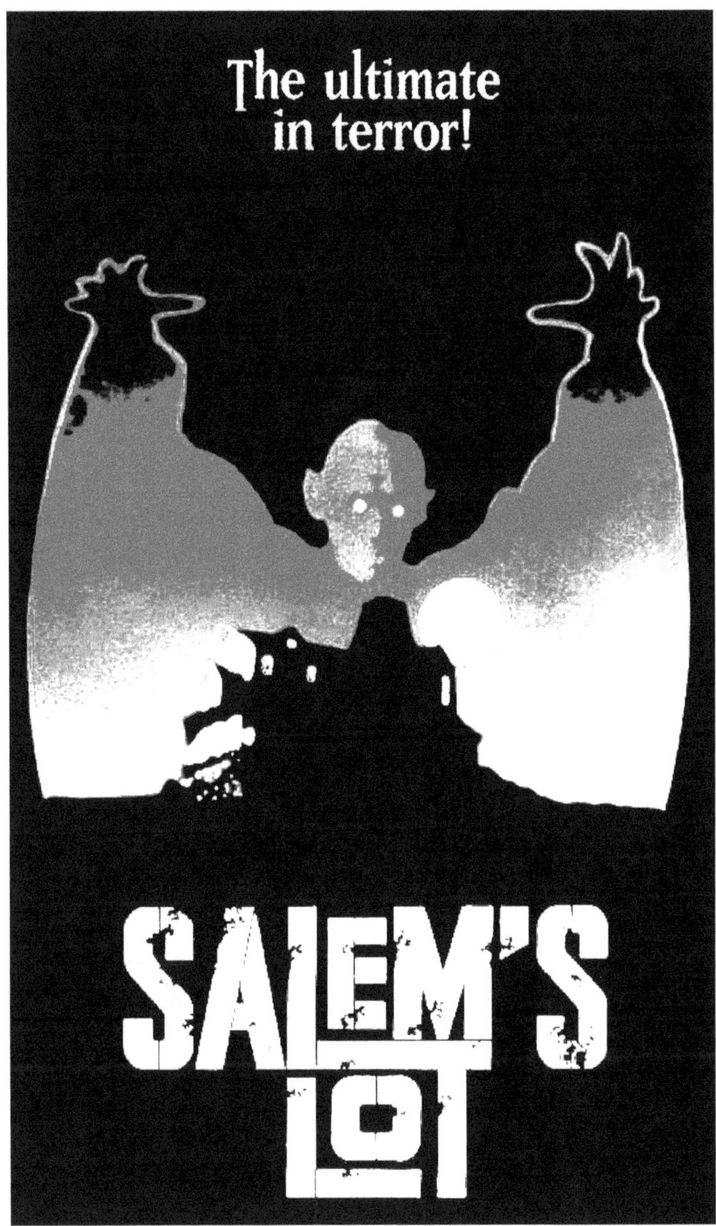

Straker is opening an antique shop within his new home and speaks frequently of his silent and absent partner Kurt Barlow (Reggie Nalder). Soon, odd happenings such as unexplainable disappearances and deaths begin in Salem. The townsfolk look to its newest residents for answers. The cryptic Straker is questioned, as is once-upon-a-time local Ben

Mears. Neither can be linked to the questionable occurrences, but Mears' interest is piqued.

Mears initiates an informal investigation of Straker, the Marsten House, and the bizarre goings on. Things become increasingly more and more clear for Mears as he discovers vampires are the culprits for these anomalies. The big problem is the vampires are increasing in numbers at an exponential rate, while the population of Salem is dwindling just as quickly.

Upon further digging, Mears uncovers the source of the town's anguish. Straker's silent and absent partner, Kurt Barlow, *has* been there, and he's the master vampire that must be destroyed.

Scariest scene:

Any scene with the film's key vampire Barlow is up for a nomination, but his demise in the end is the most horrific. Barlow shrieks and hisses inhuman sounds as Ben Mears digs in the beast's blackened heart with a wooden stake. Finally, the hideous-looking Barlow is defeated and decomposes before Ben Mears' eyes.

Memorable dialogue:

STRAKER: You'll enjoy Mr. Barlow. And he'll enjoy you.

Did you know?

George A. Romero was originally slated to direct a theatrical release of *Salem's Lot*. When Warner Bros. caught wind of John Badham's *Dracula* and Werner Herzog's *Nosferatu the Vampyre* they opted for the television mini-series route. Romero bowed out, figuring that prime-time TV restrictions would be more than he would want to deal with. Tobe Hooper was then brought onboard.

Cast:

David Soul (Ben Mears), James Mason (Richard K. Straker), Reggie Nalder (Kurt Barlow), Lance Kerwin (Mark Petrie), Bonnie Bedelia (Susan Norton), Lew Ayres (Jason Burke), Julie Cobb (Bonnie Sawyer), Elisha Cook Jr. (Gordon "Weasel" Phillips), George Dzundza (Cully Sawyer), Fred Willard (Larry Crockett).

What the critics say:

Felix Vasquez Jr., *Cinema Crazed*: "A masterful vampire film barely aged that will keep you up nights, and away from your window during the midnight hours."

Leonard Maltin, *Leonard Maltin's Movie Guide*: "A well-made hellraiser."

Staff, *Time Out*: "A surprisingly successful small screen adaptation of Stephen King's vampire novel. Edited down from the 190 minute, two-part TV movie, this cinema release version is slightly gorier and tighter than the original. Paring away the excessive plot exposition of Paul Monash's teleplay, it places the emphasis on Hooper's fluid camerawork, creepy atmospherics, and skillful handling of the gripping climax."

If you liked this, you might also like:

Return to Salem's Lot (1987).

#91 *The Stepfather* (1987)

Daddy's home and he's not very happy.

Why it made the list:

With a screenplay by noted crime novelist Donald E. Westlake and a keenly observed lead performance from Terry O'Quinn, *The Stepfather* offers a twisted take on the family dynamic when the male parental figure is also a dangerous psychopath. The suspense builds and builds as the stepfather's lies are exposed one by one, leading to a tense, brutal climax.

Synopsis:

Jerry Blake (Terry O'Quinn) seems to be the perfect new husband for the recently widowed Susan Maine (Shelley Hack). Jerry's new stepdaughter, Stephanie (Jill Schoelen) isn't convinced, however, and she has every right to be suspicious. Jerry, under the name Henry Morrison, brutally killed his former family, then changed his appearance to elude capture and started a new life with Susan. Stephanie's suspicions blossom after she witnesses Jerry have an uncontrolled outburst of rage when a story about the killings appears in the newspaper. Meanwhile, the brother of the woman Jerry killed before moving on to Susan is still searching for her murderer. Stephanie's therapist, Dr. Bondurant (Charles Lanyer) also has questions for Jerry. As the pressure builds from all sides, Jerry realizes that the perfect life he sought to build with Susan and Stephanie can never be, and he begins making bloody plans to move on once again to a new family.

Scariest scene:

When Jerry's secret is finally revealed, he drops his placid, happy family face and reveals the raging beast within. He attacks Susan with the phone, knocking her down the cellar stairs, then methodically begins hunting Stephanie throughout the house, planning to put an end to the new family that has so disappointed him.

Memorable dialogue:

> **JERRY:** This is very upsetting. If old man Grace is still there …
>
> **SUSAN:** No, forget it, honey. Forget it. She probably just got the name wrong or something.
>
> **JERRY:** Hodgkins! What's to get wrong?
>
> **SUSAN:** What did you say?
>
> **JERRY:** Huh? Wait a minute…who am I here?
>
> **SUSAN:** Jerry?
>
> **JERRY:** Jerry. Jerry Blake. Thank you, honey.

Did you know?

The Stepfather is loosely based on the story of John List, a New Jersey man who killed his family in 1971, and was on the run until 1989, when his profile on the television show *America's Most Wanted* resulted in his capture.

Cast:

Terry O'Quinn (Jerry Blake), Jill Schoelen (Stephanie), Shelley Hack (Susan), Charles Lanyer (Dr. Bondurant), Stephen Shellen (Jim Ogilvie), Stephen E. Miller (Al Brennan), Robyn Stevan (Karen), Jeff Schultz (Paul Baker), Lindsay Bourne (Art Teacher), Anna Hagan (Mrs. Leitner).

What the critics say:

John Beifuss, *Memphis Commercial Appeal*: "A model of economical suspense, *The Stepfather* demonstrates how clever writers and filmmakers can transform a potentially sensationalistic thriller premise into a movie that's not just scary and stylish but also smart (and occasionally smart-aleck); in fact, *The Stepfather* functions as both an efficient scare machine and a satirical critique of Reagan-era 'family values.'"

Staff, *Variety*: "An engrossing suspense thriller that refreshingly doesn't cheat the audience in terms of valid clues and plot twists. O'Quinn gives a measured, effective performance balancing the normalcy and craziness of the character, while Shoelen is powerfully empathetic as the young heroine. "

Staff, *TV Guide*: "Just when it looked like slasher movies were wholly irredeemable, director Joseph Ruben came along to prove there is some intelligent life in this otherwise bereft subgenre."

If you liked this, you might also like:

Stepfather II (1989).

#92 *The Exorcism of Emily Rose* (2005)

What happened to Emily?

Why it made the list:

The Exorcism of Emily Rose is the most creepy, effective film about exorcism since, well, *The Exorcist.* Fueled by an extraordinary performance from Jennifer Carpenter as Emily, the movie successfully marries courtroom drama to tension-filled terror, delivering both a troubling mystery and plenty of scares.

Synopsis:

A young woman named Emily Rose lies dead at her parents' remote farmhouse. After authorities determine that the cause of death cannot be laid to "natural causes," the parish priest, Father Moore (Tom Wilkinson), is arrested and charged with negligent homicide after it is discovered that he had attempted an exorcism on Emily, and had advised her to stop taking anti-seizure medication. Veteran defense lawyer Erin Bruner (Laura Linney) has just come off a high-profile case, and is hired by the archdiocese to oversee Father Moore's defense. He insists that Emily was not sick, but rather possessed, and that there was nothing medicine could have done to help her. Although the archdiocese and Bruner's law firm want the case to go away quickly, Father Moore refuses a plea bargain, insisting that he must tell Emily's story to the world. Bruner reluctantly allows the priest to present his defense—even though a conviction may mean years in prison. Bruner, an agnostic, begins to experience strange events as the trial moves forward, while Emily's story is gradually told through the testimony of those who were with her during the last months of her life.

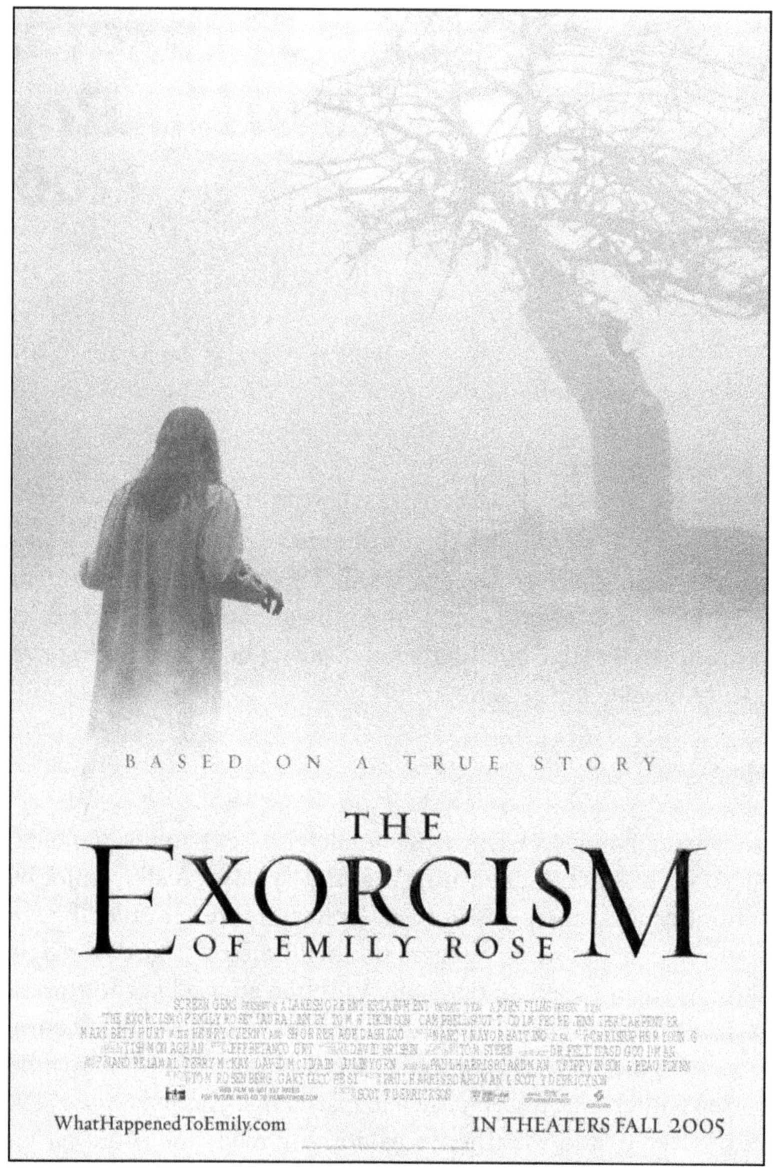

BASED ON A TRUE STORY
THE
EXORCISM
OF EMILY ROSE
WhatHappenedToEmily.com
IN THEATERS FALL 2005

Scariest scene:

Father Moore, with the help of Emily's father, her boyfriend and a doctor, attempts to perform the ancient Roman rite of exorcism at Emily's home. The tension mounts as the forces in control of Emily's body and soul resist Moore's efforts, and the exorcism begins to go horribly wrong. Despite being restrained, Emily escapes and leaps through the second floor window of her bedroom, into the stormy night outside. Moore and the others follow her to the barn, and attempt to continue the ritual, but prove no match for the demonic presences that have possessed Emily.

Memorable dialogue:

> **FATHER MOORE:** I now command you! Give me your name, demon!
>
> **EMILY:** Names! Names! One, two, three, four, five, six!
>
> **FATHER MOORE**: Ancient serpents, depart from this servant of God! Tell me your six names!
>
> **EMILY:** We are the ones who dwell within!

Did you know?

The movie was based on the true story of Anneliese Michele, a young German woman who died in 1976. Her parents and two priests who attempted an exorcism were arrested and charged with negligence.

Cast:

Laura Linney (Erin Bruner), Tom Wilkinson (Father Moore), Campbell Scott (Ethan Thomas), Jennifer Carpenter (Emily Rose), Colm Feore (Karl Gunderson), Joshua Close (Jason), Kenneth Welsh (Dr. Mueller), Duncan Frasier (Dr. Cartwright), J.R. Bourne (Ray), Mary Beth Hurt (Judge Brewster).

What the critics say:

Stephen Hunter, *Washington Post*: "*The Exorcism of Emily Rose* is full of ghostly presences who flit across the screen trailing gossamer filaments of lost possibility, dashed hopes and broken dreams. It's a haunted project, then, full of ache and loss and regret. All in all, it's a completely professional production, vivid and realistic, full of neat observations and blessedly disciplined in the nature of its special effects, which remain suggestive rather than literal and, far from going over the top, stay just a little above the bottom."

Mick LaSalle, *San Francisco Chronicle*: "In *Emily Rose* what's happening to Emily is scary. She tears her hair out, eats insects, experiences grotesque convulsions and scrapes her nails against the wall, but even as the demons are making her do these things, she remains in some way conscious and present. Talk about hell. The film gives Linney a chance to play someone sharp and aggressive again after a few years of playing softies, lightweights, witnesses and victims. She expands in the role. Wilkinson lends intensity and conviction to the priest. As for newcomer Carpenter, one could easily overlook her merely as that poor possessed girl. But that's a performance, and a strong one."

Michael Booth, *Denver Post*: "Director and writer Scott Derrickson gets extra credit for not trying to lead us all the way to the front pew. Linney is left with many questions, though not a lot of answers, and the movie's closing is a redemption for storytelling. Are we alone, or not alone, she wonders, and then like a good lawyer answers her own query: "Either thought is astonishing."

If you liked this, you might also like:

The Devil Inside (2012).

#93 *Fright Night* (1985)

If you love being scared, this could be the night of your life.

Why it made the list:

In 1985, *Fright Night* was a bit of a departure from the typical horror movie cycle of knife-wielding psychopaths. Vampires were considered "old hat" then, but *Fright Night's* revision of the genre's blueprint successfully changed all that. Director Tom Holland brought his blood-sucking vision into the 20th century with a suburban backdrop as opposed to the standard gothic settings of older horror films.

The filmmakers are quite aware of the thin line between horror and humor they are straddling. Even still, the camp values are kept at a minimum and the graphic transformations, depicted with an unflinching camera, keeps the audience firmly in the director's pocket.

Synopsis:

Horror film fanatic Charley Brewster (William Ragsdale) notices a coffin being carried into his new neighbor's house. Upon investigation he comes to believe his new neighbor, Jerry Dandridge (Chris Sarandon), is a vampire. Charley tells his mother (Dorothy Fielding), his girlfriend Amy (Amanda Bearse) and his best friend Ed (Stephen Geoffreys), but naturally they think his imagination is working overtime due to his constant consumption of horror films. Charley then turns to *Fright Night* television horror host Peter Vincent (Roddy McDowall) for assistance. Vincent had played a 'vampire killer' in many a horror film, but quickly admits to not believing in vampires or knowing anything about the destruction of them. At first the host declines Charley's pleas for help. However, in an attempt to prove her boyfriend wrong, Amy pays Vincent to go along with what she considers Charley's farce. Once everyone from Charley's best friend to his girlfriend have been transformed into vampires, Vincent feels he has no alternative but to help. With the proverbial vampire extermination tools in hand—crucifix, holy water, wooden stakes and mallets—Charley and Vincent set about the task of ridding their community of that pesky vampire Jerry Dandridge.

Scariest scene:

Like any horror film worth it's weight in fake blood, *Fright Night* incorporates a myriad of scare tactics, but Peter Vincent smashing a crucifix into Evil Ed's forehead and forging an indentation of the Christian symbol there takes the prize.

Memorable dialogue:

> **PETER VINCENT:** I have just been fired because nobody wants to see vampire killers anymore, or vampires either. Apparently all they want to see are demented madmen running around in ski-masks, hacking up young virgins.

Did you know?

Vincent Price was director Tom Holland's first choice for the character Peter Vincent. Due to Price's poor health, actor Roddy McDowall was selected for the role instead.

Cast:

Chris Sarandon (Jerry Dandridge), William Ragsdale (Charley Brewster), Amanda Bearse (Amy Peterson), Roddy McDowall (Peter Vincent), Stephen Geoffreys (Edward "Evil" Thompson), Jonathan Stark (Billy Cole), Dorothy Fielding (Judy Brewster), Art Evans (Detective Lennox), Stewart Stern (Cook), Nick Savage (Bouncer #1).

What the critics say:

Roger Ebert, *Chicago Sun-Times*: "*Fright Night* is not a distinguished movie, but it has a lot of fun being undistinguished."

Staff, *Variety*: "Director Tom Holland keeps the picture wonderfully simple and entirely believable (once the existence of vampires is accepted, of course). Chris Sarandon is terrific as the vampire, quite affable and debonair until his fingernails start to grow and his eyes get that glow. William Ragsdale superbly maintains due sympathy as a fairly typical youngster who can't get anybody to believe him about the odd new neighbor next door. Roddy McDowall hams it up on the telly as the 'fearless vampire killer.'"

Staff, *The Cult Movie Guide*: "Not content with being the greatest vampire movie of the '80s—with all due respect to ace vampire Western *Near Dark* and off-beat gem *Vamp*—*Fright Night* also stands up irrefutably as an all-time horror classic: a lively, atmospheric and most importantly frightening vampire movie. The confrontation between good and evil, living and undead, has never been so enthralling, so heartfelt, or so fun."

If you liked this, you might also like:

Jennifer's Body (2009).

#94 Drag Me To Hell (2009)

Even nice people can go to hell.

Why it made the list:

Leave it to *Evil Dead* filmmaker Sam Raimi to craft this ridiculously over-the-top thrill ride. *Drag Me to Hell* is certainly one of the better American horror films of the past decade, equal parts black comedy, camp, horror, and gross-out gusto. Not only is it filled with intermittently frightening and revolting moments, but it's incredibly well-acted and well-scripted, making it one of the most entertaining genre pictures unleashed on the public in a good long time. After taking a long hiatus from horror to make the Spider-Man films, Raimi showed horror buffs he was still capable of delivering a shock or two.

Synopsis:

Christine (Alison Lohman) is a loan officer at a bank, trying to impress her boss and get the big promotion. So when an elderly gypsy woman enters the bank crying that her house is about to be foreclosed upon, Christine must make the difficult decision to put her out in the street. When the old woman gets down on her knees and begs Christine, she feels insulted when the loan officer calls for security. This sets into motion a curse which promises to see Christine's soul dragged to hell in just a few days' time. When Christine goes to visit the old woman and beg her to remove the curse, she learns that she's too late—the old woman has passed away. Now it's up to Christine and a psychic to figure out a way to stop the demon from whisking her away to the flames of hell.

As Christine does anything she can think of to stop the curse, from sacrificing her pet kitten to holding a séance in the hopes of capturing the

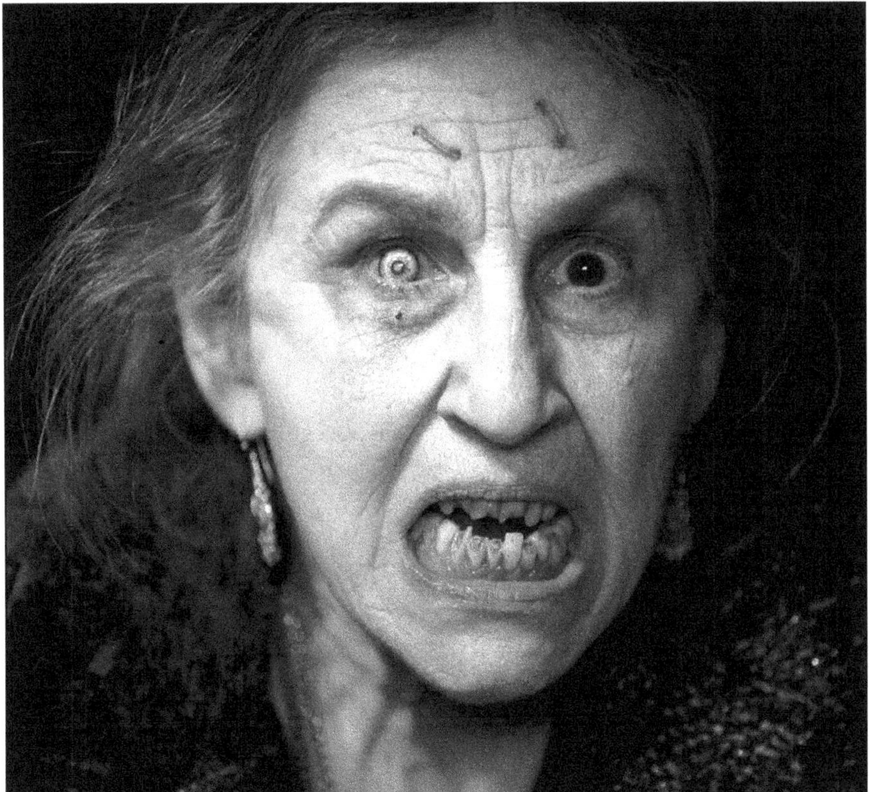

demon in a goat and slaughtering it, the stakes become higher and higher and time becomes less and less.

Scariest scene:

The film's séance scene is easily the film's most terrifying. In this scene, the demon known as the Lamia makes itself known and winds up killing the host of the séance in a frightening sequence. Runner-up for scariest scene is the film's conclusion, in which Christine realizes what is about to happen to her.

Memorable dialogue:

> **THE LAMIA:** I desire the soul of Christine Brown. We will feast upon it while she festers in the grave!

Did you know?

Clay (Justin Long) and Christine discuss taking a weekend trip to a secluded cabin the woods. This is a reference to Raimi's earlier films, *The Evil Dead* and *Evil Dead II*.

Cast:

Alison Lohman (Christine Brown), Justin Long (Clay Dalton), Lorna Raver (Mrs. Ganush), Dileep Rhao (Rham Jas), David Paymer (Mr. Jacks), Adrianna Barraza (Shaun San Dena), Chelcie Ross (Leonard Dalton), Reggie Lee (Stu Rubin), Molly Cheek (Trudy Dalton), Bojana Novakovic (Ilenka Ganush).

What the critics say:

Roger Ebert, *Chicago Sun-Times*: "*Drag Me to Hell* is a sometimes funny and often startling horror movie. That is what it wants to be, and that is what it is."

Bruce Diones, *New Yorker*: "Playful and relentlessly scary."

Dan Gire, *Daily Herald*: "The aptly titled *Drag Me to Hell* celebrates Sam Raimi's triumphant return to frightful and cheesy horror films that elicit as many nervous laughs as cringing shudders."

If you liked this, you might also like:

Thinner (1996).

#95 Scream (1996)

Someone is playing a deadly game. Someone who's seen one too many scary movies. Now he's taking his love of fear one step too far. He didn't make the rules. He just kills by them.

Why it made the list:

Director Wes Craven has always possessed panache for twisting and bending the rules of horror cinema. In 1996, *Scream* became his next feature to broaden the genre's horizons. Craven took the tired, tried, and true teen slasher flick, with all its trappings, and turned it in on itself.

It was a masterstroke for Craven as he took his characters and placed, or rather trapped, them in the very same type of horror thriller he was famous for making. *Scream* plays almost like a film within a film. It was a cinematic contrivance that Craven had explored and mined to some success in his 1994 film *Wes Craven's New Nightmare.*

Legend has it Craven begrudgingly took the violent film on as an appeasement to his fans who felt his best work was *The Hills Have Eyes.* Good or bad, *Scream* kick-started a whole new cycle of teenagers in peril horror films including *I Know What You Did Last Summer*, *Final Destination*, and *Jeepers Creepers.*

Synopsis:

Mousey Sidney Prescott (Neve Campbell) is wrapping her head and emotions around the one year anniversary of her mother's murder. Soon, a string of gruesome killings begin to occur. Sidney's friends and classmates are the stalker's primary targets.

The killer has donned a black cloak and a mask resembling Norwegian painter Edvard Munch's "The Scream." Whoever is committing the murders is unaffectionately dubbed Ghostface. Suitably outraged, the town of Westboro pressures the authorities and a witch hunt of sorts is underway.

The first suspect is Sidney's boyfriend Billy Loomis (Skeet Ulrich), who is quickly released due to a lack of evidence and another similar murder happening during his incarceration. Despite her feelings for Billy, Sidney isn't so sure of his innocence. The authorities carry on with their investigation and Sidney's friends carry on with theirs. Her friend's investigations involve applying traditional horror film rules and parameters to what is happening to their fellow students.

School is closed indefinitely until the murders are sorted out. Sidney's classmate and horror film fanatic Stuart Mach (Matthew Lillard) seizes this opportunity to throw a party. It's a tacky move on Stuart's part that half the high school student body gleefully embraces.

Stuart's house is convened upon by dozens of drinking, drugging, and promiscuous teenagers. The stage is set. Ghostface stalks about the party murdering the teenagers in a parade of appalling fashions, eventually turning his aggressions towards Sidney.

The resourceful Sidney narrowly escapes time and time again until her worst fears are revealed. Her boyfriend Billy is indeed the killer, but he is only 50 percent of the scream killing team; Stuart is his accomplice. Adding to the body count and bloodbath, Sidney kills them both in self-defense.

Scariest scene:

The opening scene to *Scream* would have to be its scariest moment. Wes Craven kills off Drew Barrymore's character, Casey, within 10 minutes of the movie's running time. This was a similar ploy to the one Hitchcock used in *Psycho* when he had Janet Leigh's character, Marion Crane, murdered during the first reel of his film. At these points, the audience becomes aware that anything can happen and ultimately both features become a cinematic runaway train.

Memorable dialogue:

CASEY: Who's there?

GHOSTFACE: Never say 'who's there?' Don't you watch scary movies? It's a death wish. You might as well come out to investigate a strange noise or something.

Did you know?

Writer Kevin Williamson based his screenplay on the real-life Gainesville Ripper. Years later, *Scream* would be accused of causing violent acts and even murder.

Cast:

Drew Barrymore (Casey Becker), Roger Jackson (Phone Voice), Kevin Patrick Walls (Steve), David Booth (Casey's Father), Carla Hatley (Casey's Mother), Neve Campbell (Sidney Prescott), Skeet Ulrich (Billy Loomis), Lawrence Hecht (Neil Prescott), Jaimie Kennedy (Randy Meeks), Courteney Cox (Gale Weathers).

What the critics say:

Roger Ebert, *Chicago-Sun Times*: "What did I think about this movie? As a film critic, I liked it. I liked the in-jokes and the self-aware characters. At the same time, I was aware of the incredible level of gore in this film. It is *really* violent. Is the violence defused by the ironic way the film uses it and comments on it? For me, it was. For some viewers, it will not be, and they will be horrified."

Dave Kehr, *New York Daily News*: "*Scream* builds to a splattering finale that should leave genre fans highly satisfied. Here's one of the year's better thrillers."

Roger Hurtburt, *South Florida Sun-Sentinel*: "It is a fright film that takes elements from classics that evoked the screamin' meemies and reinvents melodramatic applications offering a new spin to slice-and-dice antics. Gallows humor runs rampant, too."

If you liked this, you might also like:

I Know What You Did Last Summer (1997).

#96 *The Mist* (2007)

Belief divides them, mystery surrounds them, but fear changes everything.

Why it made the list:

Adapted from a novella by Stephen King, Frank Darabont's *The Mist* is a classic example of the siege film. Like similar pictures, from *Stagecoach* to *Night of the Living Dead*, the film brings together a diverse group of people and traps them together. Here Darabont and King do it right in a way that very few other films have in managing to make the people seem as frightening as the monsters which lurk outside in the mist. Divided by faith, the stranded people split into factions. When faith ultimately causes the people to react violently against one another, the film becomes far more frightening. Sure, whatever is out there in that creepy mist is scary (save for horrendous CGI which seems beneath a filmmaker of Darabont's talents), but it cannot compare to the fear-inducing, Bible-spouting religious zealots locked inside that store with the so-called faithless heathens.

The Mist also gains points for its terrific ensemble and its superb direction (again, save for some horrendous-looking CGI monsters). Also, credit Darabont for altering the novella's original ending and wrapping up the picture with a climax so dark it makes the end of *Night of the Living Dead* look like a Disney production.

Synopsis:

When a mysterious and dangerous mist envelopes their town, a group of people find themselves trapped together inside a grocery store. They don't know what's in the mist killing people, but they know something's definitely amiss. Soon they encounter strange creatures from somewhere be-

STEPHEN KING'S LEGENDARY TALE OF TERROR

FEAR CHANGES EVERYTHING

THE MIST

FROM FRANK DARABONT, SCREENWRITER AND DIRECTOR
OF 'THE GREEN MILE' AND 'THE SHAWSHANK REDEMPTION'

NOVEMBER 21 EVERYWHERE

yond the stars, and as they struggle to stay alive for another day they find themselves at odds with one another over their religious beliefs (or lack thereof). Some of the people become convinced that this is the Biblical end of times, and the captive group find themselves locked in a religious war that threatens to kill them all.

Scariest scene:

Again, no creature in this film is quite as frightening as the religious nuts who wish to sacrifice a young boy to god and keep everyone trapped inside the supermarket. However, the single most frightening scene by far is the film's shocking conclusion in which protagonist David Drayton (Thomas Jane) is forced to murder the other three survivors—including his young son. Having just done the unthinkable, David now finds himself without any more bullets to kill himself. And he hears the sounds of something approaching in the mist …

Memorable dialogue:

> **DAN MILLER:** What are you saying? What are you proposing?
>
> **MRS. CARMODY:** If we all prepare … to meet our maker …
>
> **JIM GRONDIN:** Oh, prepare to meet shit! Lady, your tongue must be hung in the middle so it can waggle at both ends.
>
> **MRS. CARMODY:** The end of times has come. Not in flames, but in mist.
>
> **JIM GRONDIN:** Come here. How about if your ass prepares to meet my size ten work boot! How about that?

Did you know?

Director Frank Darabont later became the show-runner for the popular television series *The Walking Dead*. For that project, he would enlist three of the film's actors—Laurie Holden, Jeffrey DeMunn, and Melissa McBride—to appear as series regulars.

Cast:

Thomas Jane (David Drayton), Marcia Gay Harden (Mrs. Carmody), Laurie Holden (Amanda Dunfrey), Andre Braugher (Brent Norton), Toby Jones (Ollie Weeks), William Sadler (Jim), Jeffrey DeMunn (Dan Miller), Frances Sternhagen (Irene Reppler), Nathan Gamble (Billy Drayton), Alexa Davalos (Sally).

What the critics say:

Peter Hartlaub, *San Francisco Chronicle*: "One of the first images you'll see in *The Mist* is a movie poster of John Carpenter's *The Thing*. That 1982 classic was arguably the creative peak of the last generation of horror filmmaking, filled with more than the requisite amount of gore, but also intelligence and a sense of building paranoia that you hardly ever see today. The latest Frank Darabont-directed movie based on a Stephen King book does a decent job of replicating that experience … "

S. James Snyder, *The New York Sun*: "The fact that *The Mist* cracks the two-hour barrier, at a time when most horror movies struggle to stitch together enough superficial jump-cuts to crack 80 minutes, should suggest that Frank Darabont's new film has more than just a few silly scares on its mind. And though it takes far too long to get to that more sober, serious place—leaping beyond a routine horror formula with a healthy dose of *Twilight Zone*-caliber what-if hypothesizing—the film's final few minutes are genuinely haunting and provocative."

David Edelstein, *New York Magazine*: "This film builds toward a climax so wrenching that I hesitate to recommend this film, but I think Darabont earns his vision."

If you liked this, you might also like:

Bait (2012).

#97 *The Phantom of the Opera* (1925)

The greatest horror film of modern cinema!

Why it made the list:

In 1925, the feature-length motion picture was still in its infancy. There was no ratings board yet, and movie-makers were free to explore virtually every cinematic avenue available. Horror in American movies had been sparse, but was considered fertile ground for mining.

Universal Studios spared no expense at bringing to the screen what would later be considered "A masterpiece of horror that shocked cinema for decades!" As with all older horror films, whether or not *The Phantom of the Opera* would scare an audience today is subjective and highly unlikely. However, in 1925 it riveted nearly scared-to-death moviegoers to their seats.

Synopsis:

Erik (Lon Chaney), a man physically deformed at birth, takes solace in the catacombs of the Paris Opera House. He is an aficionado of opera music and also quite adept at music composition and playing the pipe organ. He takes a fancy to apprentice opera singer Christine Daae (Mary Philbin).

Erik skulks about the opera house and has become known as its resident ghost or phantom. He insists on Box # 5 being saved for him, but is seldom seen there. He also insists that Christine Daae take the starring role in their current production of "Faust". This is much to the chagrin of Mme. Carlotta (Virginia Pearson), the production's prima donna and current star.

The Phantom sends threatening notes to the Opera's management and Mme. Carlotta outlining what could happen if his demands are not

met. The opera star refuses to step down for her understudy. The Phantom's "curse" is unleashed in the form of a falling chandelier. The chandelier crashes into the audience and forces the opera's producers to re-think the Phantom's threats.

Christine is kidnapped by the Phantom and taken to the depths of the opera house. He declares his love for her. Christine does not reciprocate and faints from the shock of it all. Later, she is released from the dungeon and tells her sweetheart Raoul (Norman Kerry) what has happened. A jealous Phantom overhears the exchange and devises a plan to rid himself of the proverbial third wheel.

The Phantom kidnaps Christine once more, thus luring Raoul and his partner Ledoux (Arthur Edmund Carewe) down into his subterranean lair on her behalf. The captor shows his captive two secret levers: one in the shape of a scorpion, the other a grasshopper. He explains that one lever will save her lover while the other will blow up the opera house.

Unwittingly, Christine chooses the scorpion lever that will drown Raoul, thus "saving" him from the opera house explosion. The duped heroine begs for Raoul's life. In desperation, the Phantom takes Christine and flees the scene. Raoul manages to save Christine. An outraged mob hunts down the Phantom and throws him into the Seine River to drown.

Scariest scene:

With little doubt, The Phantom's removal of his mask revealing his deformed face would be the film's ace in the hole. The scene was so effective it was said to have caused fainting in some movie theaters.

Memorable dialogue:

> **ERIK:** Feast your eyes! Glut your soul on my accursed ugliness!

Did you know?

Lon Chaney's make-up for the role of The Phantom was so shrouded in mystery that it was kept secret even on the set. When Christine (Mary Philbin) shrieks in horror at the sight of her antagonist's unveiled face, no acting was necessary as the actress was truly shocked and horrified.

Cast:

Lon Chaney (The Phantom/Erik), Mary Philbin (Christine Daae), Norman Kerry (Vicomte Raoul de Chagny), Arthur Edmund Carewe (Ledoux), Virginia Pearson (Mme. Carlotta), Gibson Gowland (Simon Buquet), John St. Polis (Comte Philip de Chagny), Snitz Edwards (Florine Papillon).

What the critics say:

Staff, *Time*: "Universal made a brave attempt to duplicate the success of *The Hunchback of Notre Dame* with another picture of Lon Chaney and Paris. They built the imposing facade of the Paris Opera House and constructed on various sets a series of ingenious interiors and dungeons. They took their story from the novel of Gaston Leroux and depended on horror chiefly for their entertainment. Though Mr. Chaney wears a more grotesque make-up than ever, the film play seems only pretty good."

J.R. Jones, *Chicago Reader*: "Lon Chaney's performance as the hideous organist prowling the sewers beneath the Paris Opera is still a cornerstone of gothic horror."

Jamie Russell, *Total Film*: "It succeeds in spite of itself and it's all thanks to Chaney. The man of a thousand faces imbues this character with bravado and menace, whether sitting on a statue of Apollo on the opera house roof or snorkeling through underground sewers.

With his lank hair, black-ringed eyes and stretched nostrils as deep and dark as open graves, this Phantom is the missing link between Max Schreck's cadaverous Nosferatu and the shambling corpse Boris Karloff played in Frankenstein. He's the stuff that bad dreams are made of."

If you liked this, you might also like:

Phantom of the Paradise (1974).

#98 Open Water (2003)

Who will save you?

Why it made the list:

Just when we finally felt it was safe to go back into the water—three decades after *Jaws* left an indelible mark on our psyches and made us forever afraid of sharks—*Open Water* came along and reinforced our fear of these killing machines with fins and sharp teeth. Filmed over two years with a crew of only two people (director Chris Kentis and his wife, Laura Lau), *Open Water* is a highly-effective horror film. The first 20 minutes drag on a bit, but once its protagonists find themselves stranded in the middle of the ocean, all bets are off. Shot on digital on a shoestring budget, the film has a documentary-like feel to it that only makes it feel all the more frightening. And the ending … don't get me started. The ending is as frightening and dark as anything the genre has ever seen.

Synopsis:

A young yuppie couple, Susan (Blanchard Ryan) and Daniel (Daniel Travis), go on a vacation in the Caribbean. This should be the vacation of their lives, but it soon turns into possibly the final vacation of their lives. While enjoying a scuba diving jaunt in the middle of the ocean, their boat inadvertently leaves without them, leaving them stranded and at the mercy of sharks and other sea life. The couple must endure storms, fish bites, and hunger before finally coming face to face with a pack of hungry sharks.

Scariest scene:

The final five minutes of the film are some of the darkest moments ever committed to celluloid. Having already floated for a full day, Daniel succumbs to his wounds and dies. Susan is crushed, and eventually can do nothing but watch a huge swarm of sharks eat at him as though he were nothing more than J. Crew-clothed chum. This moment is terrifying, and only leads up to the scarier moment when Susan gives up and lets herself go, giving herself over to the waters and the sharks. This is one hell of a bleak ending, right up there with the end of films like *Night of the Living Dead* and *The Mist*. It sticks in the mind long after the film has finished playing.

Memorable dialogue:

> **SUSAN:** Daniel, where's the boat?
>
> **DANIEL:** That's a good question.
>
> [Takes a moment to look around.]
>
> **DANIEL:** I guess it's one of those.
>
> **SUSAN:** You gotta be kidding me.
>
> **DANIEL:** It better be one of those.
>
> **SUSAN:** Well, which one do you think?
>
> **DANIEL:** I don't know.

Did you know?

Open Water was financed by director Chris Kentis and his wife, cinematographer/producer Laura Lau, for approximately $130,000. It was later purchased by Lion's Gate for $2.5 million after its Sundance screening.

Cast:

Blanchard Ryan (Susan), Daniel Travis (Daniel), Saul Stein (Seth), Michael E. Williamson (Davis), Cristina Zenato (Linda), John Charles (Junior), Estelle Lau (Estelle), Steve Lemme (Scuba Diver).

What the critics say:

Jacob Jester, *UTK Daily Review*: "The purpose of this film in not to keep its audience guessing, but to keep them terrified (and perhaps to carry out Kenti's elaborate scheme to cripple scuba-tourism) and at this the film fares surprisingly well. Initially the pace of the movie is sluggish. The opening 20 minutes play out like a dull Discovery Channel special. The footage almost seems to have been added as filler for an already less-than-feature-length feature. But once the main action begins, the apprehension rises to surprising levels. Kenti has an effective way of making the mood oscillate like the waves on screen, promising comfort and hope at one moment and providing only terror and disaster the next."

Peter Travers, *Rolling Stone*: "*Open Water* is open season on an audience's nerves. As in the best scare flicks, what eats at you most is what you don't see. … [F]rom the first bite—on Susan's leg (ouch!)—Kentis never lets up on the tension. You can feel the water, stretching against an unsheltering sky, seep into your bones. The ending—a more devastating surprise than *The Village* could manage—caps 80 sweat-job minutes of imaginative, jolting suspense."

Staff, *DVD Verdict*: "*Open Water* wants to be the new *Jaws*, to take Steven Spielberg's classic cat-and-mouse aquatic thriller and bring it back to its anthropomorphic roots. It also wants to celebrate the newfound freedom and creative dexterity in the emerging digital filmmaking format. It so vehemently craves to turn its home movie handcrafting (it was made over two years by a crew of two, with an equally tiny cast) into something special and epic that it only barely succeeds on sheer force of will alone. That it occasionally comes up short, never completely immersing the audience in its lost at sea tenets, is not really important. In the wide range of attempts at reinventing genres and instilling innovation into the most tired of cinematic situations, *Open Water* comes out on top."

If you liked this, you might also like:

Frozen (2010).

#99 Friday the 13th (1980)

They were warned ... They are doomed ... And on Friday the 13th,nothing will save them.

Why it made the list:

The original *Friday The 13th* offers up plenty of chilling, bloody special effects expertly delivered by FX master Tom Savini. The movie also keeps viewers guessing about the nature of the curse at Camp Crystal Lake. And, of course it spawned one of the longest-running, most successful horror movie franchises in history, and set the stage for the appearance of one of filmdom's most well-known villains, Jason Voorhees.

Synopsis:

Camp Crystal Lake has been abandoned for over 20 years, since the murder of two camp counselors in 1958. The killings came just a year after a young boy drowned at the camp, and helped the spot earn a cursed reputation. Businessman Steve Christy (Peter Brouwer), however, is unconcerned with the history of the place, and has spent $25,000 on renovations to bring Crystal Lake back to life, despite the protestations of some local townspeople. Steve and a group of young counselors are hard at work at the camp on Friday the 13th to finish the restoration project. What Steve and the others don't know is that the camp cook, Annie (Robbi Morgan) has been already been killed by someone who doesn't want the camp to re-open. As night falls on Crystal Lake, the killer begins to target the others one by one, determined that none will survive this Friday the 13th.

Scariest scene:

Blithely unaware that a killer is stalking the camp, a pair of counselors, Jack (Kevin Bacon) and Marcie (Jeannine Taylor), spend some time together away from the group in a bunk in one of the cabins. The two are soon dispatched in grisly fashion, as Jack's throat is pierced by an arrow from below as he lays in bed, and Marcie gets an axe to the face in the women's bathroom.

Memorable dialogue:

> **ENOS:** Quit. Quit now.
>
> **ANNIE:** Quit? Why would I wanna quit?
>
> **ENOS:** Camp Crystal Lake is jinxed.
>
> **ANNIE:** Oh, terrific. Not you, too! You sound like your crazy friend back there, Ralph.
>
> **ENOS:** Did Christy ever ever tell you 'bout the two kids murdered in '58? Boy drowning in '57? Buncha fires. Nobody

knows who did any of 'em. In 1962, they was gonna open up … the water was bad. Christy'll end up just like his folks, crazy and broke. He's been up there a year fixin' up that place. He musta dropped $25,000, and for what? Ask anybody, quit.

ANNIE: I can't.

ENOS: Dumb kids. Know-it-alls. Just like my niece, heads fulla rocks.

Did you know?

The movie was filmed at Camp No-Be-Bo-Sco in New Jersey. The camp is still in operation, and it has a wall of paraphernalia to honor that the movie was set there.

Cast:

Betsy Palmer (Mrs. Pamela Voorhees), Adrienne King (Alice Hardy), Jeannine Taylor (Marcie Cunningham), Robbi Morgan (Annie), Kevin Bacon (Jack Burel), Harry Crosby (Bill), Laurie Bartram (Brenda), Mark Nelson (Ned Rubinstein), Peter Brouwer (Steve Christy), Rex Everhart (Enos the Truck Driver).

What the critics say:

Kevin Carr, *7(M) Pictures*: "What makes the movie work is that the slasher genre hadn't been set in stone yet, and there are some choices that director Sean S. Cunningham makes in the film that work against type. Not all the deaths are shown on screen, and the use of Harry Manfredini's haunting theme is the only thing that identifies a kill is on the way."

David Grove, *Film Threat*: "The director Sean S. Cunningham does a great job of creating discomfort and tension when the characters start vanishing. Scenes like the one where Kevin Bacon gets an arrow through his Adam's apple are so dominant that we forget about the tense scenes where King and Billwalk around the camp, searching for the others. They find a bloody axe. The car won't start. The girl feels something is wrong. Then the guy goes down to the generator room. That's cool. *Friday the 13th* invented camera stalking, and it reminds us that killing and gore doesn't necessarily have to take place in that order."

Matt Ford, *BBC*: "It was not the first teen 'stalk-n-slash' film and certainly not the most creative, but it was undeniably a hugely influential film that contributed to the 1980s horror boom. The film's success was in its ability to understand what made audiences tick, and then manipulate it ruthlessly"

If you liked this, you might also like:

Maniac (1980).

#100 Saw (2004)

How much blood would you shed to stay alive?

Why it made the list:

In many ways, *Saw* is a terrible movie. The acting is as horrific as any film listed in this book, and its plot and payoff are ridiculous and convoluted. While many people might admit to *Saw* being a guilty pleasure, not many will defend it in terms of quality. Despite these shortcomings, *Saw* is (at times) a genuinely frightening film. With a new *Saw* film coming out each year for seven years straight, it also represents the horror genre—for better or worse—for an entire generation of moviegoers.

Synopsis:

Two flawed men, Dr. Lawrence Gordon (Cary Elwes) and Adam (screenwriter Leigh Whannell), wake up to find themselves chained to pipes inside a dirty, abandoned warehouse. They soon learn that they have been captured so they may participate in a grisly life-or-death game of difficult decisions in which the wrong choice may ultimately lead to their death(s).

Scariest scene:

The most traditionally scary scene in the film finds Adam using his camera's flashbulb to illuminate his darkened apartment. With each flash, we prepare to see something unexpected and creepy in the darkness. Ultimately, this scene does not disappoint as Adam flashes the flashbulb one too many times and finds something/someone waiting to capture him.

Memorable dialogue:

> **JIGSAW:** Dr. Gordon, this is your wake-up call. Every day of your working life you have given people the news that they're gonna die soon. Now you will be the cause of death. Your aim in this game is to kill Adam. You have until six on the clock to do it. There's a man in the room with you. When there's that much poison in your blood, the only thing left to do … is to shoot yourself. There are ways to win this, hidden all around you. Just remember, X marks the spot for the treasure. If you do not kill Adam by six, then Allison and Diana will die, Dr. Gordon … and I'll leave you in this room to rot. Let the game begin.

Did you know?

Detectives Tapp and Sing track down a fire alarm to a building on Stygian Street. This is a reference to director James Wan's first film, *Stygian*. Interestingly, that film also features Leigh Wannell, who wrote and starred in *Saw*.

Cast:

Leigh Whannell (Adam Faulkner-Stanheight), Cary Elwes (Dr. Lawrence Gordon), Danny Glover (Detective David Tapp), Ken Leung (Detective Steven Sing), Mike Butters (Paul), Paul Gutrecht (Mark), Michael Emerson (Zep Hindle), Benito Martinez (Brett), Shawnee Smith (Amanda), Tobin Bell (John).

What the critics say:

Roger Ebert, *Chicago Sun-Times*: "*Saw* is an efficiently made thriller, cheerfully gruesome, finally not quite worth the ordeal it puts us through. It's a fictional machine to pair sadistic horrors with merciless choices, and so the question becomes: Do we care enough about the characters to share what they have to endure? I didn't."

Stephen Holden, *New York Times*: "As long as it's dreaming up diabolical challenges, *Saw* displays a certain steely nerve. But the movie is seriously undermined by the half-baked, formulaic detective story in which the horror is framed. Poor Danny Glover's talents are wasted as a dogged sleuth who becomes so obsessed with the so-called Jigsaw Killer that the movie briefly toys with the notion that his character is the killer. The more it plays such silly, manipulative games, the more *Saw* blunts its own cutting edge."

Crystal Morgan, *The UTK Daily Beacon*: "The movie does have its scary moments. These moments make a person jump, crouch down or even flinch just a little. For the most part, *Saw* is more suspenseful than scary."

If you liked this, you might also like:

X Game (2010).

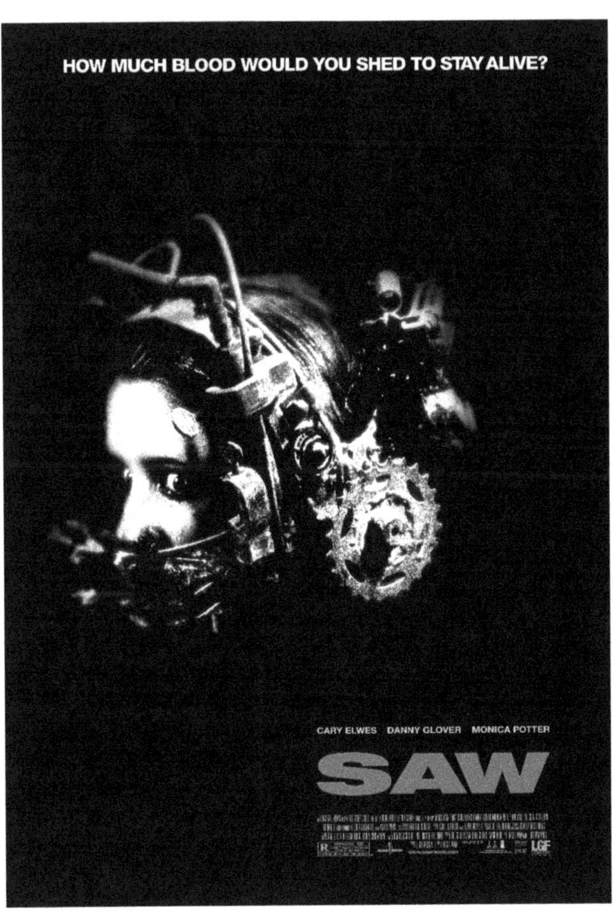

#101 The Blair Witch Project (1999)

What was supposed to be a fun trip, becomes a hunt. You are the prey.

Why it made the list:

Due to a clever, pre-release, marketing campaign involving Internet missing persons reports and possible sightings of the protagonists, most people believed that *The Blair Witch Project* was factual. Supposedly the film was edited together from the found footage left behind by the deceased filmmakers. The producers' unique scheme worked tremendously well, and for the summer of 1999 *The Blair Witch Project* was the talk of the town.

The cast is so convincing that it's truly difficult to imagine that the film isn't actually real. The viewer becomes completely immersed in what is happening to these three young people, whether they are being terrorized by an unseen entity or leisurely sitting around a campfire roasting weenies. Every word uttered, every conversation or argument and every bit of their body language is executed with just the precise amount of conviction expected from three people in their dogged predicament.

Possibly no movie in history has lived and died by its own hype like *The Blair Witch Project.* Once the proverbial cat is out of the bag, the film becomes little more than a curio. However, for a brief time it was considered the most horrifying film since *The Exorcist.* It was the first of its kind, leading to other films such as *Cloverfield, Paranormal Activity,* and *Diary of the Dead.*

Synopsis:

Three young filmmakers, Heather Donahue, Josh Leonard, and Mike Williams, convene upon the small town of Burkittsville, Maryland, to make

"SCARY AS HELL."

— *Peter Travers, ROLLING STONE*

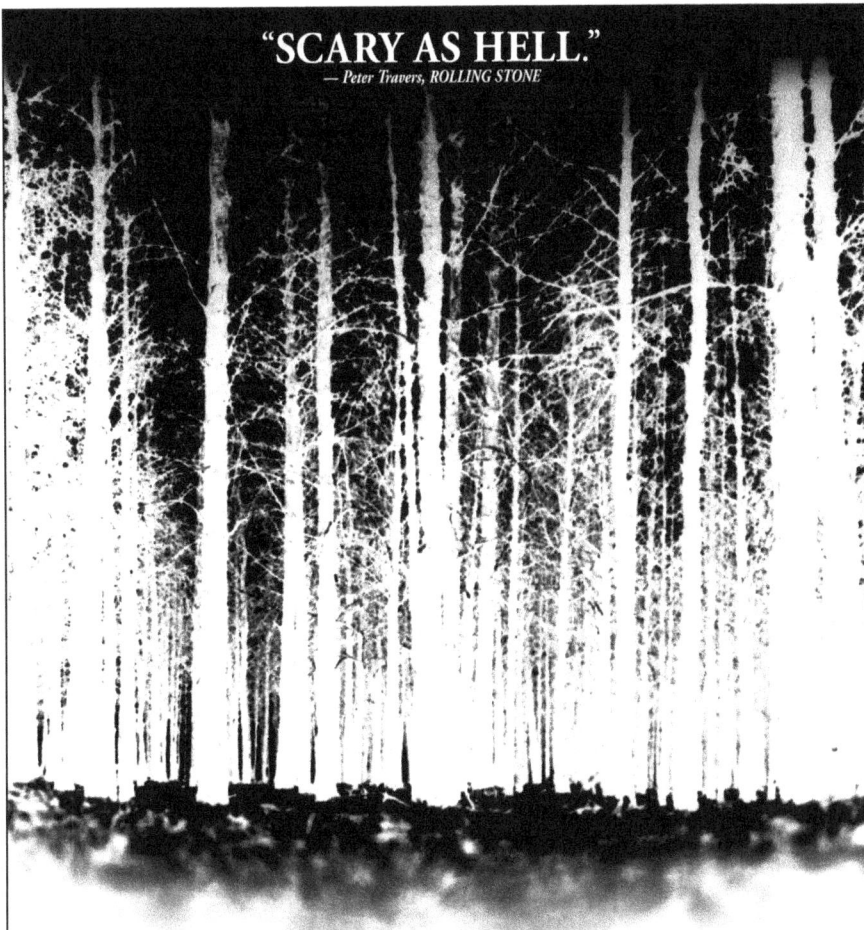

In October of 1994
three student filmmakers disappeared
in the woods near Burkittsville, Maryland,
while shooting a documentary...

A year later their footage was found.

THE BLAIR WITCH PROJECT

www.blairwitch.com

a documentary on the legendary Blair Witch. Townsfolk are interviewed using a 16mm film camera while the production is chronicled through the lens of a video camera. Once the interviews have been conducted, the three take to the woods in search of hard evidence to prove the existence of the Blair Witch. With little knowledge of the area, they are soon lost. They pitch camp and in the night hear odd crackling sounds. At daybreak they continue their journey and yet again find themselves held captive by the dense and foreboding forest.

They set up camp again and the crackling sounds become more intense while moaning and groaning intonations have been added to the unseen antagonists' arsenal of terror. The three are truly terrified, but somehow manage to sleep. Upon awakening, Heather and Mike discover Josh missing. Frantically the two search for their friend and their way out of the imprisoning woods. That night they hear the agonized screams of Josh.

Heather and Mike follow the sound of a male voice, presumably Josh's, into a burned-out, abandoned house. With the video camera on, Mike leads the way. Heather, with the 16mm camera running, follows in haste. The two wind up separated. We watch, through the camera lens, something or someone knocking Mike unconscious or worse yet killing him. The video camera drops to the floor. Heather, frantic and completely out of her mind, screams and screams for Mike as she descends the stairs still filming her every step. We watch the same scenario befall Heather as we did Mike.

Scariest scene:

Since the majority of the film is a lead-up, the ending is without a doubt its scariest moment. Watching Heather and Mike's demise through the lens of their own cameras was a unique and disconcerting twist on the ending of a horror film. Furthermore, Heather's convincing and continual screams coupled with the "shaky-cam" generally leads viewers to a near disoriented state.

Memorable dialogue:

> **HEATHER:** Everything had to be my way. And this is where we've ended up, and it's all because of me that we're here now—hungry, cold, and hunted.

Did you know?

The filmmakers took their cue from Italian exploitation movie-maker Ruggero Deodato. His 1980 gross-out *Cannibal Holocaust* contained a film-within-a-film entitled *The Green Inferno. The Green Inferno* is the found footage of a documentary film crew who are studying cannibalism in the Amazon. They do, indeed, find cannibals, and one by one, in front of the camera, die horrible and gruesome deaths.

Cast:

Heather Donahue (Heather Donahue), Joshua Leonard (Joshua Leonard), Michael C. Williams (Michael Williams), Bob Griffin (Short Fisherman), Jim King (Interviewee), Sandra Sánchez (Waitress) Ed Swanson (Fisherman With Glasses), Patricia DeCou (Mary Brown), Mark Mason (Man in Yellow Hat), Jackie Hallex (Interviewee with Child).

What the critics say:

Desmond Ryan, *Philadelphia Inquirer*: "You can dismiss *The Blair Witch Project* as a trick. Or you can give in to the treat and savor that rarest of accomplishments in a field notorious for tedium and repetition—an original horror movie."

Peter Travers, *Rolling Stone*: "I have seen the new face of movie horror and its name is *The Blair Witch Project*, a groundbreaker in fright that reinvents scary for the new millennium."

Lloyd Rose, *Washington Post*: "*The Blair Witch Project* is the scariest movie I've ever seen. Not the goriest, the grossest, the weirdest, the eeriest, the sickest, the creepiest or the slimiest … Just flat out the scariest."

If you liked this, you might also like:

The Last Broadcast (1998).

www.ingramcontent.com/pod-product-compliance
Lightning Source LLC
Chambersburg PA
CBHW060326100426
42812CB00003B/895